Boys at Sea

Also by B. R. Burg

RICHARD MATHER OF DORCHESTER

SODOMY AND THE PIRATE TRADITION: English Sea Rovers in the Seventeenth-Century Caribbean

AN AMERICAN SEAFARER IN THE AGE OF SAIL: The Erotic Diaries of Philip C. Van Buskirk, 1851–1870

GAY WARRIORS: A Documentary History from the Ancient World to the Present

Boys at Sea

Sodomy, Indecency, and Courts Martial in Nelson's Navy

B. R. Burg

palgrave
macmillan

First published in 2007 by
PALGRAVE MACMILLAN
Houndmills, Basingstoke, Hampshire RG21 6XS and
175 Fifth Avenue, New York, N.Y. 10010
Companies and representatives throughout the world.

PALGRAVE MACMILLAN is the global academic imprint of the Palgrave Macmillan division of St. Martin's Press, LLC and of Palgrave Macmillan Ltd. Macmillan® is a registered trademark in the United States, United Kingdom and other countries. Palgrave is a registered trademark in the European Union and other countries.

ISBN-13: 978–0–230–52228–2 hardback

This book is printed on paper suitable for recycling and made from fully managed and sustained forest sources. Logging, pulping and manufacturing processes are expected to conform to the environmental regulations of the country of origin.

A catalogue record for this book is available from the British Library.

Library of Congress Cataloging-in-Publication Data

Burg, B. R. (Barry Richard), 1938–
Boys at sea : sodomy, indecency, and courts martial in Nelson's navy / B. R. Burg.
p. cm.—
Includes bibliographical references and index.
ISBN 0–230–52228–9 (alk. paper)
1. Great Britain. Royal Navy – Conduct of life – History. I. Title.

VD57.G86 2007
359.1′334—dc22 2007016233

10 9 8 7 6 5 4 3 2 1
16 15 14 13 12 11 10 09 08 07

Transferred to Digital Printing in 2009

For Shag, Jill, Alice, Lucky, and Rupee

We tars are all for fun and glee, –
A hornpipe was my notion;
Time was I'd dance with any he
That sails the salt sea ocean

– From "Jack at Greenwich"
by Charles Dibden

Contents

Acknowledgments

The very nature of the historian's craft requires the support of many individuals and organizations. Those who have assisted me with my study of proscribed sexuality in the Royal Navy are numerous. I wish to particularly thank G. S. Rousseau, who provided extensive commentary on the manuscript, and Clifford L. Egan, Thomas Camfield, Benjamin D. Rhodes, and Richard A. Yasko, all of whom have offered suggestions on various chapters over the years. Roger Nixon and Ellen Poteet have assisted me in many ways with my research, and I am deeply grateful to both of them for their efforts. Others who have offered encouragement, insight, and aid are A. L. Beier, Janet Bloom, Eddie Campaigne, Victoria L. McLaughlin, Elizabeth Oldham, Daniel C. Palma, Roland Pietsch, Roberta F. Rosenberg, Kiri Ross-Jones, Ashley M. Smith, Janet L. Soper, and the staff of the Camelback Road Alphagraphics in Phoenix, Arizona. Any remaining errors of commission and omission, of course, are mine alone.

Organizations that have helped with my research are the Brown University Library, the Inter-library Loan Service of Arizona State University, the John Carter Brown Library, the National Archives and Record Service of the United States, the National Archives of the United Kingdom, the Nantucket Historical Association, the National Maritime Museum, and the William L. Clements Library.

Special thanks are due to the Provost's Research Fund at Arizona State University, which generously supported my work.

Transforming a manuscript into a book is always an agonizing process. In the case of *Boys at Sea*, the pain was considerably reduced by the advice and assistance gently offered up by Palgrave Macmillan's Ruth Ireland and Michael Strang. I am also deeply indebted to Vidhya Jayaprakash at Newgen Imaging Systems, who kept the production process moving forward with care and dispatch.

And, most important, I want to thank my family, Judy Shelton-Burg, Jenny Burg Davis, and John E. Burg, for their encouragement and support over the years I have worked on this book.

Editorial Note

In dealing with documents generated over a period of almost one hundred and fifty years, I have adopted several tactics to provide constancy, clarity, and convenience to quotations, pagination, and citations. In general, I have used modern spelling and corrected minor spelling errors. I have, for example, changed words such as "sworne" to "sworn," "embroider'd" to "embroidered," and "trowsers" to "trousers." I have also spelled out or modernized most abbreviations and variations of ordinary words: "sd" to "said," "ye" to "the." Abbreviations of rank are generally spelled out. I have also followed modern usage with punctuation in most cases. Underlining and italics within quotations are as in the original documents unless otherwise noted.

Courts martial transcripts are sometimes paginated, sometimes not. The systems of pagination also vary from one document to another. When the pages of trial records carry page numbers, those are the numbers I have used in citations. When unnumbered, I have assigned numbers to the pages beginning with the first page containing substantial information. I have not assigned numbers to sheets used as untitled covers or wrappers, even when the wrappers carry the names and dates of courts martial. In citations from the verso of leaves numbered only on the recto, I have used the recto numbering. Oftentimes, because of the way sheets were folded together or otherwise assembled, only every fourth page carries a number. In such situations, I have used the same page number for the page on which the number is inscribed and all subsequent pages, until a new page number appears. In ADM 1/5453, for example, after page 11 are three unnumbered pages, then follows page 12. References to page 11 and the three trailing, unnumbered pages are all cited as page 11. In a few unusual circumstances, I have located material in documents by reference to the names of witnesses or to dates that would best facilitate locating the cited item or passage within a cited document. The figure "/s/" is used in quotations to indicate original signatures in documents I have consulted. Many of the items in Admiralty records are copies of originals, and those making the copies usually indicated signatures they copied with the notation "(Signed)" followed by the name of the signatory written by the copier. When I have used such copied signatures in quotations, I have quoted the copied document exactly, including both the copier's notation "(Signed)" and the name following the notation.

When quoting trial testimony, I have in most cases adopted a standard format, using Q to indicate a question, and A to signify the answer. The names of the interrogator and respondent are given when they first speak. Then the Q-A format follows until another speaker begins. His name is then inserted. Oftentimes speakers are identified in the records by function rather than by name – "prosecutor," "witness," "prisoner," "judge advocate," etc. When speakers are unnamed members of courts martial, I have identified them as "Court." Courts martial transcripts are for the most part found under the classification ADM 1/_ _ _ _ in the National Archives at Kew. It is usual for each court martial to have its own reference number. For example, the number for the trial of Lieutenant Richard Morgan is ADM 1/5484. The number for the trial of Henry Bicks is ADM 1/5296. There are some numbers that contain within them numerous courts martial. ADM 1/5301 for example contains transcripts of four trials. When I have cited individual courts martial, both those having their own ADM 1/_ _ _ _ number and those filed under omnibus numbers, I have included the names of the men being tried and the dates of the trials to assist anyone wishing to locate the original documents. Abstracts of many courts martial are also available in items numbered ADM 12/21 to ADM 12/26. I have cited both the abstracts and complete transcripts, often in the same note, when appropriate to do so. There are duplicate copies in Admiralty archives of the court martial record for the case of Martin Billin and James Bryan. In citations to the case, I have included both of the numbers under which the trial transcripts are filed.

In references to courts martial where pairs of mariners were tried, the names are in alphabetical order, that is, ADM 1/5354 (Beauchamp-Bruce court martial, 6–15 January 1816) or ADM 1/5301 (Garbut-Pyle court martial, 23 October 1762).

Introduction

The Admiralty records that preserve almost one hundred and fifty years of Royal Navy prosecutions for sodomy and other sexually proscribed acts provide an arresting chapter in the history of human sexuality. The defendants, witnesses, victims, observers, and conspirators called before courts martial during the age of sail not only told of lust, rape, pain, exploitation, betrayal, retribution, and terror on the darkened decks of His Majesty's ships, but their testimony offers profound insight into the broader workings of the vast enterprise that was for centuries the worlds largest, most powerful, and most costly military organization. The details of the shipboard universe provided by courts martial transcripts go far beyond what was needed for criminal prosecutions. The material contained on daily routine, nautical politics, seafaring folklore, mens' social and sexual entanglements, religion afloat, sailors' discourse, and a thousand other details substantially enrich what is already known of life at sea in this huge and exclusively male institution.[1]

The purpose of courts martial are to determine innocence or guilt, and prescribe punishment for those judged guilty. The questions I have asked in examining the trial records of those accused of sodomy or other sexual infractions deal with matters other than whether defendants actually committed the offenses for which they were charged. I have sought instead to define the social parameters of sexuality on board the navy's ships. In short, my intent was to discover the when, where, how, why, and with whom mariners committed sodomy and allied offenses. A secondary aim was to assess the qualitative and quantitative aspects of sexual relations among ship's companies, and chart the Royal Navy's shifting responses to shipboard sexuality. At least one leading naval historian has suggested that the documentary data on sodomy has been tightly squeezed and already yielded up most of its significant content. This is hardly the case. It is surprising, in fact, that the few investigators who have dabbled with the Admiralty's attempts to punish sodomy and other manifestations of sexual conduct in the fleet have missed the central themes of erotic life in the Royal Navy. The most conspicuous feature of shipboard sex revealed by the courts martial from the earliest records in the eighteenth century until such prosecutions ended in 1830s is that a large majority of the defendants were officers and that in almost every case the officers were accused of forcing sodomy and indecent acts on unwilling boys. Ordinary sailors customarily found partners among their peers, as did midshipmen, but no officer was ever called to account for buggering another officer. Neither did men holding commissions or warrants select those immediately below them in rank as sexual partners. They chose only those in the lowest tiers of the naval hierarchy. Captains did not have sex with lieutenants, lieutenants did not have sex with warrant officers, nor did warrant officers have sex either with petty officers or with the "ratings" or "the people," as seamen were variously called by those in posts of authority. The preferred partners for officers of every level were the boys that comprised between 8 and 10 percent of ships' crews.

Not only does a study of sodomy trials provide a new perspective on the lives of boys at sea, but it explores for the first time the unique fellowship that evolved among the lads who served king and country on the nation's warships. As a hierarchal organization, separate societies were mandated throughout the Royal Navy. Officers, foretopmen, waisters, idlers, marines, and virtually every other man on board belonged to one or more groups that were defined by rank, job title, training, skill level, and various other distinctions. Among boys, it was no different. They were most obviously set apart from others on board by age, and they very likely reveled in such segregation. Although their jobs varied and there were several status levels among them, they played, chatted, ate, and lived together in close proximity, interacting in a myriad of ways on a daily basis, every day for years at a stretch. They evolved their own entertainments, nurtured friendships, fought amongst themselves, and engaged in the full range of interactions typical of youngsters. Boys do not customarily keep diaries nor did many of them write home. Other than the notices in naval records, the occasional and abbreviated recollection of a youthful experience or two contained in memoirs of adult naval careers, and a few surviving notes and letters, the lives of man of war's boys have left little trace. Fortunately, many youngsters provided substantial quantities of testimony at courts martial. The lengthy and precise accounts offered by juvenile witnesses and their cross-examinations by courts, prosecutors, and defendants provide a large measure of previously unknown detail about their lives, their hopes and thoughts, their work, the interactions among them, and their relationships with adults, particularly the men they directly served.

In denominating the sexual nexus between adult seafarers and their boys I have avoided many familiar terms such as sexual predator, molester, child abuser, pedophile, and psychopath, particularly that of "child abuser," which has been employed only since the 1970s. All are recent classifications when used in reference to adult-child sexuality. No court martial board would use such words to describe the men they judged, nor, in fact, would they recognize any legal or moral distinction between sodomy committed by two adults and sodomy involving an adult and a child.[2]

Although current scholarship often uses adult-child relationships in ancient Greece as a starting point for discussions of intergenerational sexual activity, there is no indication that any participants in Royal Navy courts martial ever took official cognizance of such engagements. Trial transcripts contain no mention of homoeroticism from earlier ages even though practices in the ancient world were surely familiar to those officers who had at least a tenuous acquaintanceship with classical literature. Despite the failure to associate the asymmetrical power and status relationships on board ships to earlier Greek practice in any surviving record, some similarity exists. This is apparent when comparing patterns of phallic penetration and attempted phallic penetration. As was the case among the Greeks, in sexual contacts involving adults and boys trial transcripts reveal not a single instance of a boy entering a man.

Courts martial not only reveal boys to have been a central focus of seaborne sexuality, but they fill in the small and large details of how personnel of all ranks in Nelson's navy actually courted and copulated. The trials indicate various sets of organizing matrices for sex on board ship. The details of each matrix – the location of the acts, the time of day, the possibility of reciprocity or discovery, and a dozen other aspects of the encounters – were determined by the niches in the shipboard hierarchy occupied by the participants. Transgenerational engagements followed models imposed on the adult instigators by naval life, naval architecture, the geography of the decks, and the proximity of one hammock to another. The manner of seduction or rape involving adult ratings had its own unique characteristics.[3] Courts martial for ratings who engaged boys revealed a pattern of behavior sharply distinct from that of adult pairs of sailors engaging one another. Trials for officers and warrant officers reveal that they, too, followed separate scenarios for acquiring partners. The leisurely and expansive script for copulating with boys in captains' great cabins differed substantially from that defining the ways warrant officers lured boys into their cramped quarters, unceremoniously bent them over sea chests, yanked down their trousers, and buggered them.

In addition to extended and graphic descriptions of specific sex acts, trial records also provide information on how mariners engaged in sodomy or other indecent acts were discovered, who discovered them, the manner in which accusations moved upward through the chain of command, and the roles of admirals, captains, lieutenants, judge advocates and expert witnesses in the judicial process. Another useful contribution to understanding sex in the Royal Navy is the sharp and clear definitions provided by courts martial of imprecise or previously ill-understood terms such as such as "uncleanness," "attempted sodomy," and "frigging."

More important than definitions are the perceptions on display in the proceedings. The thousands of pages preserving sworn testimony for scores of prosecutions reveal seafarers' attitudes on sodomy and sexual crimes with a transparency and honesty that cannot be obtained by examining regulations, published diaries, memoirs, or official pronouncements. Not only do courts martial records provide insight into the thinking of men from captains to coxswains and cooks' helpers on all-male sex, but they also trace the gradual shifts in attitudes over the decades. The salty, but crude and specific language of earlier trials was gradually replaced as the service became a softer, gentler place under the influence of a gradually increasing number of zealous Christian officers, and the harsh and usually inflexible approach to proscribed sexual conduct typical in the mid-eighteenth century was mitigated to some degree as spirituality made inroads into shipboard life in the post-Nelson navy.

Judicial proceedings by their very nature impress their own brand of order on events, and the narratives drawn from them emerge distorted in many ways.[4] That men arguing to save their lives will craft their own versions of truth is hardly surprising, and similarly other men hoping to hang them will do the same. Despite the flexed and disfigured reality presented in courts martial records, the combative atmosphere of the trials provides fascinating reading, as is usual when sex and death are juxtaposed. In like fashion, the records themselves, the sheets of paper written over from top to bottom and side to side, also help reveal how matters worked in the sailing navy. Sodomy and sex offense courts martial transcripts effectively document the modernization, consolidation, and bureaucratization of the Royal Navy from the earliest years of the eighteenth century until almost the mid-point of the nineteenth. Trial records produced during the reigns of Queen Anne and George I are pitiful things. They preserve condemnations and executions in the most cursory fashion. In two or three or four manuscript paragraphs, men could be accused, tried, judged, sentenced, and hanged. By the time of the Seven-Years War, the expanded navy, the increased size of the British government, the explosion in literacy, and the need to gain administrative control of the rapidly burgeoning bureaucracy meant more paperwork was required for every task, courts martial for sodomy and indecency included. Trial records by the 1760s are no longer three-page affairs set to paper by half-trained scribes. They run fifteen to twenty and thirty pages, and the beautiful, flowing script is the product of well-trained, professional penmen. Included are details of the accusation, the testimony of witnesses, the defense, cross-examinations, and only then the judgment. At the inception of the Victorian era, even this level of administrative complexity had been superceded. Trial documents from the 1830s run to one hundred pages or more, and are in many respects the equivalents of modern trial transcripts.

I hope the following study will not only expand and greatly amplify what is already known of naval life in the age of sail, but that it will contribute to an understanding of sodomy and other assorted sexual transgressions in military organizations. There is, of course, always much more to be done. Investigating sex between men in uniform emerged as an academic cottage industry only in the late 1970s, and its expansion has continued to the present without any signs of diminishing vigor. In the future its documents and sources may turn out to be, as G. S. Rousseau suggested in reference to the eighteenth century, "one of the richest untapped archives in our period."[5]

1
Law, Literature, Sodomy, and Royal Navy Officers

Scrawled at a forty-five degree angle on the lower left corner of an unnumbered page in the transcript of Hepburn Graham's 1806 court martial is a note reading "17 Dec. Warrant to be prepared for his execution on board the *St. George* at Portsmouth on Saturday next."[1] If all went according to standard procedure, elaborate preparations were made for Graham's hanging. On the appointed day the crew of HMS *St. George* was mustered at quarters, the death signal, a yellow flag, was raised to the masthead, and boats from every vessel in the squadron came alongside the ship to witness the day's odious business. On nearby ships all men were called up to listen as their captains read aloud the *Articles of War* laying out the crime for which Graham was to die. He stood convicted of violating the twenty-ninth article: "If any person in the fleet shall commit the unnatural and detestable sin of buggery and sodomy with man or beast, he shall be punished with death by the sentence of a court martial." Shortly before 11:00 a.m., a pair of the *St. George's* sailors, probably two of the most troublesome members of the crew, went aloft to reeve the hanging rope through a block at the fore yardarm. It had a knot twelve or fifteen feet above the condemned man's head so that when crewmembers at the waist of the ship ran with it, it would be quick-stopped at the block, speeding his end with a sharp jerk. With the preparations completed, all on board stood waiting for the firing of the signal gun. At its report, half a dozen men ran with the rope end, and Graham was hauled up to his death. He was then left swinging like a pendulum high above the deck for as long as an hour to make certain no life remained in his body.[2] George Parr, the boy whom Graham had forced into sodomy, was very likely present to witness the execution.

The *Articles of War* under which Graham was convicted and sentenced were applicable only to men serving in the Royal Navy, but despite being limited to naval personnel, article twenty-nine did not evolve independently from the vast and complex body of English civil and ecclesiastical jurisprudence.[3] Sodomy had initially been the province only of church courts throughout the medieval era. It was not made contrary to English civil law until the reign of Henry VIII, when the king's premier facilitator, Thomas Cromwell, engineered the passage through parliament of an anti-buggery statute in 1533. The new law was not crafted primarily to criminalize a specified sexual act. It was enacted as part of Henry's continuing battle with the Roman Catholic Church. Before the Henrician legislation, neither sodomy nor buggery was a crime in statute or common law. What was once an offense against God became a civil crime of the most serious kind in Henry's successful bid to extend royal authority and strike a blow against the church, its courts, and its clergy, whom he suspected of being especially dissolute.[4]

The prohibition against buggery was reenacted several times during the remainder of Henry's reign, although in the records of parliamentary actions it no longer commanded its own chapter as it did when first promulgated. Instead, it appeared in broadly expanded sections of statutes regulating wool, cattle, rope making, the export of horses, brass and copper trading, the conduct of beggars and vagrants, and the maraudings of Welshmen. By the time Henry's parliaments completed work on buggery, they had reaffirmed it as a secular offense, specified that conviction allowed for the forfeiture of property, and abrogated the right of members of holy orders to be tried in church courts.[5]

The laws passed during Henry's reign did not lead to sustained or rigorous efforts to hunt down sodomites. There were few prosecutions or convictions in the years that followed, and outside of legislative pronouncements little evidence survives to indicate any serious desire to extirpate sodomy. Nicholas Udall, a headmaster dismissed from Eton in 1541 for a series of offenses including buggery went on to assume another post as a schoolmaster and finally became, appropriately enough, the Master of Revels at the court of Edward VI. Parliament eliminated the forfeiture provisions during Edward's reign, and the secular anti-sodomy laws were repealed entirely under Mary, who returned jurisdiction to ecclesiastical courts. Later, when Elizabeth came to the throne, parliament reenacted Henry's draconian laws, and sodomy remained a capital crime in England until 1861.[6] Still, if Henrician and Elizabethan legislation did little to prevent sodomy or restrain sodomites, it had a lasting effect in the power struggle with religious authorities. By the 1690s, London's ecclesiastical courts rarely entertained cases involving sexual misconduct. They were reduced to dealing with marital disputes and charges of defamation. In the eighteenth century, when morally outraged laymen moved against sodomites they had to rely on civil officers, magistrates, and justices of the peace for the most part, to enforce their views of sin and morality.[7]

Sir Edward Coke, in his vast, seventeenth-century compendium of legal practice, expounded at length on the intricacies of the enactments against sodomy. Copying the words of the various statutes then in force, he wrote in the *Institutes of the Laws of England* that it was a crime "adjudged felony without benefit of clergy" and "a detestable and abominable sin, amongst Christians not to be named."[8] In his discourse, Coke explained that, like rape, the commission of sodomy required both penetration and emission. Tudor laws specified that those convicted of such heinous crimes be hanged. The prescribed penalty was merciful compared to ancient times, Coke noted, when "sorcerers, sodomers, and heretiques" were burnt.[9] Coke also explored the sources of English sodomy. Following the lead of tenth-century poet and playwright Roswitha of Gandersham, he classified it as an import. "Buggery cometh of the Italian word" and it was "complained in Parliament, that a Lombard did commit the sin that was not to be named." The eminent jurist was not alone in his perception that Italians were exporters of sodomy. The idea of its foreign origins was appealing enough to last well into the next century. Daniel Defoe maintained in 1701 that "Lust chose the torrid zone of Italy/Where blood ferments in rapes and sodomy." Thirty years later, the anonymous author of *Plain Reasons for the Growth of Sodomy in England* agreed with him, explaining that the adoption of southern European manners and the introduction of Italian opera were substantial factors in the spread of the contagion.[10]

Another of the legal scholars to offer up opinions on sodomy was Sir Matthew Hale. He expressed doubts about Coke's interpretation of the law and his constancy. "But the least penetration maketh it rape or buggery," he said, "yea although there be not *emissio seminis* ... And therefore I suppose the case in my Lord Coke's 12 *Rep* 36.5 *Jac.* that saith there must both ... to make rape or buggery is mistaken, and contradicts what he saith in his pleas of the crown." One hundred years after Coke, the eminent eighteenth-century jurist Sir William Blackstone continued the rhetorical condemnation. It was "an infamous crime against nature" he wrote, a "horrible crime not to be named among Christians." "I will not act so disagreeable a part to my readers as well as myself as to dwell any longer upon a subject the very mention of which is a disgrace to human nature," he said. Fellow jurist William Eden articulated the same sentiment, denouncing "crimes of a very detestable nature; the mere mention of which is disgraceful to the human species."[11] Undoubtedly aware of the danger of false accusations and the potential for blackmail, Blackstone paraphrased Hale's words on rape in his now familiar caveat to potentially overzealous prosecutors.[12] Sodomy is, he warned:

> A crime which ought to be strictly and impartially proved, and then so strictly and impartially punished. But it is an offense of so dark a nature, so easily charged, and the negative so difficult to be proved that the accusation should be clearly made out; for, if false, it deserves a punishment inferior only to that of the crime itself.[13]

I

When English jurists wrote of sodomy and buggery they treated it as an act of anal intercourse committed by two persons. In none of their writings is there any implication that practitioners of the vice were in any way particular sorts of individuals, nor was it ever implied that they might have belonged to any similarly inclined groups set apart from the majority of humanity by a preference for same-sex partners. The practice of classifying sodomy only as a closely defined physical act was followed by writers throughout the seventeenth century, although most were less aggrieved by it than were the men of the law. When Robert Burton cataloged the afflictions of mankind in his massive *Anatomy of Melancholy*, a best seller in Stuart England, he did not classify buggery as the apocalyptic scourge later generations would consider it. Sodom and Gomorrah rated only passing references. Their sins harbored no more danger in his way of thinking than constipation, an overmuch love of learning, or the additional host of ailments, misdeeds, and misfortunes he chronicled. In the concluding section of his work he lumped buggery in with "mastupration [*sic*], satyriasis, priapismus, melancholy, madness, fornication, adultery ... theft, murder, and all manner of mischiefs."[14] Neither did Burton's near contemporary, William Prynne see sodomy as a consuming threat. In his equally massive *Histrio-Mastix*, published a dozen years after Burton's work first appeared, Prynne claimed that the theater encouraged "love-passions, lusts, adulteries, incests, rapes, impostures, cheates, conspiracies, treacheries, murders, thefts, debates, and other abominable villainies." Actors and play-haunters became "mimical, histrionical, lascivious, apish, amorous, and unmanly, both in their habits, gestures, speeches, complements, and their whole deportment."[15] Prynne occasionally denounced sodomy, sodomites, and Sodom, but the sins of the "City of the Plain" rated less opprobrium in quantitative terms than singing, dancing, dicing, and other such entertainments. Effeminacy and men donning the raiment of women were, according to Prynne, two of the most noxious of the manifold evils fostered by the stage. He denounced them regularly and at length throughout his work, but he linked them to sodomy on only rare occasions. Publication of *Histrio-Mastix* brought him before the Star Chamber, stood him in the pillory, cost him both ears, and forced him to witness the public burning of his book, but it was his tendentious polemics and subversive theology rather than his treatment of anal intercourse that triggered the summons.[16] In his diatribe of over one thousand pages, he devoted only a few paragraphs to denouncing sodomy.

The persecution of Catholics spawned by Titus Oates and the Popish Plot during the reign of Charles II may have in some manner indicated the existence of loosely associated, all-male sexual groups, but that is far from certain. The earliest firm evidence that such bands existed in England dates from the reign of William and Mary, when political opponents of the king – a combination of large land owners and an increasingly powerful mercantile class – charged the sovereign and his closest associates at court with being regular visitors at "*Chateau Derrire*." William's naming his putative lover, Arnold Joost van Keppel, as Earl of Albemarle, and his lavishing favors on another favorite, William Bentinck, were widely seen by the king's detractors as proof of his bedroom preferences. The Piccadilly house of the Earl of Sutherland also served as a center for all-male sexual activity during the period, at least according to rumors.

By the 1720s, the visible nature of all-male sexual activity had changed dramatically in England. The alleged sexual antics of the royal court, which had been the public face of sodomy throughout most of the seventeenth century, gave way to a general awareness that there had grown in London and possibly elsewhere a conspicuous and widespread homoerotic network that included participants from all levels of society.[17] Scholars in Britain and the United States have over the past several decades written extensively on this phenomenon, but in early Georgian England it was not a reflective few in the academy who gave it visibility.[18] The mass of English readers learned of it from the sensationalists who wrote of secret languages and rituals, marriages among males, buggery, transvestism, and dens of iniquity where concupiscent males could revel in lust and perversion. Many of the participants in this newly revealed demimonde lent veracity to the information available in print by making little effort to disguise their inclinations. They dressed as women, flaunted their effeminacy, patronized the many inns and ale houses that catered to their erotic tastes, and were a conspicuous presence at a multitude of public areas, including the Royal Exchange, Lincoln's Inn, Petticoat Lane, the south side of St. James's Park, and Covent Garden.[19]

It is not entirely understood why a large and conspicuous all-male, homoerotic confraternity proliferated in London during this period, but the causes most probably lay in the city's huge size – over 700,000 people early in the 1700s – and the concomitant features of urbanization that encouraged diverse avenues of artistic, cultural, political, economic, and sexual expression. Whatever the reasons, there is general agreement that such groups burst upon England and became part of the public consciousness in the early years of Anne's reign.[20]

The word "homosexual" was not used in early eighteenth-century England. It would not be coined until a century and a half later, first appearing in two German-language political pamphlets written anonymously by Karl Maria Kertbeny in 1869. The term remained confined to the European continent for two decades, not crossing the Channel until the late 1880s when it appeared in the first English translation of Richard von Krafft-Ebing's *Psychopathia Sexualis*. Georgian Englishmen were not deterred by lack of nomenclature to identify the homoerotically inclined groups revealed to exist among them. They had their own word to classify effeminate, cross-dressing men. They called them "mollies," from the Latin "mollis" – meaning soft, tender, pliant, or woman-like.

Wide public awareness of the existence of mollies and the molly houses that hosted them heralded the emergence of a new sexual perspective in Britain. Practitioners of sodomy were no longer mere sodomites or buggers. Under the new dispensation, they projected a persona – a particular role – and adopted practices that sharply distinguished them from ordinary Englishmen. By congregating at establishments amenable to their sexual proclivities and adopting conspicuously effeminate manners, habits, affectations, and garb, mollies created a genuinely homoerotic presence in a single generation. Writers of every stamp along with raging moralists generated successive waves of scathingly negative publicity for London's now-conspicuous, homoerotic manifestation. The climate created by mollies and their detractors quickly became a permanent part of the nation's legal, social, and cultural milieu. Both landsmen and seafarers from the reign of George I forward would label mollyish attire, behavior patterns, and sexual practices degenerate, perverse, and disgusting.[21]

II

Naval officers attempting to evaluate charges of sodomy in early eighteenth-century courts martial, no matter what their degree of familiarity with the literature on homoeroticism, had only limited historical precedents to guide them. A number of the men who served at such trials may have had at least a measure of familiarity with some of the earliest prosecutions in secular courts, knowing perhaps of the famous cases of the first Lord Hungerford and the seventeenth Earl of Oxford. Yet even if they knew of the two proceedings, the knowledge would have been of only of limited utility. The first took place during the time of Edward VI and the second in Elizabeth's reign. The fact that both cases involved noblemen rather than commoners or naval personnel made excavating helpful information from either virtually impossible. Then, too, the prosecutions of Hungerford and Oxford involved constellations of issues encompassing religious deviation, possible treason, and spousal abuse, complications not to be found in charges levied on board ship under the *Articles of War.* Another source of historical knowledge with which some officers might have been familiar was the information on sodomy trials carried by word of mouth from courts of assize into general circulation. Still, such trials were few, and not likely to provide precedent or procedural examples to assist officers dealing with issues arising in shipboard courts martial.

Naval officers familiar with specific sodomy prosecutions ashore in all probability obtained what information they knew about them from reading the copious rogue literature available to them and to almost every other literate person. By the dawn of the Georgian era, writers and printers in Britain and Ireland discovered that a vast market existed for true crime tales laced with salacious innuendo and a leaven of aristocratic gossip. They responded to the public taste with an enthusiasm that could only be driven by the certainty of profit. There has hardly been an era in which old and new crimes were more often written up, printed, and anthologized.

The earliest sodomy case in England that might have been known to any significant number of eighteenth-century Royal Navy officers was that of the Earl of Castlehaven. The 1631 prosecution was a *cause célebre* from the time it occurred to the early years of nineteenth century. Three editions of the Castlehaven trial were published between 1699 and 1719, along with a book on another famous 1698 case, that of the notorious and effeminate navy captain, Edward Rigby, who proposed sodomy to a youthful Edward Minton. In the decades after 1720, new books and anthologies on prosecutions for assorted crimes appeared continuously, and sodomy cases, including the Castlehaven scandal, were part of every one of them.[22]

Those who read of crime and criminals had easy access to a vast array of small, cheap books and pamphlets on the two subjects. Trials and the certain administration of justice described in popular crime literature regularly included graphic, though hardly pronographic, accounts of adultery, rape, and sodomy. Over two dozen crime narratives under the title *The Ordinary of Newgate* (with many variations) were published in the eighteenth century, while the narrative of a separate 1751 sodomy case at the court of King's Bench, and involving multiple defendants, sold well enough to go through at least two editions and perhaps multiple printings. Francis Plowden in 1789 brought out a twelve-volume set of trial narratives dealing only with adultery cases in the ecclesiastical and civil courts. The work was so popular that only a few years after it went on sale an abridged but more explicit version appeared. Entitled *Cuckold's Chronicle*, it included the carnal specifics of Plowden's volumes without the legal rigmarole that provided earlier editions with a façade of respectability. An American edition followed in 1798.

Naval officers who would not deign to peruse the low-priced pamphlet-sized, trial accounts published for the ordinary sort of people might have preferred popular, multi-volume works containing true-crime narratives. One of the best known of these compilations, *The Complete Collection of State Trials*, contained an accumulation of major legal actions from the fourteenth century forward. Amid the collection of proceedings that ranged from high treason through murder, slander, bigamy, popery, and on down to stealing cows in Ireland was included the story of the Earl of Castleheaven's crimes, his trial, and his Tower Hill execution. The *Complete Collection* drew a tremendous audience for the numerous editions, supplements, and more-moderately priced abridgments published in multi-volume folio and quarto formats throughout the eighteenth- and into the nineteenth century. The publisher did not intend his volumes for scholars or lawyers. The hope was that it would be a profitable venture, gaining sales from its contribution to the era's rage for gallows confessions, scabrous tales, ghastly crime stories, and accounts of the piratical adventurers of celebrity marauders like captains William Kidd and John Quelch. Five editions of the *State Trials* appeared in the years between 1719 and 1826, and the later versions provided some of the most accurate and accessible accounts of major cases available. Another of these collections, *Select Trials at the Sessions-House in the Old Bailey* attracted enough readers to persuade its investors to back several printings, even though its four-volume original edition contained crimes committed only from 1720 to 1741. The last major edition containing seven volumes was published in 1818. The printer believed so strongly that there existed a large audience willing to pay for tales of true crimes that he or his backers willingly supported the production of the two-volume *Old Bailey Chronicle or Malefactors Register Containing Circumstantial Accounts ... of the Most Notorious Offences ... 1700 to 1783.*[23]

The book-purchasing public, which included officers of the Royal Navy, was as much attracted to sodomy cases outside the established judicial system as it was in prosecutions before the law. When a pair of Oxford divines, Reverend John Swinton and Dr. Robert Thistlethwaite, found themselves facing accusations of buggery and attempted buggery at Wadham College in the 1730s, two newspapers, the *Daily Advertiser* and the *London Evening Post,* quickly publicized the accusations against them. A number of books, hilarious poems, and at least one satire followed, all dwelling on the discomfiture of Wadham officials and the embarrassment to the college itself.[24] The story of the travails of a Mr. W. French, an undergraduate at Wadham College in the 1730s, illustrates how news of proscribed sexual conduct was presented to readers:

> When supper was over, Mr. French, with two or three more, adjourned to a gentleman's room in the college to spend the evening, where Mr. French was taken very sick and vomited, to the surprise of the company. He afterwards sat down, and, behaved during the rest of the night as if he had been distracted, calling the warden the worst of scoundrels and villains. Such uncommon behavior amazed the company, who begged to know what was the matter. *The matter,* said he, *the murder of one's father, or whole family is nothing to it; you can't conceive of anything bad enough.* But he would not tell them what it was ... . Mr. French, however, could not sit in peace during the whole night; but seemed full of horror and amazement. All *Sunday* he continued in the same condition, sometimes shedding tears, and sometimes calling the warden the worst of names in the most public manner; often saying that it was in his power to expel him.[25]

After witnessing this extraordinary display, two of the observers departed, according to one of the narratives, and later over dinner speculated on what had so agitated their comrade. The men, George Baker and Charles D'Oyly, both students at Wadham College "concluded it most probable that the warden had made a sodomitical attempt upon

Mr. French."[26] It was the only crime they could imagine that exceeded patricide in horror and revulsion. Additional testimony to the widespread interest in sodomy prosecutions among English readers came with the resurrection, rewriting, reprinting, and reissue of several Stuart-era pamphlets on the 1640 trial in Ireland of John Atherton, the Bishop of Waterford and Lismore. He was convicted of bestiality, incest, and buggery, and hanged along with his lover. The sermon preached at the bishop's funeral by Nicholas Barnard, Dean of Armagh was republished in 1709, prompting the issue of a rebuttal pamphlet the next year. The subsequent editions of the trial narrative that followed in 1710 and 1711 indicate that there was profit to be made from the case. Atherton's execution had more to do with his high-church politics than his sexual proclivities, but the careers of the men who produced the later editions of the books dealing with the bishop's misfortunes suggest that they were published for a readership with salacious tastes rather than any interest in seventeenth-century history. Two of the four books were printed by Edward Curll, a man notorious in early Georgian London for producing scandalous books for large audiences. A later edition in 1754 shows that the case had continuing appeal for readers interested in pulchritude, who it seems likely, far outnumbered Englishmen concerned with the century-old and long-forgotten political issues that bore on Atherton's prosecution.[27]

Rogue literature and occasional exposés were only partially responsible for bringing sodomy directly into public cognizance during the reigns of Queen Anne and George I. Organizations dedicated to moral reform in England provided a major thrust for anti-sodomy crusades of the era, and not surprisingly energized the resultant waves of interest and publication on the subject. The most well-known of these groups was the Society for the Reformation of Manners, founded in 1690. Two similar bodies, the Society for the Promotion of Christian Knowledge and the Society for the Propagation of the Gospel in Foreign Parts, came into being some years later. In the first decades of the eighteenth century, there may have been as many as twenty such evangelical bodies functioning in London and various provincial cities, including Bath, Exeter, Bristol, and York. These organizations, often millennian in character, viewed England much as had Puritans a century before. Theirs was a providential land, chosen by God to exemplify observance of His commands and to demonstrate the benefits of submission to Holy Writ. They had little doubt that their nation, so favored by divine blessing, must be purged of corruption. They sought comprehensive moral reform, and directed their zeal as much against idleness, blasphemy,

Sabbath breakers, disorderly conduct, vile language, drunkenness, common criminals, and prostitutes as they did against sodomites or mollies.[28]

The societies were uniquely successful in pursuing their anti-molly crusade. In one 1707 surge of activity, over one hundred alleged mollies were arrested, at least seven were convicted, and three committed suicide. A series of raids conducted on several molly establishments in 1726 were the most extensive ever made before the nineteenth century. Three men died on the gallows and others were convicted on lesser charges before the matter reached its sorry conclusion. Margaret "Mother" Clap, the proprietor of one of the houses raided, received a sentence of two years in jail and an unspecified time in the pillory. All those found guilty were ordinary folk. If any of higher station fell into the clutches of the reformers they rarely faced trial let alone conviction. The incursions of 1726 seem to have been the first attempts by English authorities to persecute mollies *en masse*, as members of a particular group rather than as individual sodomites. The new approach reflected the transfiguration of sodomy from an act of individuals into a collective crime, and the intensive multi-directional nature of the reform societies' efforts produced a spread of documentation on homoerotic customs, practices, interrelationships, and activities in London and elsewhere in England that has proved to be of incalculable value for modern-day scholarship.[29]

The publication of legal treatises, trial stories, true crime tales, and sodomy prosecutions in single and multi-volume editions in a wide variety of price ranges slaked the broad-based reading public's voyeuristic appetites by providing glimpses of life in the nether reaches of English society. For officers of the Royal Navy, as for other Englishmen from the literate and semi-literate classes, it would have been difficult by the eighteenth century to have no awareness of sodomy and attitudes toward it, but it was not only the literature of law and crime that treated the subject. The reading public, or a substantial portion of it, provided a ready market for many other sorts of materials treating all-male sexual activity. Authors and publishers produced a constant stream of broadsides, newspapers, poetry, plays, scientific and medical books, novels, and assorted pamphlets on sodomy, mollies, and other homoerotic themes. Many were accented by doggerel, satire, and humor, but despite the lighter character oftentimes evident, the one constant in virtually all of the literature was hostility.[30] It was palpable, pervasive, and unvarying from the closing years of the seventeenth century to the death of George IV in 1830 and afterward. Unlike the rare and scattered defenses of sodomy, the attacks on it were constant.[31] Homoerotic sexual manifestations, whether casual couplings by isolated pairs or group encounters among the large and flourishing legion of mollies, blighted its practitioners, those who approved of it, those who tolerated it, and the entire nation as well.[32] Every decade witnessed the production of at least an item or two cataloging the evils of homoeroticism. The navy was not an institution isolated from the land of Britain, and its courts and judicial procedures did not operate independently of public opinion or isolated from statute or common law. The evils ascribed to homoerotic sexual practices, along with a measure of knowledge about legal issues impinging on sodomy prosecutions in assize and quarter session courts, were parts of the cultural context officers carried with them into the trials where they judged the guilt or innocence of men accused of violating the *Articles of War*.

Playwrights, poets, and broadside versifiers who wrote to amuse, entertain, and occasionally outrage Englishmen, like the writers and compilers of true crime accounts, not only demonized male-male sexuality but they also affirmed the transformation of the way Englishmen perceived, classified, and practiced homoerotic relations. Descriptions of men engaging in sex with other men were no longer the sodomites of previous centuries. Every literary genre reflected the fact that what once had been the dark, infrequent, and secret sexual practices of an isolated few had now become a public spectacle. The "crime that no Christian dare name" was widely named and expanded upon. Men no longer met with other men only in shadows for hasty, furtive couplings and then sneaked away to resume their seemingly blameless and uncorrupted lives. The mollies who thrived in London and elsewhere were exposed in all their garishness and flamboyance. The material coming from the presses revealed how they organized their erotic lives, exercised their sexuality in parks, public bogs, theaters and promenades, and regularly subjected ordinary citizens to demonstrations of their often outrageous behavior.[33] The fop of the Restoration stage was reinvented for the new century. He became the effeminate, mincing, exorbitant creature that has survived into the present day. A nameless wag in 1733 neatly caricatured this newly-revealed androgynous being:

> Our eye thy mingled form does so perplex
> The midwife must be called to vouch thy sex;
> Which from thy air and habit none can know,
> A spritely youth above, a maid below:
> Awful by turns and soft, how seldom one;
> Today a daughter, and the next a son!

> Say, will this female *boy*, this manly *miss*,
> When next we visit, give or take the kiss?[34]

Novelist Tobias Smollett was one of the most widely-read authors who condemned sodomy. In 1748 he offered a tongue-in-cheek defense of it in the picaresque novel *Roderick Random*. One of the book's characters, the decadent Earl Strutwell, provided a list of the virtues in male-male sex to youthful Roderick in an effort to seduce him. Among the truths enumerated by the Earl were that it prevented bastardy, preserved the virtue of young maidens, and offered "exquisite pleasure." The younger man well knew Strutwell's game, and knew him to be a rascal.[35] He rejected the putative suitor with lines quoted from an earlier Smollett work:

> Eternal infamy his name surround,
> Who planted first that vice on British ground!
> A vice that 'spite of sense and nature reigns,
> And poisons genial love, and manhood stains.[36]

The rejection of Strutwell's reasoning typified the views Smollett expressed at various points in his novels *Roderick Random* and *Peregrine Pickle*, and in the poetic satire *Advice*. Sodomy was an imported vice, he claimed, certain to corrupt the British nation and people if it were allowed to flourish.[37]

Another to satirize the mincing, effeminate molly was actor-playwright David Garrick. In a two-act comedy, *Miss in Her Teens*, staged at both the Theatre Royal, Drury Lane and at the Royalty Theatre there could be little doubt that his character, Mr. Fribble, was not the sexually ambiguous or bisexual fop of an earlier era.[38] He sought only partners of his own kind, and exuded timidity, cowardice, and a gaggle of affectations ranging from a high-pitched voice and white gloves to knowledge of "who is the best milliner" and "where they sell the best tea."[39] The final act of the play concluded with one of the characters denouncing Fribble as "a species too despicable for correction" and driving him from the stage.[40]

Miss in Her Teens was immensely popular. It went through at least six editions and perhaps twenty reprints in London, Edinburgh, Glasgow, Belfast and Dublin between the time of its first publication in the mid-1740s until the end of the eighteenth century, but the stages that hosted performances of the play and the print versions did not circumscribe boundaries for Mr. Fribble. The character was appropriated by Nathaniel Lancaster in his work, *The Pretty Gentleman: or, Softness of*

Manners Vindicated. Although costing only a sixpence, its popularity never equaled that of Garrick's play. It died after only a single edition in 1747. Still, despite its lack of readership, it was another in the continuing progression of books, plays, and pamphlets drawing their humor from denigrating mollies.[41]

The theater not only put molly-like characters on stage, it provided a few purported real-life sodomites for public consumption. Garrick's fellow dramatist-actor, Isaac Bickerstaff, fled England after his attempt on a guardsman at the Savoy Barracks became a public scandal. A short time thereafter playwright Samuel Foote faced charges for attempting sex with a male servant. Foote was known to have fathered a covey of illegitimate children, but as a bachelor who played the part of mollies on stage, as did Garrick, he invited suspicion. Foote's case became a minor sensation, and he the victim of a vicious assault entitled *Sodom and Onan: a Satire Inscribed to __________ Esq. Alias The Devil on Two Sticks*, a work that also skewered several leading noblemen and political figures for their homoerotic proclivities. Foote was acquitted, but even having been accused of sodomy, in eighteenth-century England, could weigh heavily. He deteriorated rapidly after the trial and died within a few years, surely a victim in some measure of his unwelcome notoriety.[42]

The theater and musical entertainments were integral parts of life in Georgian England, and men of the Royal Navy were ardent theater patrons on ship and ashore, both at home and abroad. Officers regularly encouraged on-board plays and entertainments at sea, and sailors participated and attended these shows with considerable enthusiasm, on several occasions attempting to write for their own productions. Even English prisoners of war from time to time produced plays or shows of various natures. Theatrical performances were easily available to all ranks not only in London, where regularly licensed theaters competed with minor performance houses, but in other port towns that hosted major naval installations. William Dillon, on one occasion in his long and distinguished naval career, ordered a production of *The Taming of the Shrew* at a Sheerness theater and offered £10 worth of tickets to his men, which pleased them mightily. Dillon also recorded traveling with a personal copy of Shakespeare in his baggage. In 1744, the London *Daily Advertiser* estimated that of 500 patrons who attended a performance of *The Sorceress: or Harlequin Savoyard* at the New Wells Theater in Clerkenwell, 100 were sailors. Prices for performances varied with the desirability of seating. Officers usually purchased the best seats, often in boxes, while sailors were restricted both by purse and dress to the galleries. Excessive alcohol consumption was usual for all ranks in preparation for visits to the theater, which often led to rowdiness and occasionally to mayhem. In 1802, an inebriated, disrated midshipman led an impromptu boarding party from the cheap seats onto the stage of London's Surrey Theater, disrupting the entire production. Captain John H. Boteler wrote of several rows started by midshipman at theaters in Rochester.[43]

Many of the Royal Navy's higher-ranking officers held posts in London, giving them continuous access to the city's many theaters, and as playgoers they absorbed a constant stream of the ideas and attitudes being considered, debated, absorbed, and rejected by their non-seafaring countrymen. Most plays did not deal with homoerotic themes or characters, but those that did probably had at least some influence on members of the Admiralty, the Navy Board, and other powerful administrative units in that they reinforced the same negative message that was transmitted to the general population in every format from broadsides to extended treatises on law and morality.

One aspect of the virulent and pervasive attacks on mollies that may have resonated particularly with naval officers was the assertion that effeminate men represented a threat to the national security that the Royal Navy was charged with preserving. This is nowhere more apparent than in the work of Thomas Newcomb, who satirized dandified, effeminate males in a 1732 exposé of English manners and character. Such men as these, he argued, endangered Britain and its far-flung imperial possessions. What would they be like in war, Newcomb wondered rhetorically. His speculations offered little cause for optimism:

> But, say, brave chief, who dost the trade possess,
> Can heroes charge before they learn to dress?
> On valor trusting, daringly presume
> To meet a foe, without a cane or plume?
> Rashly a passion for battle feel,
> E'er yet they know their buttons are genteel;
> And they themselves well armed to take the place,
> With bombs and snuff – with cannon, and with lace?
> To shield the warrior now in dire alarms,
> The sempstress and perfumer find his arms:
> And, ah! What terrors must the foe invade,
> To view his ladyship a general made!
> No scented curl, or single hair amiss,
> Seeming at distance a fierce fighting miss.[44]

There was no way that the country's well-being could be compromised by the activities of an expanding, effete, and outrageous minority. The equation of sodomy with effeminacy and Italians and to a slightly lesser extent with the French and Spanish, meant it embodied special dangers for Britain's economy, politics, religion, and the country's military establishment. The Royal Navy, every officer and seaman knew, held the responsibility for protecting the nation. Any such debasement within its ranks reflected not only immorality and indiscipline, but also threatened the very survival of the realm.

Alarmists, writers of every stamp, wags, and a wide segment of the public were not the only elements of society concerned with the coteries of mollies coursing through London and various provincial cities. Courtiers and politicians discovered, as had their predecessors a century earlier,[45] that accusations of sodomy could be useful for clubbing opponents. Large numbers of officers, especially those with connections to the government and the Admiralty solid enough to underpin expectations of advancement to the loftiest levels of rank and precedence (membership in parliament, knighthoods, and even titles of nobility) could not have ignored the problem. Any whiff of sodomy connected with their names could be disastrous for their careers as well as their reputations. Indeed, one of the most famous political scuffles in British history involving unorthodox sexual appetites may have given some of them concern, even though it was a purely political matter involving no navy personnel. It began when John, Lord Hervey produced a scurrilous pamphlet attacking two of Robert Walpole's most abrasive opponents, William Pulteney and Henry St. John, Viscount Bolingbroke. Pulteney responded in kind to his attacker. Writing under the name of Caleb D'Anvers of Grey's Inn, he wrote *A Proper Reply to a Late Scurrilous Libel*. In it he denounced Lord John at length and in kind for the earlier attack.[46] There was no doubt among readers of *A Proper Reply* that the pamphlet's Mr. Fainlove stood in for the flouncing, heavily made up Lord Hervey. Pulteney described Hervey's first entries in the pamphlet war as works of "a forward little boarding school miss who was ambitious of becoming, one time or other, a maid of honor."[47] He then went on to compare him to Sir Fopling Flutter in George Etherege's comedy, *Man of Mode*, written during the reign of Charles II, but popular well into the time of Walpole, going through at least four editions between 1711 and 1725. Part of the reason for the play's continued and enthusiastic acceptance half a century after it was written may have been that it addressed a contemporary issue. As concern mounted over the apparent growth of the molly population, Sir Fopling Flutter was easily changed from a Restoration-style, rakish dandy to an effeminate, flouncing molly for readers and playgoers who were coming to believe in the dangers posed by a class composed of what Pulteney called master-misses and delicate hermaphrodites.

Newspapers throughout the eighteenth century actively reported the antics of mollies to assuage the prurient curiosity of a large segment of the reading public.[48] At least one periodical carried multiple sodomy-related stories during the summer of 1719. *The Original Weekly Journal* reported in June that a traveler lodging in a Surrey ale house "was surprisingly awakened with the impudence of a fellow who stole into the bed ... and was committing the abominable crime of sodomy on his body." The man's servant fired his pistols into the air, the alarmed landlord seized the "buggerer," and he was dispatched to the Marshalsea. The following month, the paper told of William Holdbrook who attempted to sodomize young Thomas Penderel. He atoned for "so foul a crime" in the pillory at Bloomsbury Market. While subject to public ridicule, he was pelted with cucumbers and rotten eggs, and "a hackney coach was tore to pieces that took him up to carry him to Newgate."[49]

The idea that sodomites, those once stigmatized only for engaging in a proscribed act, had acquired an identity and evolved into a brotherhood of like-minded men was present early-on even in the literature of the street. In *The Woman-Hater's Lamentation*, a 1707 broadside written to be sung to the tune of "Ye Pretty Sailors All," stereotyping is readily apparent, and the cognizance of a homoerotic fellowship emerges clearly. Mollies were to the anonymous author of the broadside an amorphous band, a group, a gang, a tribe of "woman haters" who intrigued "with one another," and despised the "fair sex."[50]

Edward "Ned" Ward, one of the most popular and prolific humorists of the age, also emphasized the effeminate nature of mollies in *The Modern World Disrobed*, published in 1708. It was sufficiently popular to be issued in a second edition half a dozen years later.[51] In the work, Ward wrote of a man who:

> Has so cool a sense of female favors that he has less respect for the charms of a petticoat than for the loathsome condescensions of a fricatizing catamite who is beast enough to ease his sodomitical desires with anti-venereal exercise.[52]

Another of Ward's anti-homoerotic sorties came in an account of London social life that first appeared in 1709 and went through at least seven editions or printings by mid-century. It contained an entire chapter devoted to the "The Mollies Club."[53] His description emphasized not only the female affectations but the associative character of the men. They met at "a certain tavern in the city" and there acted out lavishly described girlish charades. Ward explained that "they" were "so far degenerated from all masculine deportment, or manly exercises that they rather fancy themselves women, imitating all the little vanities that custom has reconciled to the female sex, affecting to speak, walk, tattle, curtsy, cry, scold, and to mimic all manner of effeminacy."[54] The author closed with a lengthy poem that expanded on the mollies' manifold perversions, compared them unfavorably to horses, cattle, and pigs, and concluded with an explication of the unnatural cast of their passions.[55] The notion that mollies possessed group characteristics was even more firmly established later in the century, when one broadside author and anonymous poet expanded on their deficient masculinity:

> Press ye sailors, persist, come ye soldiers, insist
> By land or by sea make 'em fight,
> And then let France and Spain call their men home again,
> And send out their wives to be right.[56]

Even contemporary historians were not immune to taking swipes at those suspected or accused of homoerotic preferences. Although Thomas Gordon, a widely read political commentator, had once written a book on Lord Chancellor Francis Bacon and another on the Catiline conspiracy, he did not concentrate on his subjects' predilections for sodomy. The profoundly negative treatment of Bacon used his early seventeenth-century bribery conviction as a metaphor for government corruption in the eighteenth-century collapse of the South Sea bubble. In that context Gordon had no need to examine the Lord Chancellor's preference for male sexual partners.[57] He chose to do it, perhaps, to add a modicum of sexual interest to his narrative hoping to attract a wider audience of readers. In similar fashion, Gordon did not focus on sexuality in his popular account of the Catiline conspirators, nor did he take the opportunity to name Italy as the nursery of exclusively-male debauchery.[58] He alleged that "all the vices of Asia were improved at Rome" but did not suggest they were being exported to England. Greed drove most of Catilinean plotters, according to Gordon. They embezzled, manipulated prices, sold justice to the highest bidder, bribed public officials, and sought to poison "the state with a general taint of debauchery." His book on the conspiracy was wildly popular, going through as many as ten editions or printings in both London and Dublin during the early 1720s. As in the account of Bacon's evil doings, he added sexual specificity as a gratuitous gesture. Only the leader of the conspirators was a notorious sodomite, according to Gordon. Nothing in Catiline's appearance suggested effeminacy, even though feminiinity was being more and more associated with homoerotic activity by the time the account of the conspiracy appeared. He was described as fat, homely, and with "a fixed and settled sourness in his face which made an impression upon the beholders at first sight much to his disadvantage."[59] Despite the lack of vanity and mincing affectations, no doubt existed about his erotic tastes:

> He married several times, but chiefly as people suspected, for the convenience of strengthening himself by alliances with great men rather than out of any affection for the ladies ... . Tis certain, however odd and unnatural his lewdness was, (yet it was a notorious practice among some great men of that age) and some of his Ganymedes were pampered and supported at a high rate at his expense, and this profuseness, excepting only in briberies, was the kind in which he most indulged himself.[60]

While Gordon's treatment of sodomy constituted no more than a negative aside within his larger themes and purposes, another historical writer, the anonymous author of *Sodom's Catastrophe: A Poem* concentrated his examination on the biblical city. Sin and general excess were denounced in the eighty-plus-page, one shilling, stitched epic rather than particular politicians or events, but contemporary perceptions intruded from line to line. The poetry draws substantially from Old Testament accounts to undergird much of the story it tells, and a virulent anti-Popish bias occasionally surfaces. Although the account of Sodom's sins and destruction in Genesis 19 contains no descriptions of unmasculine, fawning, or affected males, femininity and an absence of military spirit are some of the evils ascribed to the city's residents by the poet:

> These drones who squander all their time away,
> In careless negligence or wanton play,
> Effeminate themselves with soft delights,
> Or feast their own voracious appetites.
> Will these impaired sots pretend to fight,
> Who spend the volvous [*sic*] terms of day and night

> In riot and excess, the sure decay
> of martial vigor lets no longer stay.[61]

Even epistolary anthologies managed to disparage effete, effeminate mollies. In a one-shilling pamphlet containing a series of letters exchanged between an anonymous nobleman and his putative male lover, the editor described their connection as of an "odious and criminal a nature," adding along with virtually every true-blooded English writer that it was an imported vice, likely from the Mediterranean, "a sin which is not familiar to our northern climate."[62] Another one-shilling diatribe dating from 1732 railed against an expansive catalog of "the most flagrant enormities" ranging from atheism through stock-jobbing schemes and on to whoring. Not surprisingly, sodomy appeared along with incest and rape in a cobbled-together paragraph denouncing not only sexual deviation but profanation of the Lord's day, gaming, and the indifference of civil magistrates to such offenses.[63]

Clerics of the Church of England, the church to which a preponderant majority of the Royal Navy's Officers belonged, rarely dealt with homoeroticism. They preferred to castigate sinners guilty of more ordinary transgressions like pride, everyday lust, covetousness, anger, gluttony, envy, sloth, and occasional Romanism. Josiah Woodward's sermon preached before the Lord Mayor and aldermen of London at Guildhall Chapel in 1697, printed that year and reprinted in 1700, told how "Sodom's vices [were] destructive to other cities and states." The list of sins practiced by the residents of the doomed city was taken from Ezekiel 16:49: "pride, fulness of bread, and abundance of idleness ... neither did she strengthen the hand of the poor and needy." Since a central purpose of the sermon was to persuade the city's rulers of the need for public workhouses, the preacher purposefully dwelled on "idleness," explaining that it nurtured the biblically condemned vices of wantonness and baseness. Then, responding to a more contemporary concern, he added "effeminacy" to the results of idleness.[64] Not until page seventeen in the twenty-two-page pamphlet did Woodward mention the verse in Ezekiel dealing with "abominations," which he equated with the "uncleanness" that "was notoriously visible in Sodom's streets." Lest the mayor or aldermen misunderstand, he made it obvious that "uncleanness" meant "carnal transgression," not the wastes and refuse accumulated in the paths or thoroughfares of either Sodom or London:

> So that if the sin of uncleanness be but obscurely represented in the text, it was notoriously visible in Sodom's streets, and alas, in ours,

> too; with this shameful difference on our part, that whereas the Sodomites deferred the prosecution of their lusts till the evening, hoping to veil their unseemly sin by the black curtains of the night, with us, alas, it is prosecuted in the noon-day and in the thickest concourse.[65]

When John Wesley neared the latitude of Sodom in a 1756 sermon half a century later, he did not catalog or denounce proscribed penetrations with vague biblical terminology. He only suggested that monumental wickedness brought down the wrath of God on Lisbon and several Mediterranean cities through the great earthquake of 1755. "The whole city of Catania in Sicily and every inhabitant of it perished together," he proclaimed, "Nothing but heaps of ashes and cinders show where it stood. Not so much as one Lot escaped out of Sodom!"[66]

While an assortment of clerics, writers, dramatists, humorists, lawyers, poets, and societies for moral uplift raged against England's mollies, and popular literature gleefully chronicled their arrests, trials, convictions, and punishments, pederasty remained one aspect of sodomy that went largely unremarked beyond the occasional mention of a Ganymede or a youthful partner. Only Sir Edward Coke treated the topic, but he wrote in the sixteenth century, and only touched on it in a peripheral way. Although Italians bore the primary responsibility for exporting sodomy to England, he claimed, they were not responsible for all of the permutations that had been foisted upon the land. The Greeks were almost as culpable, he claimed, having added their peculiar twist to the imported Mediterranean corruption. "Pederastes" is a Greek word, "*amator puerorum*," wrote the great scholar, and it meant buggery with boys.[67] Coke did not pursue the legal aspects of men engaging boys in sexual conduct much further than his comment on geographical roots of such practices, but at the time he wrote English jurisprudence already contained provisions dealing with transgenerational sex. Enactments proscribing relations with juveniles, like those against sodomy and buggery, dated from the reigns of the Tudors. An Elizabethan statute of 1575 defined sexual intercourse with girls under ten years of age as rape, since they were deemed too young to consent. There were no specific provisions against the rape of boys, but jurists agreed that if one of two persons accused of buggery was under fourteen years and another past that age, only the elder committed a felony.[68] Very few examples exist of prosecutions on land from which to draw generalizations or principles about the operation of English law on the subject. A Somerset case indicates that an adult having sexual relations with any child was deplored, but it dates from 1826, when attitudes and practices had already diverged in some respects from the standards of fifty or one hundred years earlier. As a rule, pubescent boys who served as sex partners for adult males were thought to be guilty or at least partially complicit in the deed, even though in every surviving case record they served as receptors rather than insertors. Neither do these transgenerational sexual engagements exhibit any defined pattern in their resolution. Most often charges were preferred by victims, often adolescents of lower social and economic status than the men they accused. Sometimes the courts believed them, other times they appear to have been less credible. William Dillon Shepherd died on Gallows Hill for sodomizing a boy in 1762. Five years later another man about to be hanged on the word of a thirteen-year-old apprentice gained a reprieve when the boy and his mother declared they had wrongly testified. Richard Manning spent only an hour in the pillory, a year in jail, and received a one shilling fine in 1752 for the same crime. In a 1743 case, both man and boy were pilloried for an hour and sentenced to six months in jail. The next year an insertor and a receptor each received only whippings for their buggery. It appears, however, that testimony from those hailing from the same middling social levels as the jurors would more likely be believed than the apprentices, errand boys, and juvenile dross that lodged complaints. Artillery lieutenant Robert Jones was convicted of sodomizing a thirteen-year-old boy in 1761, and pardoned in 1777. Michael Levi, a Jew and a dandy, was convicted for raping a boy, condemned to death, and pardoned, all in 1751.[69]

In the navy, officers appointed to courts martial understood that although regulations contained no provisions relating to the age of sodomites, those under fourteen could not be brought to trial for the crime even though they might have been complicit. Rape was another matter. Although no boys under ten years of age appeared in any shipboard prosecutions (and the statute on child rape applied only to female children in any case), men sitting in judgment agonized more over whether buggered boys told the truth in their accusation and testimony than they did over the possibility that sex was forced upon them.

Commissioned officers of the Royal Navy were for the most part men of middling to upper-class roots, literate, well educated in terms of their professional attainments and skills, socially adept, often sophisticated, and integrated with the cultural and intellectual context that nurtured their class. They occupied the same professional strata in some respects as lawyers, schoolmasters, clerics, physicians, apothecaries, and surveyors, and in all likelihood their literary preferences went in tandem with the tastes and reading habits of men of similar social status who lived and worked ashore. Even junior officers who served long years at sea absorbed greater and greater segments of urban civil culture as they rose in rank to become captains and admirals. There were numerous among them whose careers paths, although less illustrious, paralleled that of Admiral Sir George Cockburn. In his first years as an officer, his friends and associates were his brother officers. At age thirty, he had spent sixteen years at sea with only one long leave in that period. Later, as he rose in rank, he acquired a house in London's Cavendish Square, entered parliament, dined frequently at the Carlton Club, and had a wide circle of cultured and influential friends outside the navy.[70] Little is known of what transpired among commissioned officers at sea when not engaged in shipboard duties. Certainly they talked much among themselves throughout the long months and years afloat. A considerable proportion of their conversation surely dealt with their work, sailing the ship, maintaining her, managing the crew, navigation, and the like. Of their conversation on other matters virtually nothing survives. Their idle chatter over meals or casual talk on the quarterdeck when their ships glided smoothly over calm seas or were safely at their moorings is entirely lost.[71] In like fashion, while much is available on contemporary books relating to naval topics with which they were undoubtedly familiar, it is difficult to know of their recreational reading habits. Space on board warships was limited for all but those holding the highest ranks. Most had little room to stow substantial numbers of books for whiling away idle hours. The non-nautical literature officers brought with them to sea probably circulated within their ranks over the duration of long voyages, giving each man an opportunity to sample the tastes of his colleagues and to some extent homogenizing their reading experiences, but the titles of the books for the most part remain a mystery. One naval officer told of perusing Sir Walter Scott's *Rob Roy* and suggested that numerous other officers were familiar with Captain Frederick Marryat's sea classic, *Peter Simple*, but beyond such fragments, there is almost no information.[72]

Access to the broad range of printed material presented no difficulty for commissioned officers while ashore. The middling levels of society from which they were drawn provided the base of support for the growth of subscription and circulating libraries and the burgeoning newspaper and book trades.[73] Although there is no indication in the fragmentary records of English libraries and reading clubs that they had noticeable numbers of admirals, captains, commanders, or lieutenants on their rolls, the rich and diverse book market in London served officers posted in the capital and at naval installations in the Thames valley from the Tower, past Greenwich, and down the river to the sprawling dockyard at Sheerness. The huge naval installations at Plymouth and Portsmouth, too, were served by numerous local booksellers. By mid-century, in fact, books could be obtained without difficulty in all but the tiniest villages and hamlets in England.[74] Neither did commissioned officers have difficulty affording their reading. Naval pay varied over the eighteenth century and was often in arrears, but it was more than adequate to support a modest reading habit, although not a gambling addiction. The captain of a first rate, the largest of warships, drew approximately twenty shillings per day while the lieutenant of a third or fourth rate received a quarter of that amount. Officers were easily able to purchase items from the entire range of available reading material except for the most sumptuous editions in the most extravagant of price ranges.[75] Before 1780 book prices were reasonably constant. Quartos and folios sold for between ten and twelve shillings, octavos at about half those prices, and duodecimo volumes brought between two and three shillings. The same book often appeared in a variety of price ranges, depending on the quality of paper, manner of binding, and guilt embellishments. Pirated editions of popular works printed in Ireland and Scotland also lowered expenses for frugal readers by about half, and the truly impecunious could buy their books a few sheets at a time over a period of weeks or months. Abridged chapbook versions of popular works like *Clarissa*, *Pamela*, *Reynard the Fox*, *Henry Fielding*, and *Tom Jones* could be had for a shilling. The two pence commonly charged for borrowing a library book was only slightly more than one of the penny broadsides that were widely available in larger towns and cities.[76]

Although there were only a few works devoted entirely to sodomy available in eighteenth-century Britain, discussions of the subject appeared in a wide variety of literary forms ranging from crime anthologies to sermons. How many of any of these varied materials naval officers read, and how often they mentioned the apparently growing numbers of mollies to one another in conversation defies any attempt to derive an estimate. There exists neither anecdotal nor quantitative information on the subject. Still, naval officers undoubtedly read many of the same works read by men of equivalent class, status, and occupation on shore, and they, too, ingested the attitudes toward sodomy and the concurrent fears it generated. No matter the month, the year, the decade, or the type of publication – single sheet, pamphlet, play, book, treatise, or newspaper – the sentiments almost always reflected ill on the all-male sexual practices that seemed to be spreading at the speed of a fast-moving squall.[77] Most important in all of this, however, is neither the quantity nor the variety of officers' encounters with homoeroticism in the written word. The central feature of their literary experiences for a study of naval courts martial is what they retained from their reading and what they later brought to the trials of men accused of violating the *Articles of War*. The manner in which they evaluated their reading and the constraints it placed upon them as members of what Stanley Fish identifies as "interpretive communities" with shared bases of agreement provides a key to the operations of courts martial throughout the age of Nelson and afterward.[78] Undoubtedly, there existed a wide range of literary tastes and preferences among British naval officers in an age where the amount, variety, and format of available reading materials expanded exponentially almost by the decade. Yet even for the dullest among them or those with no more than a modicum of aesthetic sensitivity or social sophistication there was one written work familiar to every member of their seaborne interpretive community. Whatever their particular Christian inclinations, the Bible bound them together in a broadly circumscribed spiritual sodality sharing common values and beliefs. This single volume placed before them incontrovertible proof of that which their entire social and cultural experience affirmed. Sodomy was a bad business. Some or even many naval officers may have found a lack of precision in the biblical story of Sodom's destruction. The Book of Genesis fails to denominate the city's sins as anal intercourse, homoeroticism, or bestiality. If any required clarification beyond that point, they could find it elsewhere in Scripture. According to Leviticus, "If a man also lie with mankind, as he lieth with a woman, both of them have committed an abomination: they shall surely be put to death; their blood *shall be* upon them."[79] For any not yet sure of the divine message, God's word appeared entirely without ambiguity in the New Testament. Paul made it plain enough in his epistle to the Romans that God gave up to "vile affections" men who "leaving the natural use of the woman, burned in their lust one toward another; men with men working that which is unseemly, and receiving in themselves that recompense of their error which was meet."[80] Still, for officers and men of the eighteenth-century Royal Navy, the crime of sodomy was not the failure to extend hospitality, as indicated in Genesis, nor was it any other of a number of lapses that might be inferred from the Bible. It was the specific sex act enumerated in the twenty-ninth of the *Articles of War*.

2
Regulating Sodomy in the Pre-Nelson Navy

England's Commonwealth government produced the first modern code for regulating the navy. The *Laws of War and Ordinances of the Sea*, enacted in 1652, contained thirty-nine articles governing all aspects of shipboard conduct deemed important by members of parliament. As might be expected in a time when Englishmen were firmly committed to expanding seaborne trade and deeply concerned over the threats posed by commercial rivals, particularly the Dutch, the *Laws of War* complemented earlier Navigation Acts and other maritime regulations adopted to enhance the nation's economic strength. Pressing mercantile concerns were manifest in provisions of the *Laws of War* that governed passports, bills of lading, prize money, piracy, privateering, pillage, and convoying of merchant ships. A good many of the items, over a dozen, were aimed at maintaining good order on board ship. There was to be no quarreling, theft, or embezzlement of the navy's property. Murder was proscribed along with threatening admirals. At least two of the provisions inadvertently testified to the poor conditions of service in the Commonwealth fleet. One explained that having pay in arrears was not an acceptable reason for refusing to fight, and the other prohibited seditious commentary about the quality of the food. Ten regulations dealt with treasonable activities, spying, sedition, desertion, encouraging others to desert, and aiding the enemy. Several more governed conduct during combat at sea. The punishment most often prescribed for violations of the *Laws* was death, although it could be mitigated by courts of admiralty or councils of war, both of which had extensive powers in capital and non-capital cases. The Commonwealth was concerned with the spiritual well-being of its officers and men as well as with temporal matters. The opening article prohibited profaneness and irreligion, enjoined crewmen to prayer and, not surprising for an enactment from a Puritan parliament, mandated regular preaching and ordered that the Lord's day be rigorously observed.

Courts martial were mentioned only twice in the *Laws of War*, both times in connection with minor violations. They had power to levy fines or imprison anyone who spoke menacing words or made objectionable signs or gestures during trials. They could also, at their discretion, punish officers or seamen who failed to find or apprehend an assortment of malefactors. One of the laws cataloged proscribed immoral behaviors such as "unlawful and rash oaths, cursings, execrations, drunkenness, uncleanness, and other scandalous acts." The councils of war punished breaches of the moral code as they saw fit. There was no compulsory or suggested death penalty for such transgressions, as was the case with most of the other articles.[1]

The restoration of the monarchy in 1660 negated legislation passed during the Commonwealth and Protectorate. Those laws adopted during the decade of Puritan dominance and that were adjudged useful had to be re-enacted by the newly installed parliament. England's commercial rivalries and overseas economic interests changed little with the ascension of Charles II, and earlier measures dealing with seaborne trade, the merchant fleet, imports and exports, ships' crews, tariffs, and the like were reaffirmed with only minor alterations. In like manner, the 1652 *Laws of War and Ordinances of the Sea* were slightly revised and then renewed under the title *An Act for the Establishing Articles and Orders for the Regulating and Better Government of His Majesty's Navies, Ships of War and Forces by Sea*. The "King's most Excellent Majesty" and the Church of England of necessity replaced references to the Commonwealth in the text, and the number of articles decreased from thirty-nine to thirty-five, largely the result of combining several of the provisions in the original 1652 legislation. The councils of war disappeared from the new document, but the functions of courts martial were greatly expanded. They were empowered to determine punishments in over a dozen of the revised articles. Specifications were included for constituting courts martial, staffing them, and denominating the bounds of their authority.[2] Martial law had been invoked occasionally in times of emergency during the reigns of Mary, Elizabeth, and Charles I, but the thirty-five naval regulations of 1661 provided for their regular and systematic employment. Over the next century, occasional complaints were lodged challenging the legality of such courts in times of peace, but they were largely ignored. Courts martial became a standard method of administering justice in the navy after 1660, and those writing in their defense, if not more persuasive than those who disparaged them, emerged victorious even though their victory bore little or no relationship to the merits of their arguments.[3]

The most startling alteration amid the tinkering, rewording, and revising that distinguished the Restoration *Act for the Establishing Articles and Orders for ... Ships of War and Forces by Sea* from its 1652 prototype came in its revised thirty-second article. It read, "If any person or persons in or belonging to the fleet shall commit the unnatural and detestable sin of buggery or sodomy with man or beast he shall be punished with death without mercy." The sentence made sodomy at sea a capital crime, as it had been on land since the time of Henry VIII. There were at least half a dozen additional measures dealing with discipline added to the *Articles and Orders* during the reigns of Charles II, William and Mary, Anne, George I and George II, but it was not until 1749 that parliament undertook a substantial overhaul of the document. While the updated version introduced significant modifications in the governance of the navy, the provisions concerning all moral lapses, including sodomy and buggery, remained largely unaltered. The only change being to shift the article prohibiting sodomy and buggery from number thirty-two to number twenty-nine. This latest version of naval regulations, officially titled *The Articles of War of 1749*, remained in force with only slight amendments until 1866.[4]

The new *Articles* contained several general categories. The first consisted of instructions to officers for conducting the affairs of the navy, admonishing them to hold regular divine services and aggressively pursue the enemy. It also declaimed on the nature of treason, and added a dozen or more pronouncements relevant to naval operations. The remaining classifications related to various crimes against king and country, acts against individuals such as theft and murder, and offenses against morality. Cursing, execrations, drunkenness, uncleanness, and scandalous actions remained proscribed under the second article. Buggery and sodomy in the 1749 version remained capital offenses.[5] The *Articles of War* made no distinction between the terms "sodomy" and "buggery," regarding them as synonymous, as was the case on land over the preceding centuries. The crime was defined in practice although not in the twenty-ninth article's text as anal intercourse, but whether the navy considered the act involving only males as serious as the same act involving a male and a female cannot be discerned. If anal intercourse took place with the prostitutes who frequently visited warships when they were at anchor or in port, it was neither noted nor prosecuted. Bestiality was also included under the twenty-ninth article. In the only such case in Admiralty records, John Blake, a marine of HMS *Rippon*, received a death sentence in 1758 for "buggery upon the body of a she-goat." No indication survives on whether Blake entered her vaginally or anally, but it appears from the record of his case that he faced a court martial only for having sex with the goat, not because of his use of a proscribed orifice. In any case, the marine did not hang for his transgression. Only the goat paid with her life. At the captain's order, her throat was cut and she was pitched over the side of the ship within an hour after the discovery of the crime. A Mr. Ozanne, the chaplain of HMS *Princess Royal*, testified that Blake "who was then under his care was the most illiterate, ignorant, stupid young fellow that he ever saw, being unfortunately deprived of all natural capacity and next to an idiot, and that he therefore thought him a very great object of pity and compassion." The matter was referred to the king, who in due course extended his mercy. Blake was released from confinement and set at liberty.[6]

Even though the prohibition of sodomy had been moved from number thirty-two to number twenty-nine in the *Articles of War*, the wording remained largely unaltered. It read, much as before, "If any person in the fleet shall commit the unnatural and detestable sin of buggery and sodomy with man or beast, he shall be punished with death by the sentence of a court martial." The distinctions between earlier texts and the version enacted under George II were that the mandatory death sentence could be handed down only by a court martial and the phrase "without mercy" disappeared.[7] The article contained no mention of the age of any of the persons involved in acts of sodomy, nor did it mention rape. The regular reading of the *Articles* to ships crews was required by naval regulations not only to inform men of forbidden behaviors, but to make them fully aware of the consequences of any transgressions. As Charles McPherson, a sailor on board the seventy-four-gun HMS *Genoa*, remembered it, "The commander read the articles of war while we all stood, hat in hand, to hear the dreadful penalties we had bound ourselves under if we broke any of the prescribed laws."[8]

The harsh penalty for sodomy reflected not only provisions of the nation's statutes, but the widely-held notion that offenses against God could severely impede the Royal Navy's ability to defend the nation. Divine favor would naturally accrue to the fleet most closely cleaving to His commandments. The truth of this was never in doubt among officers or sailors. Josiah Woodward was only one of the authors who emphasized how Christianity formed a constituent part of the formula for victory at sea. Over twenty editions of his pamphlet entitled *The Seaman's Monitor, or Advice to Seafaring Men* were distributed throughout the navy over the course of the eighteenth and early nineteenth centuries.

Ignoring Holy Writ not only dishonored the individual, he assured his readers, it imperiled Britain and her distant possessions.[9]

There is no indication that the Restoration prohibition against sodomy reflected a response to homoeroticism run rampant in the navy. No sodomites were prosecuted under it during the final forty years of the seventeenth century, or at least no records of such prosecutions survive. Charles II and his ill-starred successor James II were long in their graves by 1706 – the first time there is evidence that a man of the Royal Navy stood trial for buggery.

I

Officers were classified under three separate headings in the eighteenth-century navy: commissioned officers, warrant officers, and petty officers. There is little confusion or ambiguity identifying the first group. Commissioned officers included admirals, captains, commanders, lieutenants, and officers of marines. All of them held their commissions from the Admiralty, which was superintended by the Lord High Admiral and his deputies, known collectively as the Lords Commissioners of the Admiralty.[10] Admirals and captains occupied commodious cabins by shipboard standards. Lieutenants generally berthed in the wardroom, an area occupying the aft portion of the main deck and usually partitioned off from it by a temporary bulkhead. Down each side of the wardroom and between the guns, cabins were provided to lieutenants. The partitions were of wood until 1757 when the Admiralty ordered they be made of canvas so that they could be quickly triced up when clearing the decks for action. The first lieutenant traditionally occupied the aftermost cabin on the port side. A door in the wardroom led to the quarter galleries where the officers' toilets were situated. The cabins were scarcely large enough to hold their occupants, a sea chest, a cot or bedframe suspended from the beams, and a few personal belongings,[11] but they did have privacy, a benefit increasingly prized by the middling and upper classes of the age.[12]

The situation of warrant officers, or standing officers as they were regularly called, was not as precisely defined as that of their commissioned superiors in part because status of some types of standing officers shifted over the decades. At various times during the period between 1700 and 1850, warranted men on board ships of the Royal Navy included boatswains, masters, gunners, carpenters, sailmakers, surgeons, pursers, chaplains, schoolmasters, and cooks. While the distinctions of rank and precedence separating commissioned officers from one another were sharp and clear, among warrant officers such matters were sometimes ill-defined. Still, a marked division existed between the seafarer warrant officers, the boatswains, masters, gunners, and carpenters who helped sail and fight the ship, and those holding warrants for what were essentially civilian occupations practiced at sea. This latter, subordinate class included surgeons, pursers, chaplains and schoolmasters. Complicating matters were the variations in where standing officers berthed on board ship and where they messed. Their perquisites, especially for those on the lower end of the scale varied over the decades and often differed from ship to ship.[13]

Seafarer warrant officers usually began their naval careers as boys, slowly learning their skills, then earning promotions as they excelled at their application. Generally speaking, they earned their warrants by long years of exemplary service, although securing positions on the most desirable ships required at least a measure of political influence on some level. Once appointed, whether to plum posts or not, warrant officers occupied exceedingly comfortable niches within the service. They received decent pay and rations, one-eighth of any prize money to divide among them, directed their own departments, were well positioned to start their sons off on careers leading toward naval commissions, and were more secure in their appointments than the lieutenants, commanders, captains, and admirals who outranked them. Even being invalidated for incompetence did not preclude a later shipboard assignment. Commissioned officers were often put on half pay for years or even decades when they were not serving on board ships but warrant holders experienced no such inconvenience. They were usually assigned to their ships at the time when they were ordered built and they remained for the most part with the same ships throughout their careers. The only situations that ended their postings was when their ships were lost or they obtained transfers to other more desirable ships. When vessels were undergoing dockyard refits or repair or were laid up in ordinary, their standing officers stayed on board to supervise maintenance, and all the while drew full pay. Sometimes wives and families lived with them when their ship was in port or dockyard for extended periods. Occasionally, superannuated standing officers were borne on the books of very old or even unserviceable ships or ships not-yet-built to secure their pensions.[14]

Warrant officers received their appointments from the Navy Board, an organization subordinate to the Admiralty, but less politically sensitive. Its staff consisted of career bureaucrats often with far more experience than high ranking officers of the Admiralty. Although warranted members of ships' companies followed all commissioned officers in precedence, they shared with them a common situation. The men of both groups, commissioned and warranted, were permanent members of the navy, unlike petty officers and sailors who signed on for specific cruises and were paid off and released when their ship returned to port. Standing officers and senior admirals were in fact some of the oldest men in the service. Along with being permanently on the navy pay list, standing officers shared another enviable situation with their commissioned superiors. They had private quarters on board ship.[15]

Vessels from the smallest sloops, bomb ketches, and sixth rates up to the largest ships of the line carried dozens of petty officers, ranging from the armorer and his mates to an assortment of yeomen, and including among them the master at arms, the quartermaster, and the captains of the tops. Among the petty officers were a bevy of mates assigned to the boatswain, gunner, sailmaker, carpenter, and to other departments or occupational specialties.[16]

Immediately below the petty officers stood the ordinary sailors of the Royal Navy. The "ratings," or "the people," comprised slightly over half of any crew. The proportion varied somewhat depending on the size of the ship. In general, they were ranked and paid according to their experience. Those new to the navy, classified as landsmen, were at the base of the status ladder. A year or so of service allowed a man to be taken on as ordinary seaman, and those with a voyage or two behind them customarily signed on as able seamen.

Large numbers of boys also served in the Royal Navy. No accurate approximation of the total number exists, but at least 31,000 were placed with the fleet between the beginning of the Seven Years War in 1756 and the final defeat of Napoleon in 1815. Thirteen years was set as the minimum age to serve on board His Majesty's ships according to the navy's *Regulations and Instructions Relating to His Majesty's Service at Sea*, but an exception was made for the sons of officers who could be at sea when as young as eleven. Some captains ignored the regulations entirely and made no objection to boys as young as six or eight years old sailing with them. Occasionally, commanders on some stations ordered the ages of crewmen recorded in muster books. Admiral Edward Vernon did so in 1740, but his purpose was to aid in locating deserters rather than to deter the employment of underage lads. Boys in the navy ceased to be boys and became men at approximately eighteen years of age. The percentage of youngsters among crews varied from ship to ship, but generally constituted about eight or ten of every one hundred souls in any crew. Every officer had at least one boy to assist him, boatswains, gunners, and carpenters often rated two, and each captain was authorized four boys per one hundred of his ship's complement. Boys were never subject to impressment, and throughout most of the eighteenth century they were classified as "volunteers." Youngsters were not simply a convenience to the navy. They were essential to manning the king's ships not only for the duties they performed but because when they became adults many of them remained in the service.[17]

Navy lads came from a number of sources. In addition to the genuine volunteers and those driven into the service by hunger, want of shelter, or other privations, there were waifs, orphans, juvenile criminals, troublemakers, and ne'er-do-wells sent to sea by a variety of local officials, most often in port towns, where the service provided a convenient repository for refractory male children. Another source was the Marine Society, a philanthropical organization founded in 1756 by Jonas Hanway, the umbrella pioneer. Hanaway and his friend, Bow Street magistrate Sir John Fielding, saw dual utility in the organization. It could mitigate the manning needs of the navy and at the same time rid London of at least some of the undesirables roaming the city's streets. The Society fed and clothed the boys it took in, sheltered them for periods ranging from a few days to a few weeks, provided them a modicum of education, then sent them out on merchant ships or placed them in the navy. Unlike so many eighteenth-century humanitarian schemes that foundered for a host of reasons, the Marine Society succeeded admirably. The organizers originally intended to bring 10,000 boys into the service. By the end of the Seven Years War they had sponsored 10,625, a huge majority of whom continued their maritime careers in the merchant service when peace returned. Boy volunteers assigned to warships became either "apprentices" or "servants" before the term "boy" officially replaced both titles in 1794. Apprentices at sea were like apprentices ashore. They had legal articles binding them to naval service, usually for a period of five years, and the navy was obligated to teach them an appropriate trade. "Servants" had no articles of apprenticeship, and usually attended the personal needs of officers, most often standing officers. Youths also came on board naval vessels in the capacity of "young gentlemen." They hailed from officer families or families having some degree of political influence. They began as servants to commissioned officers, but it was understood in most cases that they and their parents expected them eventually to be commissioned when they had gained sufficient experience. Boys' wages were paid to their shipboard masters until 1794, when regulations changed to allow them to keep their earnings.[18]

II

Sodomy prosecutions in the navy began long before Horatio Nelson first set foot on the deck of a warship. Two of the earliest cases involved officers, James Ball and John Coise, who were brought to trial for buggering boys. Ball, a petty officer, ran afoul of the prohibition against sodomy in 1706. The record of his trial is typical in most respects of the documents preserving all of the naval courts martial for sexual offenses held during the first decade of the eighteenth century. It runs a mere sixteen hundred words spread out over ten manuscript pages. The penman who produced the document used generous margins and an ordinary-sized script, with no evidence of crabbing or compressing in any way to save paper. Much of the space on the pages is taken up with lists of the officers who sat in judgment. Questions asked by the court, testimony, cross-examination, attempts to establish innocence, and mitigating circumstances are recorded only in the most cursory fashion. The ideas, opinions, beliefs, frustrations, and the scores of emotions characteristic of later trial transcripts are absent from these earliest records.

As a petty officer holding the post of ship's quartermaster, James Ball was a man with a measure of authority and a corresponding amount of privilege. Although petty officers messed with ratings and slept with them as well, they could often hang their hammocks along the sides of the ship, which gave them more space than ordinary crewmembers, whose hammocks were slung fourteen inches apart, allowing each man twenty-eight inches of space since watches alternated. It would have been unusual for a petty officer to have the luxury of extra space to hang a cot rather than a hammock though not impossible. In any case, whatever the general pattern in the navy for petty officers' sleeping arrangements, Ball had his own cabin where, away from the prying eyes of fellow crew members, and "betwixt the hours of 9 and 10 o'clock of the night" he was accused of committing the act which brought him before a court martial.[19]

> James Ball obliged him [Jones] to lie with him in his cabin and ... the said James Ball thrust his finger into his arse which he said hurt him very much but notwithstanding he afterwards forced him and put his cock in his arse. Mr. Rook [the lieutenant present at the surgeon's examination] then asked him what he did further, the boy answered he wriggled about and pissed in his arse.[20]

When Ball had the opportunity to defend himself, he first denied the charge, then claimed he thought the boy was a hermaphrodite. Later said he was drunk at the time he committed the act, and concluded by stating that one of the witnesses against him testified out of malice. None of the defenses worked. The defendant was convicted and sentenced to hang.[21]

Ball's sex partner, thirteen-year-old Walter Jones was protected by his youth against charges arising from any suspicion he was complicit in his own buggering. Although naval regulations contained no specifications dealing with the ages of those involved in buggery, English law established that those who were thirteen years or younger were ineligible to be felons, and courts martial never challenged the immunity conferred on boys by age.[22] Only shipboard lads attaining the age of fourteen were "equally liable to suffer as a person of the full age of twenty-one."[23]

Even if young Walter Jones had been a year older, however, it is unlikely he would have been condemned since testimony made it obvious that James Ball had raped him rather than seduced him into sodomy:

> It having appeared to the court by the course of the evidence that the said James Ball did by threatening and by force oblige the said boy to submit to this his wicked action. The court is of opinion that the said Walter Jones was not consenting to the said act of buggery committed upon him, and therefore the court does acquit the said Walter Jones from this charge.[24]

In this form or in others similar to it, such proceedings followed a distinct pattern over the decades. Officers customarily released boys and young men up to seventeen years of age who had been forced into sexual relations by older, higher-ranking, stronger men.

Three years after the execution of James Ball in 1706, Boatswain John Coise of HMS *Looe* became the first warrant officer known to be tried for sodomy. On board ship, boatswains were men to be reckoned with. Ned Ward's 1707 overdrawn caricature contained in his half-shilling pamphlet, *Wooden World*, gives some impression of their way of doing business at sea:

> He's a damned thundering fellow, that's certain, and oft gives the purser a fair pretext for his bad beer, alleging that the boatswain sours it with his bellowing.
>
> He's as noisy about trifles as the lieutenant, and it much better becomes him. He shall roar forth death and destruction about the hoisting of a water cask, and makes as much clamor about the dropping of a dog's turd as the falling of a topmast.

> He may boast with Caesar that he can call every man by his name, for he dignifies all his umbras with the title of dog, rogue, or rascal; and they will answer to it more readily than if he gave them more Christian epithets.
>
> He has a thousand pretty phrases and expressions picked up at Billingsgate and elsewhere, which he never sends abroad without bedecking them with all the embroidered oaths and curses that can be had for love or money.[25]

Coise was accused of breaching the twenty-ninth article of war by John Davis, a boy of the ship.[26] As a boatswain and a senior member of the crew, Coise probably found it easy to arrange a shipboard sexual encounter. In all likelihood he had his own cabin located near the forecastle, close by the cabin of the carpenter, and near the galley, where the stove kept him warm in winter and the gun ports were located far enough above the water line so they could often be left open in the summer to admit light and fresh air. His cabin was most probably convenient to the roundhouses, the enclosures that offered a measure of privacy to warrant officers and sometimes petty officers exercising their bodily functions. The nearness may have been particularly appreciated by Coise, who, because of the seniority usually required to become a boatswain, was probably far older than most of the sailors who made up the *Looe*'s crew.[27]

There is no judging from the court martial record whether Boatswain Coise's professional demeanor squares with Ward's description. Only eighteen lines in the two-page record deal with the substance of the case, hardly enough to round out the character of the accused. What is clearly indicated by the record is that surgeons from three of Her Majesty's ships, *Advice*, *Looe*, and *Pool* all examined the boy, and they concurred that there were no symptoms of sodomy. The examiners could find none of the fissures or cristæ near the verge of the anus that one of the foremost medical tomes of the period attributed to sodomy. The surgeons pronounced John Davis "unbuggered," and the charge was dropped.[28] Though the testimony of the medical men saved him from the noose, the boatswain did not leave the court martial with his reputation or innocence secured. Even though acquitted of violating the article prohibiting sodomy, the court convicted him of violating article number thirty-three, "All other faults, misdemeanors and disorders committed at sea not mentioned in this act shall be punished according to the laws and customs in such cases used at sea." The trial record is not specific on what transpired. It contains only the cryptic note, "Said boatswain cannot clear himself of some indecent actions with the said Davis." Coise was sacked from his job as boatswain, and declared "not fit to be any more employed in her Majesty's service." The record contains no mention of any punishment adjudicated against the boy Davis for levying a charge that was not proved or for engaging in whatever indecent behavior it was that turned the court against Coise.[29]

In addition to James Ball and John Coise, at least three ratings were tried for sodomy or crimes related to sexual activities during the period from 1704 to 1706. In the first court martial, at Spithead in April of 1704, John Brese a crewmen of HMS *Warspite* was accused of soliciting a twelve-year-old ship's boy, Richard Hoter, to commit sodomy. The boy deposed that he had been opportuned by Brese, but he had refused his advance. No penetration or emission took place. Since he was guilty only of indecency, a violation of the second article of war, there was no possibility of a death sentence. Brese was ordered to receive ten lashes by the side of each of the ten ships then anchored at Spithead. His punishment was to be announced at each ship by beating on a drum.[30] The two other cases of men sexually involved with boys during the period both occurred in Jamaica in May of 1706. William Hughes and young James Emmeson, both of HMS *Hector,* were discovered committing sodomy. The record contains no information on who reported them or where on board ship they were discovered. Both of the accused confessed, and the surgeon testified that the boy's anus indicated he had been entered by the man. The pair were sentenced to be hanged at either the main or fore yardarm of the *Hector*. The brief trial record does not mention James Emmeson's age, but the officers of the court martial were undoubtedly troubled by sentencing a boy to death, and passed responsibility for the hanging upward along the chain of command. They ordered "The execution of the boy to be respited for a month or further if the admiral think fit."[31] No information survives on the final disposition of the case. Later in the month, at the other trial in Jamaica, Edward Jones of HMS *Bristol* stood accused of attempting to bugger fourteen-year-old Richard Cartwright of the same ship. Since Jones was charged only with attempted buggery he could not be executed. Instead the the court sentenced him to receive seven lashes at the side of every one of the navy's ships in and around Port Royal harbor. When that portion of his punishment was complete, the order continued, he was "then to be thrown overboard and rowed ashore, his wages for the said ship to be forfeited to the use of Greenwich Hospital."[32]

A constant feature running through these early five cases, of course, is that in every one of them an adult was sexually involved one way or another with a boy. The records contain no occupational titles for Hoter, Emmeson, and Cartwright, the youths involved with ratings in the 1704–6 courts martial, but Walter Jones, the lad raped by Quartermaster James Ball, and John Davis, who accused Boatswain John Coise of buggering him, were both classified as servants. Although it is not certain that Jones was actually assigned to Ball and Davis to Coise, it is probable such was the case. The master and servant lad connection, like the adult-child linkage, is a constantly recurring feature in shipboard sodomy prosecutions over the next one hundred years. Another typical feature of these early courts martial was the introduction of expert testimony, and this, too, would become a standard practice. In the Ball and Hughes cases where defendants were convicted of sodomy, testimony of ship's surgeons helped produce the guilty verdicts, while the exculpatory word of a surgeon very likely saved Boatswain Coise from the noose. No rectal examinations were performed on boys Richard Cartwright and John Hoter because penetration was not claimed and sodomy not charged.

It is uncertain why the court martial required a trio of doctors in the trial of John Coise. It may have been that they were easily available, or perhaps the men sitting in judgment wanted multiple witnesses when it appeared there might be an acquittal. In most trials held over the years, one doctor's testimony sufficed to support a guilty verdict. It is also possible that it was merely the general lack of confidence in naval surgeons that induced the court at Coise's trial summon three doctors to give evidence. Surgeons were often disparaged in the Royal Navy during the early decades of the eighteenth century. They had been added to the fleet only a few years before Coise faced charges of sodomy and their pay and status were low. William Dillon, who rose to the rank of admiral, once wrote of an incompetent surgeon on board HMS *Defense* who was unable to amputate. He later told of another assigned to HMS *Glenmore* whose eyesight was so poor that Dillon thought him unable to do his job. A sailors' slang term for surgeon was "crocus," a shortening of "croak us" or kill us. It was not until after the 1750s and 1760s that they gained sufficient prestige to be admitted to wardrooms, and it was only in 1805, ninety-six years after John Coise's acquittal, that they finally earned official recognition as officers, were authorized their own uniforms, received tolerable pay, and acquired precedence almost equal to that of lieutenants. Although the skill level varied widely from man to man, it was their knowledge of medicine rather than their enhanced, if not lofty, status in the naval hierarchy that ultimately gained them the respect of ships crews. By the time of the Napoleonic Wars, in fact, surgeons were some of the best educated men afloat, and usually presided over departments that ranged from one to five assistants, depending on the size of the ship.[33]

III

With the end of the War of Spanish Succession, sodomy and indecency prosecutions ceased, and did not resume until the eve of the Seven Years War. Those named in a series of sexual incidents beginning in the late 1750s included two warrant officers, a midshipman, one captain, a boatswain's mate, and a seaman.

Two of the alleged miscreants belonged to the lower echelon of the warrant officer hierarchy, one a purser and the other a surgeon, but because neither ever faced trial, the surviving records on them are more fragmentary than those available for prosecutions dating from the first years of the century. Information on the purser's indiscretions survives only incidentally in a letter from Sir Edward Hawke to John Clevland, the then Secretary of the Admiralty. On 20 July 1755, he wrote from the *St. George*, anchored at the time at Spithead, to explain why he had been unable to sail as ordered. Weather caused the delay for the *St. George*, he explained, adding that the departure of HMS *Newcastle* had also been delayed. The excuse for the second ship's remaining at Spithead had no connection with the "dirty W. S. W." wind. According to her captain, "the purser of the said ship having been detected in some things not so decent to name, had run away and left her in want of necessaries." No more details survive on the identity of the vanished purser or the precise nature of his offense. A second sentence in the letter indicates that Hawke may have had an ulterior motive in making sure the absconded warrant officers' crimes were reported to higher authority. He wrote, "I appointed Mr. John Hay, my secretary, to act as purser of [the *Newcastle*], and shall be greatly obliged to their lordships if they will be so good as grant him a warrant accordingly." The purser's disappearance gave Hawke an excuse to provide a favorite with a very permanent and lucrative appointment.[34] Information on the offending medical man is even more sparse. It is contained entirely in a June 1757 note written by Admiral Thomas Broderick to Secretary Clevland. Broderick dealt with a number of topics in the note, and only incidentally forwarded a letter he received from Captain Alexander Innes of HMS *Mermaid* concerning the ship's surgeon. The letter cannot now be found, but scrawled in a non-professional hand diagonally across the corner on the back of Broderick's note is an endorsement reading: "21 June. Send a copy of Captain Innes's letter with the enclosed [2 or 3 words illegible] and direct them to dismiss the surgeon from the King's service for indecent behavior. Let him know it."[35] Why the surgeon of the *Mermaid* was dismissed from the navy rather than tried by court martial is not explained. He probably could have been charged under the second of the *Articles of War*, hailed before a court martial for "scandalous actions in derogation of God's honor and corruption of good manners," and punished "as the nature and degree of [the] offense shall deserve." Still, a measure of ambiguity in the one reference to the case hints the reason for so mild a punishment. Admiral Broderick did not know what to do in the situation, so he moved with utmost caution, passing responsibility upward. When he wrote to the Secretary of the Admiralty he explained that the letter he was forwarding from Captain Innes concerned matters "which I must beg their Lordships' directions."[36]

There is no indication in the snippets of data preserved in the cases of the *Newcastle* purser or the *Mermaid* surgeon of the status of their partners in impropriety, if indeed the purser and the surgeon had partners. While it seems likely that they were involved in some manner with fellow crew members, it is also possible that they might only have been indiscreet, solitary masturbators. Of the remaining four men accused during the period of violating articles two or twenty-nine, all did so with persons who were younger, beneath them in rank, or otherwise vulnerable. The first of these, Francis French, a "young gentleman" or midshipmen, destined for the quarterdeck, faced a court martial in February of 1756 "for sodomitical practices" with a ship's boy. The penman who drafted the written summary from the now missing trial transcript, claimed, "It would be difficult to figure a case where the charge was more completely established by a chain of irresistible evidence,"[37] and what little testimony he copied affirms his judgment:

> One night the prisoner [French] came naked to the hammock of [sixteen-year-old Henry Pomble] with a knife in his hand, and swore that if the witness would not let him enter him, or if he heard a word of it from his mouth, he would cut his throat directly. The prisoner then went into the boy's hammock and put his yard into the deponent's backside, and entered him a little way, about an inch, which hurt him very much, and the prisoner kept shoving it backwards and forwards for some little time, and then the deponent felt himself very wet, and then the prisoner went away.[38]

French repeated the act at least three more times on Pomble, and "made various attempts of a similar nature upon other young people in the ship." With evidence of this nature, it is difficult to understand why the court had difficulty judging French. A possible explanation is that although not a commissioned officer, French's rank as a midshipman indicated a sufficient measure of social prominence to save his life. In a highly unusual measure, someone recorded the votes of the court members. Six said he was guilty of sodomy. Seven stood for acquittal. Another seven-to-six majority condemned him for "uncleanness and scandalous actions." The sentence: three hundred lashes with a halter about his neck, then to be put ashore with a letter about his neck detailing his crimes. In addition, he was forever prohibited from serving in the navy.[39]

The cases of the absconding purser, the dismissed surgeon, and the flogged midshipman ended quietly and without permanent consequences for the accused. This was in sharp contrast to the fate of Captain Thomas Churchill. The captain's record is also brief, only a paragraph in a short letter sent from an officer named Smith to the Secretary of the Admiralty and dated 8 June 1757. It is best quoted in full:

> Complaint having been made to me by William Stewart belonging to the *Canterbury* buss, that Captain Churchill had committed sodomy with him several times, I wrote yesterday to acquaint him thereof, and directed him to report to me what he had to offer in his vindication that I might inform their Lordships thereof, and received the enclosed letter in answer: The gunner of the said buss has informed me that this morning about 4 o'clock, hearing the report of a pistol in the cabin, he went in and found Captain Churchill had shot himself.[40]

The writer of the letter, possibly Admiral Thomas Smith, chose neither to comment on the deceased captain's predicament nor on his solution. He continued, dealing only with the immediate difficulties the suicide created:

> I have ordered his corpse to be buried in the deep, as he was very corpulent and must prove offensive before the admiralty coroner can come down. I have ordered Lieutenant George Hamilton to command the *Canterbury*, buss, till their Lordships' pleasure is known.[41]

Smith then ended with the same matter-of-fact tone, explaining that the *Canterbury*, "with the *Medway*, buss, will sail tomorrow to attend the fishery off Hastings."[42]

The letter contains no reference to William Seward's age, but it is likely that he was a boy since no indication survives that any action was preferred against him. Further, had he been an adult, it seems unlikely he would complain of repeated acts of sodomy, knowing that his participation on "several" occasions implied consent and could cost him his life. Captains had boys as servants, and any that desired to engage them in sex had more than sufficient power, prestige, and funds to compel, compensate, or convince their young attendants to cooperate. Admiral Smith's request for the captain to provide "his vindication" rather than an explanation or an account of what took place indicates he may have been offering an opportunity for the accused to impugn the assertions of a juvenile. Testimony by youngsters against adults, and particularly against officers, almost always caused uneasiness for courts martial members, and Smith, too, might have had qualms about allowing a boy's assertions to besmirch if not destroy the reputation or even the career of a Royal Navy captain.

Although the age of William Stewart is uncertain, a 1759 incident involving George Val contains no such ambiguity. Val, who is identified as a juvenile, accused a boatswain's mate of buggering him, and the charge brought an immediate investigation. The surgeon examined Val's fundament and found it slightly inflamed, but not enough to prove buggery. The medical man's expert advice prevailed over the claims of the lad, and the accused was released without being charged. No more is known of the incident.[43]

Perhaps the saddest example of sexual relations between an adult and a boy is the case of Seaman George Newton and Thomas Finley, a Marine Society lad. A court martial tried the pair on board HMS *Princess-Royal* at the Nore on 2 July 1761.[44] Newton claimed he was drunk at the time the crime occurred, never an effective defense under any circumstance. Both defendants also objected to having the black man who discovered them serve as a witness. They insisted he could not testify against Christians. The matter was put to rest when the court learned that the witness, Charles Ferrett, had been baptized (the renowned Admiral Augustus Keppel served as one of the godfathers), he was a free man, received wages, and understood the meaning of an oath. Any defense was further vitiated when the youngster confessed that he willingly had sex with Newton, and that before entering the navy he customarily visited London's Bird-Cage Walk, suggesting he previously engaged in sex with other men or perhaps worked as a male prostitute. The members of the court listened to mitigating testimony from the boy's father, who told them he had always been a good son and used to help him in his business as a butcher, but that he had a mind to go to sea. The elder Finley's testimony proved ineffective. There is no mention of the boy's exact age in the record, but he had to have been at least fourteen to be convicted. He and Newton were judged equally guilty of the "unnatural and detestable sin of sodomy" on July 2, 1761 and sentenced to be "hanged by the neck until they are dead." On the day he died, Finley had been in the service only twenty-two days.[45]

IV

It was at about the time of the Seven Years War that at least a few judge advocates, the men who superintended courts martial, began keeping expansive and meticulous accounts of the proceedings they directed. The reasons for the gradual increase in the care with which courts martial records were kept are not hard to find. The war produced tremendous expansion in the navy. Numbers of ships increased dramatically as did the size of dockyards and the auxiliary services necessary to support the growing fleet. All facets of administration naturally grew to accommodate the requirements of the rapidly enlarging institution, and the practice of producing complete trial records gradually took hold as part of the burgeoning administrative apparatus rather than to meet any particular need to deal more effectively with buggery or indecency.[46] The earliest sodomy prosecutions in the Royal Navy for which extensive records survive date from the late 1750s, and by the next decade courts martial records dealing with sex offenses routinely covered dozens of pages. The care and precision that became standard for recording trials and for preserving the records after the 1760s would continue over the decades until the last of the sailing navy's prosecutions for sodomy and indecency on the eve of the Victoria's ascension to the throne.

The lengthy and detailed records of courts martial for sexual and sexually-related violations of the *Articles of War* dating from the final four decades of the eighteenth century and afterward make it possible not only to evaluate the effectiveness of the Admiralty's system of legal administration in such matters, but also to discover whether the King's justice weighed equally on all his mariners, scattered as they were from the home waters, southward to the Mediterranean, and around the world from the East Indies and South Asia to North America and the Caribbean. Within the fleet there existed a stable system that conformed to the expectations of all ranks. There were few surprises in terms of compensation, rations, or shelter. Wide variations existed according to rank, but on each level from the newest boy afloat to senior admirals, each person knew what to expect and the navy for the most part met those expectations. Still, circumstances could vary widely from one station to another. The British in the West Indies were nearer to the enemy, and men made good use of the greater opportunities to desert to the French and the Spanish or to sign on with merchant ships of other nations. Courts martial in home waters, where there was always an ample supply of captains to staff them and adequate administrative support, were held in greater proportion to the number of naval personnel on hand than on other stations. Pardons, too, were distributed in proportionately higher numbers in England, as might be expected, given the propinquity to the loftiest levels of government where they originated. The thousands of miles separating ships and fleets on distant stations from the Admiralty in London gave local commanders considerable autonomy in the administration of justice, and this carried with it potential for inconsistency. On stations where there were few officers, it was difficult to assemble quorums for courts martial, and that had to be a factor in deciding whether to use summary punishment on some occasions. Panels of five officers rather than thirteen were frequent in these far-distant places, and it was not unusual to find lieutenants sitting in for captains when necessary. In no naval station for which statistics are available, at least during the Seven Years War, did the proportion of courts martial vary much when compared to the number of personnel at the station. The home waters provided the only exception. There the rate was somewhat higher, which might be explained if courts martial for offenders on cruising warships were delayed until their ships reached England.[47]

Ratings charged with sodomy sometimes received summary punishment rather than courts martial, but there is no way to discern how often such justice was prescribed for sodomites and other homoerotic sex offenders or whether there was any consistency across the fleet's multiple operational areas on this matter. John D. Byrn found, in his study of discipline on the Leeward Islands station from 1784 to 1815 that summary punishment for sodomites was only slightly more severe than that prescribed for more common offenses such as drunkenness, fighting, and desertion. The captain of HMS *Perdix* prescribed six dozen stripes for William Bayly for violating the twenty-ninth article. At the same time, *Perdix* crewman Samuel Smith collected twenty-four for neglect of duty. Francis Frontain earned four dozen on board HMS *Nyaden* in 1810 merely for attempting what Bayly succeeded in doing, but he was only temporarily daunted by the sentence. Almost a year later Frontain tried it again, again unsuccessfully, and his second offense was punished more lightly than the first by a different captain. He received only forty lashes for "attempting to commit an unnatural crime" in

May of 1811. Seaman Samuel Blanchard received three dozen stripes for drunkenness and "contempt" on board the *Nyaden* the same day.[48] Still, it is impossible to generalize about summary punishment. Although patterns varied greatly for the usual sailors' offenses such as desertion, drunkenness, neglect of duty, and disobedience, the number of shipboard sexual offenses dealt with by individual captains rather than courts martial that have found their way into various studies is simply too small to make judgments about constancy of the response in squadrons across the globe.[49]

3 Ratings with Ratings, Ratings with Boys

Prosecutions for sexual relations between adult sailors occurred from time to time, although they were far fewer in number than those involving men and boys. One of the earliest such trials held under the *Articles of War* took place at Hamoaze pursuant to an order from the Right Honorable the Lords Commissioners of the Admiralty. Two seamen belonging to HMS *Thames*, Robert Pearson and John Clark were ordered to stand trial in 1763 for "the unnatural and horrid sin of sodomy together."[1]

The griffin-shaped Hamoaze estuary adjacent to Plymouth is one of the largest and most protected anchorages in the world. Fed by three rivers and accessible only through the 500-yard-wide channel at Devil's Point, its six-mile length and the extensive dockyard facilities along its shores meant that large numbers of warships, from the most powerful in the fleet to the smallest sixth rates and armed sloops, regularly found shelter there.[2] Hamoaze was an ideal location for convening courts martial. The presence of so many ships and the thousands of naval personnel necessary to man and maintain them meant the necessary manpower and shipboard venues for legal proceedings were always available. The abundance of resources was no small matter, for sodomy courts martial could be grand shows. Ship captains in the vicinity were required to participate up to a maximum number of thirteen, and the proceedings were customarily held on main decks of the most commodious ships to accommodate sizeable audiences. At major installations spectators could often attend a "Roast Beef Court," where officers donned full dress for the occasion. The trial of Clark and Pearson convened on board HMS *Ocean*, a newlybuilt second rate, with three decks, almost two hundred feet in length, and carrying ninety-eight guns. Captain John Reynolds, the president of the court, could hardly have accommodated such a proceeding on board his own ship, the much smaller HMS *Milford*, a sixth rate with a mere twenty-eight guns and only half the length of the *Ocean*. Pearson and Clark's ship was similarly deficient for the spectacle. The fifth rate, *Thames*, only twenty feet longer than the *Milford* and carrying only four more guns, was wholly inadequate for the drama played out in the judicial theater of a sodomy trial which, as with all courts martial, "shall always be held in the forenoon, and in the most public place of the ship where all, who will, may be present; and the captains of all His Majesty's ships in company, which take post, have a right to assist thereat."[3] Like floggings around the fleet, with their elaborate ceremonies performed as separate acts before every nearby ship and with accompaniment by bands playing "The Rogues March," courts martial needed expansive venues to serve up enough pomp and dignity to impress all and sundry with the Royal Navy's absolute power and unchallenged authority.

On the day appointed for the trial of the two *Thames* seamen, the president, and ten other officers, all holding the rank of captain, assembled for the grand event. The service's long-established judicial customs, processes, and procedures were undoubtedly followed with precision. At the start of the court martial, the Union Jack was run up to the peak signaling a trial was under way. The officers took their seats at the table, with the senior officer to the right of the president and the others alternating by seniority to the left and right of him.[4] The charge was levied, witnesses were heard, experts testified, the accused mounted a defense, the board of officers deliberated, then donned their hats to announce the verdict and pass sentence if the defendant had been found guilty. The transcript of the trial was then forwarded to higher naval authorities and eventually lodged at the Public Record Office in London where it would lay virtually undisturbed and unexamined for the next several centuries.

The Clark-Pearson case reveals few details of the crime. The only thing certain from the manuscript record is that the charge of sodomy lodged against them was not proved. Exactly why the prosecution failed to persuade the board of officers of the two men's guilt remains obscure. On the basis of what often occurred in other shipboard sodomy trials, it might be surmised that proof of both penetration and emission could not be had. The court's pronouncements after dismissing the charge, however, reveal that the two sailors were involved in some manner of no good. They were found guilty of "several unclean and scandalous actions in derogation of God's honor," a violation of the second article of war. They were awarded three hundred lashes each "with a cat o'nine tails on their bare backs" and dismissed from the service "with the usual marks of ignominy," punishments commensurate with their unnamed offense according to the court martial. The whippings were to be administered "at such time and in such proportion on board such of His Majesty's ships ... in Hamoaze and Plymouth Sound" as the commanding officer prescribed.[5]

The record of the Clark-Pearson trial offers no hint on the course of the deliberations among the president and members of the court martial as they weighed the culpability of the defendants and determined the appropriate sentence. Such business was customarily conducted in private, and no minutes were kept. The record of the Pearson and Clark case carried the signatures of every officer of the court martial, whether or not all of them supported it. The requirement that all members sign the record was a normal procedure. Naval courts needed only simple majorities to convict, unlike courts of assize on land that required unanimity, so deliberations were kept secret and all signed the trial records to preserve the anonymity of those voting for condemnation.[6]

Another mid eighteenth-century court martial of two men provides a more comprehensive view of how sodomy was prosecuted during the period. Martin Billin and James Bryan, both ratings on board HMS *Newark*, were tried at Gibralter Bay for the "unnatural act of sodomy" in 1763. The record of their trial is more lengthy and detailed than that produced by the court that tried Robert Pearson and John Clark that same year. Suitable facilities and an adequate number of personnel were available at Gibralter to make the trial a major legal production. In the half century after Britain acquired the Rock from Spain in the 1713 Treaty of Utrecht, the Royal Navy had developed extensive facilities there to serve the fleet that protected the Mediterranean interests of the Empire, and a full compliment of thirteen officers could usually be secured to serve as members of any courts martial. If more than that number were available, members were appointed by seniority to prevent Admiralty officials or local commanders from packing courts. Sir Percy Brett was named president of the Billin-Bryan trial, and a dozen captains were placed on the board, bringing the number of officers serving up to the specified limit. Since the proceedings were held outside England, the order authorizing the court martial came not from the Lords Commissioners of the Admiralty, but from the highest local authority, Sir Charles Saunders, Knight of the Bath, "Vice Admiral of the Blue and Commander in Chief of all of His Majesty's Ships and Vessels in the Mediterranean."[7] There was no need to designate a more imposing venue in this case. The ship of the accused men, the *Newark*, was a second rate, more than large enough to host the sodomy trial of two common sailors.

The pageant of naval discipline at Gibralter began on the forenoon of 13 May, when the provost martial brought the defendants to the main deck where the trial would be held. With the audience convened, the board members took their seats right and left of Sir Percy. The judge advocate sat facing the president at the bottom of the table. The gravity of the occasion was certified not only by the number and high rank of those present, but by the regulations and customs surrounding the event. The service of the officers participating at this or any court martial constituted part of their assigned duty rather than a supplemental task. Members attended in their "uniform frocks," and none were allowed to go ashore until the proceedings concluded. Any leaving the ship prematurely or without authorization did so under pain of being cashiered. Revisions under George III required courts martial to sit daily, except Sundays, until completion of testimony, the rendering of verdicts, and the passing of sentences if the defendants were found guilty.[8]

The trial of Martin Billin and James Bryan opened with the reading of Sir Charles Saunders's order constituting the court. The judge advocate then administered the prescribed oaths to the officers who would decide the case. Unlike judges in trials on shore, judge advocates had multiple and conflicting responsibilities during courts martial and in their aftermaths, and there was concern in some quarters over the years about the lack of formal training received by the men who held this vital post. They assembled the court, advised its members on matters of law and procedure, and superintended the operational details of the trials such as administering oaths and keeping the minutes. They also prosecuted the cases, assisted the defense, and made certain that when matters were in doubt, they were resolved in favor of the accused. When courts martial concluded, judge advocates countersigned the trial transcripts, and sent them to the Admiralty in London or, if the court were held far from home waters, they were provided to the commanders of the fleets or squadrons where the verdicts were rendered. This last, the forwarding of trial records to the proper authorities, was an especially vital function when defendants were sentenced to be hanged. Only Admiralty officials or local fleet or squadron commanders could authorize the carrying out of death sentences, and they required proper documentation to inform their decisions.[9]

Once the organizational details had been completed preparatory to trying Bryan and Billin, the court martial was under way. A letter of 9 May from Captain Charles Inglis of the *Newark* to Commander in

Chief Sir Charles Saunders was read to the assemblage. The text of the letter is not preserved, but it appears Inglis was the one who wrote to ask that a court martial be convened to try his two crewmen.[10]

The judge advocate then called the first witness for the prosecution, Seaman Joseph Britton. There were no prescribed oaths for witnesses, but officials were instructed to swear them in a manner reflecting considerable solemnity, particularly for "the lower class of seamen" some of whom might be prone to dilute the truthfulness required by their oaths by holding mental reservations or "by kissing their thumb ... [or] with other absurd and trifling evasions."[11] Britton's interaction with the court is short and bears quotation in its entirety:

Q [Court]: Declare to the court what you know concerning this affair now trying before them.

A [Britton]: On Saturday last, the 8th instant, I went upon deck at 8 o'clock in order to keep the first watch, and going down soon after with William King, on the middle gun deck by the cook room forward saw the prisoners, Martin Billin and James Bryan in the detestable act of sodomy, which I took notice of to William King, who wrung his hands and was struck with horror. I then seized them and called for a light, which not coming immediately, I a second time called for God's sake bring a light, for two men are buggering one another. Bryan, then, who was uppermost and had his leg over Billin endeavored to get up his breeches, but Billin lay still when the light came. Joshua Toner, master at arms, put down his hand and took Bryan's c - - k [*sic*] from between Billin's thighs and showed it to all present, desiring that they might take notice of it.[12]

The passage reveals the fright given to one of the sailors upon learning of the shipboard fornication. William King "wrung his hands and was stuck with horror." Britton exhibited more presence of mind. He seized the perpetrators, shouted that there was buggery on board, and called for a light to be brought. When the master at arms appeared with the light, he, too, knew what to do. He grabbed hold of Bryan's penis and presented it to the view of those who had gathered at the scene upon hearing the crime of buggery called out. He instructed the onlookers to remember what he showed them, presumably so they could testify accurately before a court martial at a later date. William King's testimony followed, and essentially reinforced what Britton had said. He added only details: the discovery of the two accused seamen came near 10:30 at night, Bryan and Billin were "in motion" when discovered, and when the master at arms seized hold of Bryan's "yard" it was "standing." When the two men were asked if either had seen whether Bryan's penis had penetrated Billin's anus, each answered with one word, "No."

The *Newark*'s master at arms, Joshua Jones, was the third witness. He confirmed the testimony of the two men who preceded him, and provided additional bits of useful information. He told how the prisoners hid behind a chest to make it less likely they would be found out, and detailed the series of events that began after their discovery. Jones first made a report of the incident to a Lieutenant Willis, who had the accused seamen clapped in irons, and informed Captain Inglis. The captain then wrote a letter to the commander in chief, Sir Charles Saunders, and it was he who ordered the court martial. When asked whether alcohol was involved, Master at Arms Jones answered that Bryan seemed to be sober, but Billin was drunk. When asked about emission and penetration, important testimony for securing conviction in any sodomy case, Jones replied to the first part of the question, saying, that when he held Bryan's penis in his hand it was moist but he could not tell whether there had been any emission. The trial transcript preserves his graphic account:

> *Q [Court]*: Did you see Bryan's yard in Billin's body?
> *A [Jones]*: No.
> *Q*: By what means are you sure Bryan's yard had penetrated the body of Billin?
> *A*: Because I laid hold of part of his yard. The other part came out with a spring, as if a cork had been drawn out of a bottle.[13]

The testimony of the master at arms firmly established penetration, but the court pressed for even more certainty. They asked Jones if, when he extracted Bryan's penis from Billin's anus, he discovered "any offensive smell." "No," he replied.

Three more witnesses were then called by the prosecution. Two of them claimed to have seen Bryan's penis penetrating Billin, the other did not. One of them, Richard Morris testified that Billin seemed drunk, but Bryan appeared sober.

The last to testify for the prosecution was John Baily, a *Newark* marine. To him, both prisoners seemed drunk, although Billin more so that Bryan.

Billin took the opportunity to defend himself, calling one witness to speak in his favor. His attempt to mitigate the circumstances or secure an acquittal, like almost all defenses mounted by ill-educated and naive mariners without assistance of counsel, proved to be of little of value. Defense witness John Cranefield, the boatswain's mate of the *Newark,* was asked if he knew anything of the affair. He answered "I do not, as I was not present at any part of it."[14] With these thirteen words of testimony the defense rested.

The court was then cleared, the prisoners taken away by the provost marshal, and the closeted deliberations began. Two questions were propounded to the court by its president, Sir Percy: Is the charge proved, and if so, what punishment should be inflicted? Since their discussions went unrecorded, it is not certain which factors influenced the judges. There could be no doubt that penetration occurred. Perhaps the failure of the prosecution to establish that emission had taken place was a vital element in the decision. The court held that the charge had been only partially proved, and so both Billin and Bryan avoided the death penalty. Each instead was sentenced to receive one thousand lashes "alongside such of His Majesty's ships at such times and in such proportion as Sir Charles Saunders, Knight of the Bath, Admiral of the Blue ... shall please to direct."[15] The unidentified penman who produced the digest of the case for the Admiralty thought the sentence in error. In a note added to his work, he wrote:

> N. B. On considering the evidence there seems reason to presume that the court, in not inflicting a capital punishment were moved by the circumstance of the prisoners' having been interrupted before the criminal act, in their apprehension,was fully performed. The legality of the sentence may, however, be questioned, penetration being clearly proved.[16]

It was not until June of 1797, almost thirty-five years after Martin Billin and James Bryan stood trial for sodomy, that another pair of ratings was charged in Cadiz with the same crime. It was an unfortunate time for John Benson and Philip Francis, two seamen of the *St. George,* to be accused of violating the twenty-ninth article of war. Officers were already deeply concerned with indiscipline in the spring of that year. Four mutinies between 1793 and 1795, three of them on ships of the line, as well as the great mutiny at Spithead in April of 1797 created an atmosphere of abiding insecurity on the quarterdeck of every ship.[17] Then, too, during the same period as the mutinies, the Royal Navy had to deal with the heavy burden of defeat. The war with France produced not a single victory of any size after a British fleet bested Admiral Louis Villaret de Joyeuse at the battle of "The Glorious First of June" in 1794. Since then, the Royal Navy had been swept from the Mediterranean, Spain and Holland were lost as allies, Belgium was in the hands of the enemy, and Austria, heavily subsidized by London, seemed on the verge of collapse. Rumors of a French invasion ran rampant, prices of food at home accelerated alarmingly, and the nation's economic stability seemed tenuous at best.[18]

There is no way to evaluate the effect the series of shipboard uprisings or the sagging fortunes of the Royal Navy might have had on those who sat in judgment of Benson and Francis, but the personal predilections of the local commander, Admiral of the Blue, Sir John Jervis, Earl of St. Vincent, may well have exacerbated the plight of the *St. George*'s accused seamen. Jervis, who had been elevated to the English peerage, given a medal with a gold chain, and awarded a £3,000 per annum pension only a short time before, may have harbored a virulent hatred of sodomy according to some testimony, but whether or not Sir John grew livid at the notion of anal copulation among his sailors, he was with good reason very much in fear of mutiny.[19] Earlier in the year, shortly after he arrived on station at Cadiz, he endured some agonizing moments due to indiscipline in his own fleet. He explained what happened in a letter of 29 March written to the First Lord of the Admiralty. "Poor Sir Charles Knowles," he wrote, "is so feeble that the very first night he received the *Britannia* from Captain [Sir Thomas] Foley, the ship's company took the command from him, and have been in a state of licentiousness ever since." Jervis undoubtedly knew of the earlier mutinies on board British warships between 1793 and 1795 when he wrote in March, but when he later learned of the April uprising in the Channel Fleet at Spithead, he realized he had to move quickly to avoid damage to his own reputation. He fell back on a technique used by centuries of successful officers. He first ducked, then covered. No Spithead had occurred under his command, he quickly proclaimed. "The disorder in the *Britannia* was nothing like a mutiny." The fault for the collapse of discipline on board the ship in March resulted entirely from the "notorious imbecility of Sir Charles Knowles."[20] Whether or not the officers under Jervis were aware of his putative hatred of sodomy, they undoubtedly knew of the various mutinies and of the situation on board *Britannia* after the captain had lost control. In such a situation it is not difficult to understand why a fear of indiscipline led them to believe that the legal truths so loved by lawyers and landsmen were irrelevant at sea.

The charges against the hapless Benson and Francis came about in the usual fashion after a sailor bumbled upon the two at night in the dark on a lower deck, one atop the other. The man who happened on them summoned a light and called others to view what he had found. In all, four men, the coxswain, a boatswain's mate, and two seamen, saw the accused pair prone on the deck with trousers down.[21] At the trial witnesses were questioned closely on whether they could vouch for penetration, indicating the court's strong interest in establishing that sodomy had taken place. No witness from the ship saw penetration or emission, nor was there a master at arms at this trial to relate how one man's penis might have come from the other's anus "with a spring, as if a cork had been drawn out of a bottle."[22] No one, in fact "could swear positively to the act of criminal connection."[23] When called to testify, even Surgeon John Brazer said he could not discern any signs of a connection or an attempted connection between the prisoners.[24] In 1762, the thirteen officers who tried Martin Billin and James Bryan at Gibralter Bay had ample evidence of penetration from a quartet of witnesses. The failure to establish emission, presumably, led them to a verdict of "part proved," sparing each of the accused a hanging in exchange for one thousand lashes. No one observed such niceties of the law in the proceeding against the two ratings from the *St. George*. "On consideration of the circumstances, [they] held the presumptive evidence sufficient for the conviction of the prisoners [for sodomy] and sentenced them both to be hanged."[25]

Similarly when a seaman and a marine, both of HMS *Invincible*, went to trial at Fort Royal Bay, Martinique in 1799 there was little inclination toward mercy. Identified only as McMaster and Callaghan, they were discovered by a marine sergeant who heard noises close to his berth. The non-commissioned officer lit a candle, ordered two men nearby to accompany him as witnesses, and proceeded to the source of the noise. The trio found two men lying on their sides close together. The sergeant "gave them a shake, and then saw Callaghan's privates come out of McMaster's fundament." The trial record contains no hint of emission. McMaster and Callaghan were hanged.[26]

The next year, another pair of sodomites from the *St. George* received death sentences when officers again opted for severity rather than leniency. At the court martial of George Hynes and Thomas Hubbard, officers exhibited no qualms over creating their own brutal style brand of shipboard justice. The case against the two accused seamen began as usual, by chance. Peter Melville, a marine, heard whispering coming from a hammock and went over to it to investigate. As he later explained in testimony before the court martial, when he approached the hammock he overheard what is one of the very few recorded examples of pillow talk preserved in any of the Royal Navy's sodomy trials. One of the men in the hammock said to the other, "You do not do it so well to me as I do it to you." At this juncture, the master at arms appeared, pulled a lantern out of a bag, and the light revealed Hynes naked and Hubbard with pants about his ankles. When discovered, Hubbard tumbled off Hynes, and two witnesses saw "Hubbard's tool come out of Hynes's fundament." Again, the lack of testimony to substantiate emission troubled no one at the Hubbard-Hynes court martial. Both men received death sentences.[27]

In 1800, a naval court martial in Jamaica exhibited a comparable lack of concern about convicting two men of sodomy on the basis of dubious evidence. The case began after sailors happened upon two seamen from the HMS *Vengeance*, identified only as Greenard and Fuller, "playing and toying with one other on deck the same as a man would do with a girl." When crewmen observed them later, Greenard was atop Fuller, at least one of them was in motion, and those present testified they thought buggery was being done. Despite the suggestive circumstances, none claimed to have seen an actual sodomitic connection, one seaman's penis entering or withdrawing from the anus of the other. In the absence of eye-witness testimony to sodomy, the board of officers called up an expert, a naval surgeon. He examined the defendants and found no symptoms to convict either mariner. The failure to establish penetration or emission did not impress the court greatly. They claimed there were sufficient grounds to ignore the surgeon's testimony – he made his observations a week after the alleged crime. The charge was proved in their opinion, and the two were sentenced to death.[28]

Greenard and Fuller's court martial took place at Port Royal, Jamaica, and the death sentence could be carried out only on the signature of Rear Admiral Sir John Thomas Duckworth, the local commander in chief, but some aspect of the trial must have raised concern and perhaps a sense of the need to temper justice with a modicum of mercy. Sir John, "a tall bony man with an enormous nose and a small quirky mouth," was reputed to possess "a large share of forbearance."[29] Whatever the nature of his concerns about the case, Duckworth thought it best to communicate with London on the matter. A scrawl at the end of the court martial summary that extends into the left margin, written in a hand much smaller than that of the text, provides the following information:

> From a letter addressed by Admiral Duckworth to the Secretary of the Admiralty and a note by the latter thereon, it appears that Fuller, on

> the recommendation of the court was pardoned but ordered not again to be received on board a King's ship. Neither this letter nor the recommendation are to be found among the records, but the letter is in possession of the Board of Admiralty.[30]

Fuller was a doubly fortunate man to have received a Royal pardon. Reviewing capital convictions on stations distant from home waters was a not only a difficult and time-consuming process stretching all the way back to London, but few sodomites sentenced to death avoided the noose. Usually it required compelling reasons to overturn a sodomy conviction. In Fuller's case, authorities presumably decided that he had been convicted on seriously defective evidence. Another, and possibly the only other pardon granted to one of the "people" following a sodomy conviction, was that given to John Blake, the mentally defective marine convicted of copulating with a goat in 1758.[31]

The death sentences pronounced on George Hynes, Thomas Hubbard, John Benson, Philip Francis, McMaster, Callaghan, Greenard, and Fuller could be interpreted to indicate that over half a dozen mutinies between 1793 and 1800 and a string of defeats at sea during the same years created a mood in the Royal Navy that brooked no inclination to split hairs or offer leniency when discipline was threatened, but there is ample evidence to the contrary. In a number of trials the law was observed scrupulously during these difficult years. The relentlessness that characterized the prosecutions of the men sentenced to hang was nowhere to be found at a court martial held in early 1797 to try John Morris and William Savage, messmates on board HMS *Adamant*, for sodomy. The problem on board the *Adamant* began at Yarmouth Roads one evening about eight o'clock when one of the ship's company, William Green, came upon the pair "opposite the bitts" and under the cable.[32] He hollered out that buggery was underway, and four other crewmen appeared in response to his call, all of whom were later summoned to testify at the court martial of the men allegedly surprised in the act. As each witness later explained to the court, the accused were found "in the following position–Savage was placed on his knees stooping forwards and supporting himself on his arms. His trousers were down as low as his knees, his backside was bare, and his shirt turned up towards his jacket."[33] Both had been drinking, but how much the two had drunk could not be ascertained. One man testified that the accused pair had divided two bottles of gin between themselves and a fellow sailor. Another witness claimed a gallon, presumably of beer, and three parts of a bottle had been consumed by Morris, Savage, and two others. Whatever the amounts, testimony indicated Morris was "groggy" and Savage may have been unconscious when they were discovered.

The Morris-Savage court martial is unusual because it is one of the few trials where ordinary crewmen expressed their emotional reactions to sodomy in words other than the stilted phrases of legal formulations. When the court asked witness John Dennett what he said to the men about him as they stood watching Morris and Savage on the deck, he replied, "I felt so hurt at seeing such a thing I could not speak." He also told another sailor, Robert Edmonds, that he "never saw the like in his life." Another, Peter Rich, who had heard of the goings on but evidently did not witness them said, "something was carried on that was not right ... it was a damned shame." Rich's indignation did not last long. He briefly observed the two after they had been taken into custody, then "went forward to the foremost berth [and] took no further notice." Even among the small group who actually stood by observing Morris and Savage copulate, all were not profoundly struck by what they saw. William Green, who first sounded the alarm, later told Savage the entire matter would be "hushed up."[34]

In the end, despite receiving conflicting testimony on whether Morris actually penetrated Savage, the court chose to ignore the ambiguousness of the evidence and temper their judgment with a leaven of mercy. Although they declared Morris guilty and sentenced him to be hanged, they did not seize the opportunity they had to execute both men. They let the "doubts hanging on their minds touching [Savage's] guilt," weigh in their judgment, and they acquitted him.[35]

The trial of Morris and Savage took place some months before the signal event at Spithead and the later, large-scale mutiny at the Nore in May of 1797, but while naval uprisings and their denouement were past by late autumn, the war with France continued. Even though Britain's fortunes remained at a low ebb well into the following year, there were at least some officers who were not inclined to manifest frustrations in punitive measures against their people. In 1798, one court martial relied far more heavily on legal precedent to obtain leniency for two men than they were required to do by precedent or regulations. When a pair of sailors from HMS *Prince Frederick*, Francisco Falso and John Lambert, "were taken in the act of sodomy" the court protected them by admitting no deviation from the letter of the law . The pair stood trial for violating only the twenty-ninth article. The court decided both that they engaged in indecent and scandalous practices which fell far short of buggery and that their behaviors were proscribed in the second article of war. Since they stood accused of violating only the twenty-ninth article, however, the court acquitted both men. The anonymous compiler of the digest of the case thought it worthy of editorial attention. In notes at the beginning of his summary, he wrote, "This case merits notice on no other account than that it is an instance of greater legal correctness than is generally to be found in the recorded proceedings of naval courts- martial."[36] In his concluding commentary, he explained:

> This decision appears to be founded on sound legal principles. Agreeably to the more general, though loose practice, however, it would not have been extraordinary, had the court in this case found the charge proved in part that the prisoners fell under the 2nd Article of War, and therefore inflicted upon them such arbitrary punishment as they had thought the offense deserved.[37]

In a similarly merciful fashion, when an apparent outburst of sodomy took place on HMS *Trident*, officers demonstrated an obvious reluctance to take the most punitive course of action open to them. In trials held on 10 June 1800 at Trincomalee, two pairs of sailors stood trial. The first to face a court martial were John Ware and John Douglas, who were discovered in a hammock together. There was enough suspicion of sodomy to call for a medical examination. It is not certain what the surgeon discovered. The brief record says only that his "deposition tended strongly to confirm" some suspicious circumstances. The evidence was not persuasive. "It might be said that the prisoners were saved by the darkness of the night and the stupidity of those who first discovered them." If such evidence had been presented to another court on board a different ship, Ware and Douglas might have forfeited their lives despite only being involved in suspicious circumstances, but they were a fortunate duo. The officers who decided their case acquitted them of sodomy, convicting them only of violating the second article of war. No details survive of the proceeding against the second pair of Seamen John Harrison and William Harries, but the charge against them was "adjudged groundless and malicious." They both went free.[38]

Ware and Douglas may have been saved by darkness and stupidity, but certainly a factor in preserving their lives was scrupulous adherence to the law. There was considerable suspicion in their case but no proof. The same was true in 1802 when a third pair of seamen from the *Trident* were seen in a situation that looked much like sodomy to a boatswain's mate named White. The boatswain's mate immediately summoned the master at arms, who hastened to the scene with a lantern. The master at arms later described what he saw before a court martial: "I ... found

Holland between Riley's legs. I drew them apart and found both their trousers loose, and Holland's yard erected. I took hold of it, and said ... 'White, look at this. It's fit for action.'"[39]

Although White's description of "Riley laying on his belly and Holland ... upon him with his backside in motion the same as [White's] would be if [he] was on a woman," strongly suggested penetration occurred, the court would have none of it. They found Holland guilty only of attempted sodomy and Riley of uncleanness. The former was sentenced to receive six hundred lashes. The latter only three hundred. Both were mulcted of their pay and discharged from the navy.[40]

In describing the deeds of the two pairs of seamen, Holland and Riley and Douglas and Ware, vocabulary in the trial records reveals much about the attitudes and perceptions of the courts. The boatswain's mate who discovered the crime described Holland's motion as akin to copulating with a woman, but there is no suggestion that the buggered Riley was in any way womanish, female, or feminine. The same is true in the court martial of Douglas and Ware. The court went beyond the usual pejoratives found in the second article of war, adding "infamous," "unmanly," "indecent," and "unworthy" to familiar description that included "scandalous" actions "in derogation of God's honor and corruption of good manners." Only the word "unmanly" in the roster of deprecating adjectives strikes a discordant tone. Although effeminacy was a stock feature of virtually every denunciation of sodomites and mollies from Ned Ward and Josiah Woodward early in the eighteenth century to Smollett and Garrick later on, this aspect of the rhetorical fusillade did not go to sea, at least in buggery and indecency trials.[41] While accused sodomites are everywhere denounced in courts martial records using various terms, throughout the corpus of trial records, the modifiers "unmanly," "effeminate," "womanish," "girl-like," or similar adjectives do not appear. Sailors had no doubt what "manly" meant. It embodied the brave, courageous, and true. Robert M. Wilson, a crewmember on board HMS *Unité*, referred to the "manly gracefulness" of the male dancers he observed at a ball held on board his ship in 1807.[42] On the rare instances when seafarers described someone as "unmanly" it meant cowardice and physical weakness not femininity. Even when sodomites were described in testimony as having assumed the positions of women in the commission of sex acts, their behavior was never described as "woman-like" or "feminine." It meant only they were receptors rather than insertors, the buggered rather than the buggerer, or that they occupied the bottom position in the sexual encounters for which they stood trial. Shipboard buggers were a different cast of men than the mollies ashore who bore the heaviest onus of criticism in every variety and form of printed matter. Royal Navy sodomites played no roles and they did not ape shoreside, bi-gendered society or flouncing mollies. On the basis of what can be discerned from trial transcripts, it appears that the actions they took to obtain sexual gratification most often held no more emotional content than the performance of other compelling bodily functions. Mariners hauled before courts martial lived in a universe with limited sexual options when their ships were at sea. There is no way to understand what these men thought or felt. Surviving Admiralty documents do not reveal if their preferences ran toward men and boys or if their choice of same-sex partners was simply the result of deprivation.[43] Trial transcripts indicate that these men only used whatever was most easily available. Any convenient man, boy, hand, or anus would do.

During the five years beginning with the prosecution of John Benson and Philip Francis at Cadiz in 1797, and concluding with the death sentence handed down for Greenard and the pardoning of Fuller in 1802, there was only one court martial dealing with a sexual offense that did not involve at least an initial accusation of sodomy. Seaman Bryan McMahan was brought to trial in 1798 for putting his hand into the trousers of two shipmates while they slept. When taken, he knocked the light from the hand of the sentinel and denounced the lieutenant who arrested him. He received five hundred lashes, but the record is sparse and it cannot be determined whether the punishment was levied only for lewdness or if his conduct after discovery was a factor in the harsh sentence.[44]

The Napoleonic wars went on for a dozen years after the Greenard-Fuller prosecutions despite the brief respite provided by the 1802 Treaty of Amiens. After the resumption of hostilities in 1803 and their continuation until Napoleon's exile to Elbe in 1814, the navy held only two courts martial for sodomy involving pairs of men from roughly equal status levels. In 1809, two faced charges of sodomy as did a duo consisting of a midshipman and an assistant surgeon. By the time the four men went to trial, the dark days for the Royal Navy had ended with Nelson's stunning victory at Trafalgar, but the lifting of the pall of defeat created no noticeable trend in the prosecutions for homoerotic adventures. The case against Benjamin Grimshaw and John Scott at the Downs began in a usual fashion when a boy of HMS *Illustrious*, William Fowles, spotted the two engaged in buggery against a gun between eight and ten in the evening. He reported what he saw, a light was brought, and the men arrested. At the trial ample testimony indicated the defendants were not drunk and three officers testified to young Fowles' good character. What sets this particular court martial apart from many others was the confession made by John Scott to a group of officers and marine non-commissioned officers. It was here the court encountered a procedural difficulty. Several witnesses were asked if Scott had been promised leniency in exchange for confessing, and all replied in the negative, except for the commander of the ship's marine detachment.[45] When testifying, he was asked:

Q [Court]: Were you present when the prisoner Scott confessed to Captain [John?] Broughton that he had been guilty of the crime with which he is charged?
A [Marine commander]: I was.
Q: Did he make that confession voluntarily or was it drawn from by any threat or promise?
A: There was no threat made use of, but I conceive the confession was drawn from him in a manner the court would not have admitted of.[46]

The questioning continued with the officers bent on extracting from the marine captain the perceived irregularities in Scott's interrogation:

Q [Court]: During the conversation which you say took place, did Captain Broughton hold out to the prisoner the hope of being himself forgiven if he made that confession?
A [Marine commander]: I was not present the first part of this examination.
Q: Was any such hope held out for him in your hearing?
A: There was no language made use of to that effect, but Captain Broughton spoke in a very kind and conciliatory manner; which might have induced the man to suppose by such a confession he would be admitted as king's evidence.[47]

The compelling testimony of a reliable, juvenile eye witness, when supported by a confession extracted without coercion although in what was possibly a devious manner, were sufficient evidence for a guilty verdict. Both men were sentenced to death on 21 June 1809.[48]

Two days later and hundreds of miles from England, on board HMS *Royal Sovereign* at sea off Toulon, Midshipman Roderick Colquhoun and Assistant Surgeon Robert Fleming faced a court martial, having been accused of sodomy by three marines from their ship, HMS *Bulwark*.[49] As a midshipman, Colquhoun stood well above common sailors and marines who picked sexual partners from among their fellows, but the friend with whom he was accused of buggery was from a status level similar to his own in the shipboard hierarchy. Midshipmen in most cases were destined to become commissioned officers, and surgeon's assistants in the navy were also men with expectations. They were required after 1790 to have passed the examinations at Surgeon's Hall, and they could look forward to becoming ship's surgeons after they had gained experience at sea. The job title for men in Fleming's post had been upgraded from "surgeon's mate" to "assistant surgeon" or "surgeon's assistant" just three years earlier, in 1806, but it is unlikely that even with the nominal promotion Fleming had private quarters below deck on the *Bulwark*. Cabins or even cubicles sectioned off with canvas were not mandated for assistant surgeons until mid-century. Previous to that time they slung their hammocks from the cockpit beams.[50]

The lack of private quarters did not mean that the midshipman and the assistant surgeon engaged in sexual activity between guns in the dark of the night like ratings. In the case of Colquhoun and Fleming, they had access to the ship's dispensary, an area cordoned off by canvas curtains. It was while in the dispensary that the three marines observed them through an aperture of some sort in the curtains. The story of what they had seen, two men cavorting, breeches down, one atop the other on a chest, circulated through the ship for a number of days before officers took notice of it and requested a court martial. Once the trial began, testimony made it apparent that the marines had seen nothing that would hang the two men. Not one of the three could swear there was anal penetration, and only two claimed to have seen either man with trousers lowered. A fourth witness, Seaman John Day, also claimed to have seen the two defendants with their pants down, and added he had seen them on other occasions in the dispensary with their private parts exposed. Like the marines, though, he at no time witnessed sodomy. In addition to the lack of evidence, at least three of the four prosecution witnesses were suspect. John Day's testimony was impugned because he was regularly drunk. One of the marines came from Italy, spoke no English, and presumably belonged to the Roman Catholic Church. Marine Abraham Benjamin was a Jew.

His testimony may or may not have been acceptable, according to what he had once been told. The court acquitted Colquhoun and Fleming of the sodomy charge, and although they had been observed one atop the other with trousers down by three crewmen, they were not punished under the second article. They went free to resume their naval careers.[51]

A century of peace in Europe followed the final British victory at Waterloo in 1815. The only conflict requiring a large commitment of British regulars was the Crimean War, but by the time the Light Brigade charged at Balaclava the sailing navy had long abandoned prosecuting its sailors for sodomy or indecency. The last court martial summoned to try a pair of enlisted men for homoerotic involvement assembled at the Royal Marine Barracks at Woolwich on 17 July 1832. The accused were both marines, their alleged misconduct occurred on land rather on board ship, and those hearing the case were marine officers rather than naval captains. Besides these differences, the proceeding was much like those on shipboard during the previous one hundred years. The president and members took their seats according to seniority, the prisoners were brought in, the audience admitted, and the order for assembling the court read aloud, probably in this case by Acting Judge Advocate Captain George Varlo. The two men named in the order, marine privates Edward McGee and John Peach, were to be tried "for immoral and indecent conduct, having been found in an indecent position in bed together on the night of the 5th instant in a barrack room at Deptford." The Commander of the Royal Marines at Woolwich, Colonel R. McCleverty, signed the single-page order.[52]

The judge advocate swore in the members of the court, the president then swore in the judge advocate, the prisoners pleaded not guilty, and their ordeal began.

Private James Lomax of the 24th Company was the first witness called. He testified he shared the same room with the prisoners on the night of the alleged incident. At around eleven o'clock at night he heard the prisoners whispering, and at first thought each was in his own bed. The sound of rustling straw and heavy breathing like that of a man with a woman induced the curious Lomax to rise and to check out the situation. He decided that the two both lay in Peach's bed. At this juncture, Private Richard Lythgoe entered the room and retired to his assigned bed. He asked Lomax if he slept, and Lomax replied not with a word, but with a noise of some sort. The two then lay quietly for about ten minutes before Lomax decided he had had enough. With encouragement from Lythgoe, he rose and went to the guard room to summon assistance. When he arrived, the corporal on duty asked what was the matter.

Lomax replied, "there was plenty the matter," and told him to come along and bring his light. When the two returned to the barrack room, Peach lay in bed on his back, and McGee sat on his own bunk. McGee grabbed up his blanket and sheets and "belted" Lomax with them, saying, "You old bugger, why did you disturb me?" At that point the corporal took McGee to the guard house.

Lomax admitted under questioning that the room was dark, and when asked how he determined the marines lay in bed together if he could see nothing, he first responded saying he "Cannot answer that question," and later explained that although he could not see the men in bed together he knew it was the case "in [his] own opinion from what [he] heard." When the court finished its questioning, Peach sprang to his own defense, asking Lomax squarely, "Did you actually see McGee and me in bed together?" The witness replied, "No, I cannot say I saw them."[53]

Unlike pairs of enlisted men tried previously for sexual crimes, McGee and Peach provided an extended statement as part of their defense. In their address to the court they explained:

> We can only rely upon your kindness to weigh well the serious charge against us and to believe that as men it is impossible we could have been guilty of any indecent intention and we do most earnestly declare our innocence. It is possible (that having drank very freely and which is admitted by the witnesses) that we may have got into the same bed but we can declare without any evil intention we throw ourselves upon the merciful consideration of the court and request to be allowed to call on Corporal Millikin and Sergeant Haywood to prove that we were in so drunken a state as not to know what we were about and from that not capable of any improper intent.[54]

A defense based on drunkenness was not likely to sway a panel of officers, but it surely proved less persuasive after the testimony of the two witnesses called by the accused. Sergeant Haywood, when asked twice by John Peach if he were drunk or sober at the time of the alleged offense, replied twice with exactly the same words, "You was neither drunk nor sober – evidently had been drinking." Corporal George Millikin provided even less support for the prisoners. When asked the ill-formulated question by Peach, "Was I perfectly sober?" he replied affirmatively, saying, "To the best of my knowledge."[55]

Had McGee and Peach been more adroit in their selection of witnesses or had they calibrated questions more effectively, it is nevertheless unlikely they would have prevailed. Officers rarely if ever rendered verdicts of not guilty when prisoners had no more to offer than the fact that they were drunk. By 1832, courts may have been more lenient than in previous decades. There was, after all, no attempt to charge the two with sodomy despite the lack of firm evidence as might have been done twenty years earlier. Still, leniency could only be carried so far. They would not escape unscathed. The court considered their defense, rejected it, then convicted them for "being in breach of the *Articles of War.*" Each man received a sentence of three hundred lashes laid on their bare backs, and when a surgeon determined them sufficiently recovered from their punishment they were ejected from the service with "branded" discharges.[56]

The court martial records of sailors and marines prosecuted for sodomy and other assorted indecent acts provide answers to a few puzzling questions about sex on board warships in the age of sail. One of the most obvious of these, of course, is where on board a vessel might men find space and privacy enough to drop their trousers, climb one atop the other, and engage long enough to induce orgasm. Dimensions of the first rates, the largest ships in the fleet, indicate they were quite commodious. The largest ran nearly 200 feet in length and were one quarter that distance at their widest points. A sagittal section of such a ship reveals strata ranging from the hold and the orlop deck, both far below the waterline, upward to a series of gun decks, and on to the main deck, a quarter deck, and a poop deck, high above the ocean's surface. While the architecture of a first rate provided considerable space in terms of cubic feet or yards of capacity, a substantial portion of it was unavailable for general usage. Long periods at sea required the hold to be filled with barrels of water and spiritous liquors, powder, shot, cable, foodstuffs, and scores of other items necessary for sailing and fighting the ship. Other decks held the sick bay, cabins belonging to officers of various grades, steering gear, cooking facilities, small arms, and the ships guns and their accouterment. When such a vessel was fully maned with eight or nine hundred men, little space remained for private sexual assignations. The same held true on smaller warships ranging downward in size from mighty second rates to sixth rates, with their two dozen or so guns, and to sloops and bomb ketches as well. No matter what the size of the vessel and its crew, there was little space available for secret acts or covert deeds when large numbers of men were on board, even if the number fell far short of the authorized strength, as was usually the case. Joseph Britton's testimony in the 1763 court martial of James Bryan and Martin Billin, and testimony like it from other courts martial, provide at least one answer to questions about where sailor couples could go to be alone long enough for sex. The obvious solution to the problem of shipboard population density for ratings seeking a secluded spot for buggery was to wait until dark. All the accused ratings and marines brought to trial had been discovered between eight and eleven o'clock in the evening, except in two cases where witnesses described covert actions occurring later at night. Ships may have been crowded with men, but after nightfall many of the crew were asleep, others were on watch, and sentries below the main deck sometimes dozed at their posts. There were many crannies and bays, or hidden spaces between guns, chests, supplies, and equipment where furtive fornicators could gain moments alone and unobserved. John Ware and John Douglas, of the *Trident*, were acquitted of the sodomy charge in part, because of "the darkness of the night."[57] Indeed, the lack of light is a constant theme in courts martial testimony. One of the first cries on discovering sodomites was for someone to bring a lantern. Even then, the levels of illumination when lanterns arrived often proved inadequate. Candles available on board Royal Navy ships were often of dismal quality, "miserable dips (twelve to the pound), and they constantly required snuffing." One sailor complained of the gloom below decks, saying "your light for a day and night is a small candle, which is often stuck at the side of your platter at meals, for want of a better convenience."[58] On a ship the size of the *Newark* there were enough spaces between the eighty guns on board to provide ample quiet and secret places for furtive trysts. Bryan and Billin were caught in the act, to be sure, as were other gun deck dyads who faced courts martial for sodomy, but their exposure does not lessen the importance of the fact in every such case, they assumed that the intervals between cannon, the spaces behind chests, or the burrows that could occasionally be located under shipboard gear would provide sufficient cover for dropping trousers, pulling up shirt tails, and stealing quick measures of gratification.

There is of course no way of estimating how many men committed sodomy or other sex acts undetected in darkened, secret spaces and were not caught. Perhaps it was only carelessness, drunkenness, or stupidity that allowed those apprehended to have chosen locations for their sexual activities that made exposure likely. Another possibility is that even with darkness and a multiplicity of shipboard nooks and recessed coves to hide, the tightly packed mass of humanity on board warships made it certain at least some proportion of the seagoing sodomists, no matter how well hidden, would be detected. There is also the final possibility that those discovered and brought to trial simply had the bad luck to be caught while their more fortunate peers escaped detection. Every instance where records show how pairs of accused ratings were apprehended is the same. No shipboard patrols wandered the decks after dark hoping to drive buggering couples from their murky lairs, nor did captains have standing orders for their men to be ever-watchful for such activities. Crewmen going about their business or intent on unrelated tasks found them by accident.

The courts that tried seamen for indecent acts or sodomy did not indulge in oratorical flights of condemnation or denunciation. They remained always low key in matters of language. When naming the crimes attributed to accused mariners they clewed closely to the words the of *Articles of War*. Among officers and men in Nelson's day there was little shilly-shallying over nouns. Sodomy and buggery were rendered as sodomy and buggery throughout the trial records. When the need to describe action arose, they spoke directly of men "buggering one another." They were as straightforward when searching for descriptive terms. Their combined dictionary and thesaurus consisted of the second and twenty-ninth article. Only the adjectives "unnatural" and "detestable," appear in article twenty-nine, and, except for one "horrid," they were only two adjectives in courts martial of ordinary sailors that were used to modify "sodomy" and "buggery." Accusations of indecency were classified in the second of the *Articles of War* using the catchall "unclean and scandalous actions in derogation of God's honor." The phrase has a euphemistic quality, suggesting that its authors sought to avoid using sexually specific terminology, but that was probably not the case. The men who wrote the article actually had little choice in their selection of descriptive terms. It would have been exceedingly cumbersome, if not impossible, for the article to enumerate every possible indecent or filthy act that mariners might devise. While the article listed no specifics, the indecent acts of which sailors were accused received much clarification in the trial texts. On occasion "uncleanness" was applied to violations of shipboard hygienic regulations, as when the Thomas Carter, a "disorderly, turbulent" marine of HMS *Lapwing* received three hundred lashes for "pissing from his hammock upon the deck," but most often the term applied to sexual offenses.[59] Bryan McMahan uncleanly slipped his hand down the trousers of two shipmates while they slept. Unclean McGee and Peach lay in bed together, rooting about in the straw and breathing heavily like a man with a woman. "Uncleanness" was also a handy term sometimes applied to those who escaped convictions for sodomy due to lack of evidence of penetration or emission. Those convicted of uncleanness under the second article of war in every case escaped hanging, but they usually received hundreds of lashes for their offenses against decency.[60]

Navy men were less direct in their nomenclature for the male member. Although the word "penis" appeared on occasion, nautical substitutes were frequently used. The male organ was most often a "yard" – a reference not to a unit of length but to a spar tapered at both ends used for spreading and providing support to the head of a sail. Court members, witnesses, and defendants alike regularly employed the term. When Joseph Britton used the word "cock" in his testimony against James Bryan and Martin Billin in 1762, the court responded with a question repeating the word. The judge advocate who prepared the trial transcript was evidently the only one who had difficulty dealing with such crude terminology, at least in writing, and put it in the record as "c - - k." He exhibited the same squeamishness with another of the trial's coarser moments. When Bryan asked Billin why he was put in irons, the penman wrote, "Billin answered "for f - - k - - g of me."[61] The man who later compiled the trial summary for the Admiralty from the judge advocate's transcript preferred to be more direct. He replaced "f - - k - - g" in the trial transcript with "fucking" in his abbreviated record of the testimony.[62] Forty years afterward, the language used by both the court and witnesses in 1798 trial martial of Morris and Savage avoided some of the earthy expressions found in such proceedings during the 1760s. No crude or explicit "cocks" or "pricks" found their way into the record of their transgressions. The court questioners, officers all, spoke of erections and penises, while witnesses from the lower deck relied more often upon euphemisms. "Yard" frequently appeared in testimony as it had in the past, but there were also more genteel references to "privates." When one man was asked about the state of Morris's penis when the two accused were apprehended, he explained that it was in the "state of that of a man that is going to have connection with a woman."[63] As a seaman, presumably with limited education, it is entirely possible he was unfamiliar with the term "erection" or, perhaps, he simply preferred to use a descriptive circumlocution in a public forum before a panel of his social betters.[64]

The directness of courts martial discourse, even as it softened and became more circumspect in the late eighteenth and early nineteenth centuries, stood in remarkable contrast to the run of references to sodomy among the works of legal, literary, and popular authors ashore. Lawyers wrote of an "infamous crime against nature," a "horrible crime not to be named among Christians," and an act that "is disgraceful to the human species."[65] Other works, from comedies by David Garrick to the sermons of John Wesley raged on about Satanic vices and unnatural crimes, and created a covey of similar circumlocutions. Nothing of the sort happened in the navy, where direct and specific speech, though softening over the years, held sway despite the literary examples of landsmen.[66]

Trial records reveal that accusations of drunkenness often accompanied charges of violating articles two and twenty-nine. Given the seriousness of sex crimes and the severity of punishments inflicted on those found guilty, it would have been pointless to pursue charges of drunkenness. Yet over-consumption of alcohol by those charged with sodomy or indecency was a topic that appeared often in the testimony of witnesses and in the ineffectual explanations proffered by the accused. What effect drunkenness had on pairs of accused sailors is impossible to assess. Without excessive drinking perhaps some or most of the acts charged against the defendants would not have been committed. More likely, without alcohol, pairs accused of sodomy or uncleanness might have been more discreet and sought out less traveled venues for their trysts or, in the case of Edward McGee and John Peach, been quiet enough not to attract the attention of fellow marines. The alcohol-induced stupors of some seamen may also have provided opportunities for their sober or more-nearly-sober comrades to force them into buggery. Although James Bryan and Martin Billin had both been drinking according to the testimony of one witness, Billin was the drunker of the two. Other witnesses at the same court martial insisted Bryan was sober. What is certain is that Bryan, who had been drinking, lay on top of a profoundly drunk Billin and broached his anus with his penis.[67] In a comparable situation on board the *St. George*, crewmen discovered John Benson lying on top of Philip Francis. When someone brought a light Benson stood up, but Francis was too drunk to rise and had to be helped to his feet. Whether Francis was a willing participant or was in his stupor too unaware or unable to or resist is unknown. The one hundred and fifty-word record of the trial reveals only that the court condemned both men to death. William Savage was another who had passed out from drink before he was buggered by John Morris. There is no suggestion that any courts martial considered sober sailors buggering their very drunk comrades in any way akin to rape. Instead, courts martial members in two or three such cases deemed both men equally guilty. None but the unconscious William Savage won an acquittal under such circumstances by explaining he had no memory whatsoever of being sodomized by John Morris. In only one case involving two enlisted men, that of Peach and McGee, did the defendants seriously employ drunkenness as a defense, and they were charged with the far less serious offense of indecency rather than sodomy.

The several cases where men totally incapacitated by drink were penetrated anally by sober or by less intoxicated shipmates suggests the question of mutuality. Did ordinary pairs of ratings who were not drunk when they engaged in buggery ever trade roles, with one man buggering another, then the two changing positions and engaging in buggery again. No such cases appear in the record of prosecutions, which may be due entirely to the way in which offenses were discovered and reported rather than to the lack or need for reciprocity between homoerotically linked sailors. Mariners stumbling on buggering pairs did not sit down on handy chests or lean against nearby guns, light pipes, and wait to discover if the two switched positions. Instead, they immediately raised the alarm, crewmen came running to witness the scenes, sentries bearing lanterns appeared to expose the malefactors to feeble, flickering candle light, officers learned of the infamous behaviors in due course, and often within a matter of days courts martial assembled. There is no indication in any of the trials whether crewmen uncovered the accused in their first or second shifts, and men on trial for their lives wisely refrained from adducing additional evidence of their culpability. Still, cases of sodomy on the lower decks may well have involved reciprocity. The trial of George Hynes and Thomas Hubbard revealed that one had been overheard saying to the other, "You do not do it so well to me as I do it to you."[68] Evidence from on board HMS *Africaine* (considered in Chapter 6) indicates the presence among some pairs of a willingness to exchange roles in both sodomy and in serial masturbation. Then, too, if modern practice can provide clues to past sexual behaviors – hardly a certainty – there are those among today's seafarers who prefer to be "tops" and others who prefer to be "bottoms," muting the matter of mutuality in at least some homoerotic engagements.[69]

No information survives on what naval officers who actually condemned ratings to death for sodomy thought about such criminal behaviors. The men who walked the Royal Navy's quarterdecks were not an introspective lot, and the few who chronicled their careers generally wrote of deeds and events rather than ruminations or mental states. The only surviving musings on such matters comes from William Dillon who, shortly after receiving his captaincy, served on the court martial that tried a marine for sodomy in June of 1809. From Dillon's account it is clear the man received a death sentence, but the newly-dubbed captain wrestled with what he had done, at least for a time:

> It was a question of mine that led to his conviction. Upon summing up, the president [of the court martial] agreed with me, and the

> criminal was condemned. The president and I, without having any communication with each other, were both sensible of this responsibility. The marine was a Romanist, and confessed his guilt to his priest. The holy man kindly waited upon the president to let him know it. The president then came to me, saying that he supposed I labored under the same anxiety as he did himself. I acknowledged it. "Then," said he, "we are both clear, for the prisoner has confessed the whole." That certainly removed a considerable oppression of mind which had annoyed me for two or three days.[70]

The number of cases in which pairs of common sailors and private marines were tried for crimes of a sexual nature number only a dozen or so from the day in May of 1763 when James Bryan and Martin Billin were given one thousand lashes to the court martial of Edward McGee and John Peach where the two received a sentences of three hundred lashes each and were sent packing with "branded" discharges in 1832. The number is far too small to draw generalizations about the frequency or extent of sodomy and sex crimes among ratings in Nelson's navy. The one thing that becomes most apparent from the cases is that they are not typical of courts martial for sexual offenses during the period. They involved only men copulating or otherwise erotically engaged with other men. A far greater number of cases, from those first brought in the early eighteenth century to the last of them shortly before the opening years of Victoria's reign, saw adults of all ranks being called to answer for sexual contacts with boys.

I

Cases where ordinary seamen stood accused of sex crimes with boys or young men were different in many respects from those involving adult couples, and they provide an abundance of information about sodomy, indecent activities, and intergenerational sexual activities among the lower ranges of naval personnel. The cases also offer insight into the hesitant manner in which charges made by juveniles against adults were usually dealt with by men in positions of authority, from corporals of marines to post-captains. Accusations of sodomy levied by adult crewmembers were likely to result in convictions and death sentences. Similar accusations laid against sailors by ships' boys carried with them considerable chance of acquittal. Discoveries of sex crimes committed by men with boys also came about most often in a manner far different from the way copulating adult seamen were exposed. While fornicating sailors were usually found by accident, men who engaged with boys were normally brought to account only when their young partners reported them to higher authorities.

The case of Seaman Henry Bicks provides an early example of both the manner in which a case involving an adult and a youth came to the notice of officers and their reluctance to hang a man on the word of a child. In 1757, John Booth, a lad of HMS *Royal William*, accused Bicks, his shipmate and messmate, of using him to violate the twenty-ninth of the *Articles of War*.[71] Booth first told his story to a mate of the watch. The mate immediately took the twelve-year-old to one of the *Royal William*'s lieutenants and had him relate what had happened. As the youngster explained, Bicks did not select him at random. He had for a time importuned Booth while the two were on board the sixty-four-gun HMS *Magnanime*, finally catching him after dark in a hammock in late May of 1757 and buggering him several times. On 5 June the seaman again adopted his "troublesome" ways. In the evening of that day when Booth went from the *Magnanime* to the *Royal William* Bicks made some excuse to a sentry in order to follow him. He cornered his quarry in the *Royal William*'s gunroom and took down both their breeches. Then, as the boy succinctly explained, he "buggered him" again. The hesitant lieutenant wanted to be certain that Booth understood exactly what he was saying, and asked him to explain what he meant by "buggered." The youth replied "[Bicks] put his thing into [my] backside." After learning the boy suffered from a sore anus, the next step was obvious. Surgeon's Mate Johnson was summoned to look into the matter, but was unable to say if there had been penetration. The lieutenant continued questioning Booth, asking why he did not cry out and why, after being buggered the first time, he did not report what had happened. Booth replied that he did cry out, but to the second question "he made ... no answer." The boy's testimony sufficed to have Bicks placed in irons.[72]

Bicks was a single-minded fellow, it seems, hardly deterred by his shackles. A short time after being confined, at about 2:00 a. m., a sentinel noticed activity under some articles of clothing laying atop the prisoner. He summoned Quarter Gunner John Chapman, Sylvanus Hopping, the master at arms, and another sentinel posted at the gunroom door to help investigate. The sentinel yanked off Bicks's covering, and discovered the prisoner holding the penis of Stephen Touhead, another miscreant chained to the same bolt. When questioned, Touhead claimed to be too drunk to remember anything that transpired between him and Bicks. Trial testimony indicated the defendant showed no signs of drunkenness at the time he was discovered fondling Touhead's yard.

Bicks mounted no defense at his trial, other than a few questions that appeared to have little purpose. The members of the court martial, for reasons unspecified in the record, rejected young Booth's allegations, and decided Bicks had not committed sodomy. The prisoner violated only the second of the *Articles of War* in their opinion, and sentenced him to receive 500 lashes with the cat, and to be sent ashore with a halter about his neck and a paper pinned to his chest proclaiming the cause of his discharge.[73] The penman who prepared the case summary from the trial transcript for the Admiralty court martial digest recognized the disparity between the testimony against Bicks and the verdict:

> It was clearly established by the evidence that the prisoner had committed the detestable crime with which he was charged upon the body of John Booth, a boy in the same ship … . The boy deposed distinctly to six several criminal acts. And without doubt the prisoner fell under the 29th article of the act 22 Geo. II, whereby is enacted that the perpetrator of that crime "shall be punished with death by the sentence of a court martial."[74]

The apparent reluctance at mid-century to sentence an adult to death on the testimony of a boy extended beyond the Bicks case. In a previously-mentioned 1759 trial, young George Val accused a boatswain's mate of sodomy. Few details of the Val case can now be recovered. The circumstances of the accusation are lost as is the trial record. The only fragment of the proceeding available indicates a surgeon examined Val's anus and found it somewhat inflamed. The boy's testimony, on which the case depended given the ambiguous medical evidence, failed to convince a board of officers of the validity of the charge, and the accused went free.[75]

In a similar situation, with evidence offered only by a juvenile, a different court martial reached the same conclusion. In what first appeared to be an ordinary series of events leading to a sodomy prosecution in 1759, boy George Veaux, a Marine Society lad, leveled a lengthy and detailed accusation against a boatswain's servant named William Tremissen. There is no indication of Tremissen's age, but it is safe to assume that even if he were only a boy (as is suggested by his job title as boatswain's servant) he was in all likelihood older, larger, and stronger than Veaux or he would not have been able to force him into submission. According to Veaux:

> He … came to my hammock one dark night … he made me lay upon my belly, and put his prick into my backside. He came to me another

> time in the gun room, and would not let me alone, but put his finger in my backside … . Another time he made me pull down my breeches behind Mr. Emmett's berth and put his prick into my backside.[76]

The boy first told the story to one of the boatswain's mates, who told the boatswain, who then told the captain, who ordered Tremissen arrested. A court martial followed. Veaux's claim that the prisoner continued "with his prick in [his] backside" for "an hour" raised doubts among those who heard the testimony, and others offered evidence throwing further doubt on the accusation. The surgeon found only a little inflamation, but did not know what caused it. Witnesses claimed the two could not have been in the same hammock together at the times specified. "The court acquitted the prisoner on the footing that the charge had not been proved," but unlike the Bicks case, no indication exists that Veaux's testimony resulted in Tremissen receiving any punishment for indecency or scandalous behavior under the second article of war.[77]

Not all of the ordinary crewmen brought to trial for sexual offenses involving juveniles were accused of sodomy. There are a number of cases where mariners' antics never even approached the level of capital offenses, and the charges preferred against them reflected this. When Seaman John Palmer came to trial, he stood accused only of attempted sodomy with a twelve-year-old. Officials at no time even suggested that he violated the twenty-ninth article of war. In his 1772 trial, the accused sailor protested the prosecution's use of testimony by a boy so young, but the court rejected his arguments. The boy testified, and the officers hearing the case convicted the seaman of the original charge, attempted sodomy, sentenced him to receive two hundred lashes, and ejected him from the navy.[78] Three years later, a sixteen-year-old reported that a sailor identified only as A. Parrott came to his hammock and began fondling his private parts. Upon conviction of attempted sodomy, the man received a sentence of three hundred lashes.[79]

Even when accusations were made against a man by a group juveniles not just a single boy, the courts martial were wary about accepting their testimony. In a 1761 case, three youths charged Seaman Michael Berry of the storeship HMS *Crown* with the non-capital crime of attempted sodomy. One of them, William Layer, particularly attracted the scrutiny of the court. Questioning revealed that the fatherless Marine Society waif from Petticoat Lane, could neither read nor understand the meaning of an oath although he was fifteen years old. He was not allowed to give evidence. No information survives on the testimony of the other two witnesses, or if they even appeared before the court and gave evidence, but Berry went free, the charges against him judged to be false.[80]

Although three lads accused Michael Berry of attempted sodomy at one time or another, the court found him not guilty, and it is very likely another court would have done the same thing the next year with Richard Chilton, a sailor from the twenty-four gun HMS *Seahorse* if there had been no more evidence against him than the testimony of ship's boys. The officers insisted on far more than the word of a band of juveniles. They wanted irrefutable evidence of guilt. The case began when crewmen objected to the public displays of affection sailor Richard Chilton lavished on a fatherless boy named William Hoskins, who had been brought to the navy after his mother entered him into the Marine Society three years earlier. Chilton was once seen with "Hoskins between his legs ... hugging the boy with his hand round his neck." Hoskins, a fifer on board the ship, offered no objection to the attention according to the trial summary. The scrutiny of the crewmen evidently made the pair uncomfortable, for they subsequently moved their fondling to a more sheltered locale behind the ladder near the door to the carpenter's store room. Still, this half-secluded spot provided too little protection from the eyes of other mariners for what Chilton had in mind. Testimony at trial revealed that he later "pulled" the boy into the galley coal hole, "cut [his] trousers open and then put his cock to [his] belly." At this point it appears young Hoskins had enough of his friend, but Chilton employed both force and the fear of punishment to bugger Hoskins, threatening to have him flogged when he attempted to cry out. The cook and his mate discovered the two secreted in the coal hole after Chilton "had done what he would" with the boy, and chased them from the galley. For reasons unknown, neither the cook nor the mate testified at the court martial, but several witnesses revealed that the cook told them of discovering the pair and driving them off. Chilton's actions, substantiated by the testimony of numerous of his adult shipmates left little doubt of his guilt "under the 29th Article of War, and [the court] sentenced him to be hanged." It is not known whether officers judging the case decided Hoskins was too young to be guilty of sodomy (there is no indication of his exact age in the surviving case digest) or if the knowledge that he was coerced had any influence on their decisions. Whatever reasons the court martial accepted, it appears no punishment was ever prescribed for the boy.[81]

A similar case occurred in 1798 when three lads from HMS *Prince*, accused Seaman David Jenness of buggering them, and a fourth boy claimed that the sailor tried unsuccessfully to induce him to share sleeping arrangements. Had there been only the word of the youngsters, it is likely Jenness would have been acquitted. In this case, though, there was more than just the testimony of mere boys. There was solid evidence that they spoke the truth. Trial records reveal that Jenness had once put his hand into one of the boy's hammocks. The boy drew a knife, slashed him, and drove him off. Although the blade-wielding thirteen-year-old later told the court that he told no one of what the sailor did because he "was ashamed to mention what had passed to anyone on board," Jenness soon afterward had to reveal the secret. He had been badly injured by his assailant and sought medical help. The surgeon who examined him obtained the information on the source of his wound and the reason for it, and sent the information forward. The doctor also testified that one of the boys the seaman allegedly buggered had an anus so inflamed that he sent him to the "sick berth." With the doctor certifying damage to one of the accuser's anus and the perpetrator's stab wound, the testimony of the juveniles was so strongly reinforced that there could be no doubt about Jenness's guilt. He received the mandatory death sentence.[82]

The case of John Black, a marine of H. M. Gun Brig *Wrangler*, provides even more evidence of the way the judicial process moved against a low-ranking crewmember accused of sodomy by a boy who was able to support his charge with evidence that was far more persuasive than his own accusation. Black was tried at Sheerness before a "roast beef" court martial held on board the *Magnanime* in 1809. A dozen captains sat in judgment. According to Garrett Phillips, the lad who claimed to have been buggered by Black, the first instance took place when the marine came across him late one night in the larboard cable tier. He put the boy's hand on his genitals, then pulled down his trousers and attempted to enter him. Even using spittle to smooth his entry, Black was unable to achieve penetration on this occasion. Phillips reported the incident to the corporal of marines, and asked him to tell the brig's captain, John Bentick Pettet, but it was never done. It is not clear why the information failed to reach the commanding officer. Perhaps the corporal was not inclined to betray one of his fellows, he could have been reluctant to act on the accusation made by a juvenile as was usually the case with superior officers, or the matter may simply have been lost or forgotten amidst the quotidian affairs of the vessel.[83]

Some time later Black managed to waylay the Phillips again, bend him over a medicine chest, and achieve both penetration and emission. This time the boy wasted no time with the proper chain of command. He went directly to the captain to complain, then told any other crewmembers who would listen. The result was not what he intended. Both man and boy were placed in irons, and it was under these circumstances that the second part of the Black-Phillips saga took place. While incarcerated, the marine at least once tried to insert his finger into the youngster's anus, but desisted when he cried out loudly for him to stop. Black later cut holes in the boy's trousers to commit what the trial record delicately calls "indecencies," and which caused Phillips considerable pain and discomfort. At the trial the young accuser not only described Black's actions, but added that the marine had given him at various times half a guinea, a seven shilling piece, four shillings in silver, and new trousers and shoes.[84] The *Wrangler*'s surgeon followed Phillips as a witness. He said that the boy's anus exhibited slight inflamation, but he could not be sure what caused it.[85]

Only Garrett Phillips's accusations directly supported the charges against the defendant. There had been no eye-witnesses to any of the alleged instances of buggery, but adult crewmembers called to testify were able to strengthen the prosecution's case by providing persuasive circumstantial evidence. Joseph Keefe and Peter Lock confirmed the boy's claim that he had called out for Black to stop trying to insert his finger into his fundament. Thomas Freer told how the accused marine offered Phillips new trousers and shoes. Corporal Adam Fisher affirmed the shoe-and-trouser story, and added that he knew the defendant once offered the boy £1 in exchange for sex.[86]

Several witness for the defense followed, but they added little if anything to Black's case. In due course, the court pronounced him guilty and sentenced him to be hanged from the yardarm of one of His Majesty's ships.

Courts martial were not only loath to convict ratings of buggering boys without hard evidence or testimony from credible adult witnesses, but in at least one case they were quite willing to acquit an accused seaman even though it appeared his captain was bent on having him hanged. An unusual 1809 case was dismissed because of something akin to prosecutorial misconduct. In that year, sailor Edward Martin took a youth, Michael James, into his hammock. He well might have been motivated by altruism rather than lust since the boy evidently lacked either a blanket or hammock, but on board ship it aroused considerable suspicion. Word of Martin's behavior spread among the crew and ultimately reached captain, who was determined to make the two mariners pay for their indiscretions. He first ordered the boy flogged then threatened to have him flogged again if he refused to swear the sailor buggered him. The testimony reads:

Q [Prosecutor]:	Did you inform me that the prisoner had committed that unnatural crime on you twice?
A [James]:	Yes, but I was afraid the captain would flog me.[87]

The narrative of the case contains too little information even to hazard a guess about the true nature of the relationship between Edward Martin and the boy, and neither is there additional evidence in the trial record, which contains only a few more than three hundred and fifty words. Perhaps the elder man only sought to assist a luckless lad, but it is equally possible that the two engaged in a consensual relationship with sufficient commitment to one another so that only one flogging and the threat of a second could elicit testimony. Whatever the truth of the matter, the members of the court martial refused in this case to sanction obviously improper conduct by one of their fellow captains. They rejected the coerced and tainted testimony, and Martin went free.[88]

The only courts martial where officers judging sodomy and indecency cases were inclined to believe juveniles was when they actively acceded to sex with older crewmen. The trust placed in the word of the boys under these circumstances is difficult to understand. They had every reason to lie to save their lovers' lives, yet their testimony apparently went unchallenged when it helped exonerate rather than convict defendants. In these trials, of course, it was not the lads who complained of their partners. Instead, the pairs were apprehended accidentally, in the manner that pairs of ratings were exposed. One such court martial is that of Seaman John Brown and his lad, Charles McCarthy. They were caught when the master at arms of HMS *Ville de Paris* happened upon them hiding under a hammock atop a chest, both with their trousers pulled down. Although it appeared likely that sodomy might be have been committed, young McCarthy confessed the next morning before the captain, a lieutenant, the captain's clerk and the surgeon's mate only that Brown "had to do with him." The absence of any further testimony in the brief summary of the court martial fails to explain exactly what occurred between the two bare-bottomed mariners when the elder of the duo "had to do" with the younger, but the court believed the boy's claim that the elder man had not buggered him. They decided the two had nevertheless committed indecencies. Brown received a sentence of two hundred lashes, and McCarthy's participation earned him sixty "in the usual manner of punishing boys."[89] A second case similar to Brown and McCarthy's in that the youth was fully compliant ended in a very different way. It began when Captain Edward Bass, captain HM Sloop *Gluckstadt* received word that Charles North, one of his marines was a sodomite. A crewman made the report after noticing North's hammock swaying and heard him say to someone else in the hammock "how nice it was" when the motion stopped. The captain explained in a letter to his superior officer at Sheerness that he had only been told that North engaged in sodomy, but thought it best he be tried for it anyway. He hoped, presumably, that the truth would emerge from the proceeding. When the court martial got under way, one of the witnesses testified to seeing North and the boy, Henry Noel, hugging and kissing on board the sloop. He also related how he had once heard heavy breathing from North's rocking hammock, and upon looking into it discovered Noel playing with North's privates.[90] The key testimony, of course, came from Noel, who confessed to visiting the marine's hammock on several occasions. He admitted involvement in sex play, but denied anything more. During their back-to-belly encounters, Noel adamantly insisted North only inserted his penis between his thighs. Again, the court believed the juvenile witness and convicted the marine of violating article number two. He received a sentence of three hundred lashes. Although Noel's complicity made him as guilty as North, he was not punished, probably because he was young enough still to be considered a child.[91]

4
Officers and Boys at Sea

By the latter part of the eighteenth century, English attitudes were easing toward sodomy and the mollies who had become a regular feature of life in at least some sections of London. Prosecutions, stays in the pillory, and executions occurred far less often than in earlier decades, when organizations opposed to vice and moral corruption made common cause with local officials to pursue practitioners of unorthodox sexual appetites with unflagging zeal. The reputations of literary and theatrical celebrities and other persons of distinction in government or the clergy could still be destroyed by rumors of engaging same-sex partners, and blackmailers remained a threat in some quarters, but the stigma of such allegations could usually be mitigated in some fashion through published denials, court action, or by denigrating accusers. Certainly the possibilities that putative sodomites might be pilloried or hanged became remote, at least for members of the middling and monied classes. While the nation relaxed its attitudes toward sodomy to some extent, the same was not true in the higher reaches of the Royal Navy. Almost a half century after Captain Churchill's suicide in 1757, the actions of a Lieutenant Dickie indicate that even the suggestion that a man engaged in sodomy had lost none of its power to elicit an extreme reaction. When Dickie and his captain, both of the bomb vessel HMS *Vulcan*, returned to the ship from dinner ashore at Trincomalee on 4 September 1800, they were met by a Mr. Munday, their ship's carpenter, who was quite drunk. He called the officers rascals and liars, then struck them repeatedly. Such conduct would have earned the offender punishment in due course, but his next words provoked the lieutenant to immediate action. The inebriate repeatedly sang out the couplet:

> Little Dickie, Little Dickie
> Damn and Bugger Little Dickie.[1]

Obviously outraged over the insult, Dickie drew his dirk and stabbed the carpenter to death. The lieutenant was brought to trial before a court that was quite willing to concede that he acted under extenuating circumstances. It is not certain whether Dickie was actually tried for murder, although the summary of his case survives in Admiralty records under the "Murder" heading. What is certain is that he was not convicted of killing the carpenter. Still, though avoiding condemnation under that most serious charge, he did not escape unscathed. The court martial panel of officers chastised the lieutenant for not following established procedure for dealing with a drunken crewmen, that is placing him in irons or otherwise confining him. He was cashiered and forbidden ever to serve as an officer again.[2]

The cases of Churchill and Dickie are only two illustrations of the importance of reputation for the Royal Navy's officers. The former had committed suicide after only being accused of sodomy, not convicted. The latter became sufficiently enraged at being taunted with the word "bugger" that he ignored established procedure for handling drunken crewmen and stabbed a warrant officer to death. The reactions of the two men, while extreme, are easy enough to understand. Throughout the latter half of the eighteenth and early nineteenth centuries the awareness of naval officers that they belonged to a unique and prestigious occupational category that carried with it considerable social responsibility gradually became part of the quarterdeck mentality. Every man from lieutenant upward strove to burnish the image of the profession and demonstrate his own worthiness to be numbered among its members. Evidence of this trend appeared not only in matters of personal conduct but also in the corporeal presence of those holding commissions. Uniforms with golden insignia and badges of rank became standard apparel shortly after the War of Austrian Succession, and over the next fifty years white lapels were gradually kept whiter, epaulettes acquired more decoration, buttons and gold braid became more elaborate, and officers sought out better quality materials and tailoring for their apparel. By the time of Trafalgar, men in the loftiest ranks expended considerable effort in securing their exalted status, appearing sumptuously attired, exhibiting assorted cultural attainments, and by entertaining their associates in styles appropriate to their position. Like noblemen or the wealthier landed gentry, they were concerned with "keeping a table" of the quality that emphasized their place in the navy and in English society. As the availability of tinned delicacies expanded and elaborate hampers could be supplied to far-distant stations by provisioners like London's Fortnum and Mason, high-ranking officers often strove mightily to outdo their associates in the professionally serious business of extending hospitality.

By the second half of the century the character of a good officer had already become a matter for extended debate. The surrender of the forty-four-gun HMS *Angelsea* in 1745 in part sparked the discussion. The commander, Lieutenant Baker Phillips, took over the ship when the captain fell before heavy fire from the fifty-gun French *Appollon*. Finding the *Angelsea* in dire condition, he struck his colors. Phillips was later tried for failing to do his duty and fight on. He was convicted, sentenced to death, and executed despite a recommendation for mercy due to his inexperience. Two years later the court martial and execution of Admiral John Byng for his failures at Minorca inserted an additional measure of intensity into the debate. In the end, all involved in the discussions agreed that men worthy of the quarterdeck needed courage, steadfastness, honesty, aggressiveness, and morality – and they needed them in profusion. In the minds of officers, homoeroticism was entirely incompatible with personal honor and the requirements of their profession.

As the Empire grew, the nation exalted in overseas expansion and trade, and the prosperity that followed. The status of the Royal Navy increased dramatically with its enhanced role as armed guarantor of the nation's imperial prestige and economic well-being. At the same time, famous commanders were lionized, the naval hospital at Greenwich became synonymous with sea power, James Thompson's *Rule Britannia* became an anthem to global expansion, and the rousing song, *Heart of Oak*, written by Dr. William Boyce for David Garrick's *Harlequin's Invasion* in 1759, quickly grew into a favorite among men of the fleet and remained popular with them well into the nineteenth century. It was played on board at least one ship as late as 1827 when "the drum beat to quarters" before Battle of Navarino.

Captain Thomas Churchill's suicide on board the *Canterbury*, not only indicates the destructive nature an accusation of sodomy could have for an officer, but because it also saved the navy the trouble and embarrassment of investigating and probably prosecuting him, those in positions of higher authority probably breathed sighs of relief. That the abject horror with which one officer regarded a charge of sodomy levied against him led to suicide was unfortunate, but at least it could be handled neatly. The navy gained another neat solution to a similar problem when in the early 1820s. Lieutenant Horatio Darby deserted his ship in South America after his homoerotic involvements became common knowledge.[3]

Not all officers reacted with measures as extreme as those taken by Churchill, Dickie, or Darby, and the Royal Navy had procedures suitable for dealing with officers accused of all-male sexual activity who chose not to flee or kill themselves. In 1759, Lieutenant Richard Beale of HMS *Polacre* repeatedly kissed two of the ships boys and engaged them in masturbation. His indiscretions came to official notice in the usual way that adults toying with boys were most often exposed. One of the thirteen-year-olds he forced "to lay hold of his private parts and to shake it [*sic*] about" had enough. Jonathan Silk "did not like such behavior and told the captain of it."[4] The lieutenant stood trial, but the transcript of his court martial is lost. Only a three-hundred-word summary of the proceeding has survived. It does not indicate whether the officers who judged Beale were concerned with the truthfulness of the two young witnesses who condemned him, but they may have been more inclined to believe what they heard because, since the defendant was not charged with sodomy, his life was not at stake. The lieutenant was convicted at Gibralter of violating the second article of war, and dismissed from the service.[5]

It was easy enough to dispose of the dishonored Richard Beale. The evidence seems clear against him, at least from what little can be discerned from the brief record of his trial. Two years later, when Captain Henry Angel chose to fight shaky accusations of sexual indecency and attempted sodomy, the result was prodigious disruption within the well-ordered navy. On 31 December 1761, Angel, of HMS *Stag*, returned to his ship from a shore visit on the island of Guadeloupe. As he came on board he was met by a delegation of his officers who informed him that they had decided unanimously to remove him from his post as captain and place him under arrest. The ship's first lieutenant, John Orde, then took command of the vessel. The shocked captain, who had sailed the *Stag* from Portsmouth to the West Indies without incident or difficulty, demanded to know the reasons for the mutiny. The second lieutenant, John Bazely responded by reading out a letter from one of the passengers who had crossed the Atlantic on board the ship. The passenger, Rice Price, who had been ordered to Antigua by Admiral Francis Holburn to work three years as a shipwright, accused Angel in the letter of a series of indecencies. Price claimed that the captain had kissed him, forced his tongue into his mouth, repeatedly groped him, and thrust his erect "yard" into his hand.[6]

On hearing this, "Capt. Angel appeared then quite shocked and said incoherently that the man wanted to extort a sum of money from him – pulled off his wig – and seemed in the greatest of agonies."[7] The captain's agitation is easy enough to understand. Beyond being accused of homoerotic sex crimes and being removed from his command, the charge seriously impugned his character as an officer and gentlemen. The imputations against him lodged by his own officers swept away the life of the *Stag*'s captain. All of what he should have been and probably held himself to be was gone in an instant. His composure disappeared with it. The ship's officers took the captain's emotional display as both a vindication of what they had done and reasonable evidence of his guilt. Angel, already removed from his command, was confined to his cabin.

The mutiny against Angel had been planned earlier in the day when at the order of Lieutenant Orde the *Stag*'s officers met in the ship's gunroom, where they were read passenger Price's letter. Dated 31 December at Basseterre, St. Kitts and addressed to Orde, it is long and detailed:

> Sir:
>
> Thinking it proper to report to the actions that I have received from Captain Angel on the 17th November, etc.
>
> First: By his calling me into his cabin and doing those actions which I think [illegible] not proper to be kept secret. By his receiving me in this manner in grasping me round the waist and kissing me the same as if a woman. Then by his forcing his hand towards my private parts which I defended. Then again by force drove his hand into my breeches took hold of my private parts which I forced away again. Then in a little time after he put his private parts into my hand and give me a hard cheg [?] to his belly which I beg of him to be easy and look in his Articles of War. Then taking and kissing me the same as before. Then seeing such actions, I beg to be excused which as last putting his hand into my bosom and then dismiss me. Then his calling me into his cabin the second time doing such like actions kissing me when at the same time put his tongue in my mouth and repeating these words. Telling me he should be glad to see me [on] shore saying I knew what he meant.
>
> From your humble servant,
> /s/ Rice Price

Price then concluded his letter with a postscript.

> Sir:
>
> The reason of my not informing you of this before is by being afraid of being ill treated from him if he heard of it again. But it was not kept as a secret, for I told Mr. Blamey the carpenter two or three days after I received the actions from Captain Angel.
>
> /s/ RP[8]

Price well knew that Angel's actions were precursors to sodomy. That is why he warned him about the *Articles of War* and the possibility of a death sentence.

After Lieutenant Orde read the letter to the assembled officers, all were immediately aware of their dilemma. Acting against the captain constituted mutiny under most circumstances, yet they feared that if they ignored the letter and did nothing the secret would soon be known and they might fall afoul of the thirty-second article, which was also read aloud to the group by one of those present. The latter part of it said:

> All captains, officers, and others in the fleet, shall do their endeavour [*sic*] to detect, apprehend, and bring to punishment all offenders, and shall assist the officers appointed for that purpose therein, upon pain of being proceeded against, and punished by a court martial according to the nature and degree of the offense.

After the article was read, and after some discussion, "it was therefore agreed by all the officers that it was absolutely necessary for the safety of His Majesty's ship as well as of ourselves, to put Capt. Angel under an arrest until we joined the admiral or a superior officer." Orde first argued that the ship's safety was not compromised by leaving Angel in command, but he later altered his stance. The verdict in the end was unanimous that he must be removed.[9] It was not only the three commissioned officers, Orde and Bazely, and Mr. Forester, the marine lieutenant on board, who supported the course of action. They were joined by each of the *Stag*'s warrant officers, Mr. Blamey, the carpenter, Mr. Dalrymple, the gunner, Mr. Macklesaith, the master, Mr. Miller, the boatswain, Mr. Prosser, the purser, and Mr. Spence, the ship's surgeon.[10]

The day after Angel's arrest, Lieutenant Orde reported what had happened to Guadeloupe's governor, Campbell Dalrymple, and then to Rear Admiral George B. Rodney, the "Commander in Chief of His Majesty's Ships and Vessels Employed and to Be Employed at Barbados and the Leeward Islands and the Seas Adjacent."[11] As the ranking naval officer in the Caribbean, Rodney now had to deal with mutiny and a post-captain who stood accused of crimes related to sodomy if not actually sodomy itself. He ordered Captain Angel tried on charges "set forth against him by letter from Rice Price for kissing him, putting his hand into his breeches, and behaving in a very indecent manner towards him on board His Majesty's Ship *Stag*, at two different times during the passage to the West Indies."[12]

The day after the mutiny, Orde talked with the deposed captain. The lieutenant said that he hoped confinement did not sit heavy on him, and Angel said, "no otherwise than its making his trial inevitable. But the letter, the damned letter, makes me blame myself for not having stopped the man."[13] At the conclusion of their conversation, Orde reported the prisoner in a disordered state, and decided it was probably fortunate for the service that he was locked away.

Angel expressed no optimism about his situation. "But to me, dying today or five days hence is immaterial," he told Orde, "every captain is my enemy, and where there is one honest man among them, there are six rogues."[14] Still, things were not as dismal as the captain thought. Though a prisoner, he had not been placed in irons by the mutineers. He continued on in the captain's cabin, just as he had done since taking command of the *Stag* months earlier in England. Neither did he need fear being hanged from the yardarm of his ship or swinging from a gibbet on shore. Price, after all, had not accused him of sodomy, only a series of indecent acts potentially leading to sodomy. Still, given his state of mind, it is easy enough to understand how Captain Angel might have seen his predicament in the darkest shades.

The court martial convened on board HMS *Devonshire*, at St. Anne's Bay, Martinique on 12 January 1762. John Barker, captain of the seventy-four-gun *Culloden* presided over the trial, and eight captains served as members of the board.[15] The chief prosecution witness, Rice Price, expounded on how the *Stag*'s commander attempted to lead him into sodomy. The kissing, hugging, and groping listed in the letter were recounted in some detail, as were Price's rejections of each advance. Price further claimed that Angel promised to try to have him released from his three-year commitment to work as a shipwright on Antigua and employ him on the *Stag* as a carpenter's mate if he would be more compliant. The captain also said, according to Price, that carpenter Blamey actually belonged to another, larger ship, and when he returned to his own ship, Price would have the post as the *Stag*'s carpenter. Then, when the ship returned to England, the captain promised to intercede to obtain a warrant for Price, ensconcing him officially and permanently as the ship's carpenter. This was a promise of considerable value. Securing a carpenter's warrant provided its holder with a well-paid, lifetime sinecure. If Angel actually made the offer, as Price averred, and if he had been able to deliver its promise, it would have been handsome compensation to the *Stag*'s passenger for bending to the captain's passions.[16]

Price also explained that the captain's attempts at seduction had not come as a complete surprise. The purser's steward, William Collins, once told him that Angel stood accused of buggery with his clerk when he served on board HMS *Deal Castle*, a twenty-gun fifth rate, earlier in his career.[17] Price claimed he had heard the tale from others as well, but they remained unnamed in the testimony. This put the steward in an awkward position, having been accused of spreading word that his captain was a sodomite. He admitted to the charge when later called to testify, but strove to mitigate his guilt by claiming that although he had heard the tale, he "believed it to be a falsity."[18]

At least some of Price's non-criminal allegations were supported by testimony of other members of the *Stag*'s crew. Mr. Blamey confirmed the captain's asking Price to be a carpenter's mate, and also that he did belong to another ship. Other crewmen supported Price's claim that he had told them about Angel's advances shortly after they were alleged to have occurred.[19]

The prosecution continued the assault on the accused captain by claiming that in his attempt to seduce Price, he allowed him special favors. Lieutenant Bazely thought Angel's familiarity with the passenger so extraordinary that he mentioned it to Lieutenant Orde, Spence the surgeon, and Lieutenant Forester.[20] In his own testimony the surgeon confirmed Bazely's judgment, stating, "I have seen him [Angel] talking very familiarly at different times with him [Price] and smiling on him."[21] A Midshipman Nichols seconded Spence's words, saying the captain walked and talked with Price on several occasions and once gave him small beer when the crew had none.[22] Price was also provided with victuals from the gunroom mess rather than the sailors' fare that was his due, according to Mr. Miller, the boatswain.[23]

The only man to testify directly concerning Angel's supposed indecent actions was his chief accuser, Rice Price. No eye-witness testimony supported any of his allegations. When the captain began his defense, he drove this point home, but he did much more to vindicate himself than merely speak to the insufficiency and dubious reliability of the evidence against him. He set out to prove that the untoward events and actions attributed to him by Price simply had not happened.

Angel's general narrative of events ran parallel to that provided by Price, but he denied making any sexual advances. In the captain's version it was his accuser who initiated and pressed the relationship between the two men. On weighing anchor at Spithead the *Stag* had a minor collision with another vessel. Price helped with the repairs, although he was only a passenger rather than a crewman. He then offered to assist with any other carpentry that might need to be done, and he also volunteered to build a model of the *Stag* for the captain. The reasons why Price attempted to ingratiate himself were two, according to Angel. He wanted to get out of his three-year assignment on Antigua and he hoped to extort money, much in the manner blackmailers famously used accusations of sodomy to fleece gentlemen in the mother country.[24] As the officers of the court martial very likely knew, blackmail and sodomy kept close company, and it is likely they would have found the captain's allegations entirely plausible from their reading or hearing about the widely publicized court cases of the age involving libel suits over such matters.[25]

It is unclear how Price intended to attain either of these goals by telling crewmen that the captain committed indecent acts and offered indecent suggestions, and Angel, after suggesting the motives, did not bother to explain how his accuser might have effected them. Instead, he launched the heart of his defense by calling a string of witnesses to testify that it would have been difficult or impossible for him to have kissed and groped Price, and placed his penis in his hand without the acts being observed.

One of the witnesses called by the defense was James Rennie, the captain's clerk. He claimed to have seen Price through the open cabin door during the entire length of his first visit, and that afterward he chatted with Price. In their conversation Price told Rennie that he wanted to remain on board the *Stag* as a carpenter's mate and that Angel told him if all went well he might be able to get him a warrant as a ship's carpenter. He mentioned nothing of any indecent behavior in their conversation. Rennie did not witness the second visit, but only talked with Price as he left the cabin. Again, the clerk heard the same story that had been imparted to him after the first visit, and again there was no mention of any indecencies. Rennie's only comments not firmly in support of the defense came in response to a question from the court about whether any officers said anything about Price being summoned to the captain's cabin. He said, "I did hear somebody on the quarterdeck say that Price was a fine smooth-faced [*sic*] and that would all come out in time."[26]

Another defense witness was William Collins, the purser's steward. His testimony supported the captain. In response to a question by the court, he explained that Price, although claiming he heard Angel was a "buggerer," denied that the captain made any sexual advances toward him. Collins continued by stating that he observed Price in Angel's cabin during the two visits he made, and the door was open all of the time on each occasion. The court questioned him extensively about what he observed during the second visit. Collins was unequivocal. He witnessed the entire second visit, which lasted six or seven minutes. The captain and the passenger were about a yard apart throughout the meeting, he said, and never changed positions during the entire time.[27] Two marine sentries also swore that the cabin door remained always open during Price's visits, but neither provided information on the relative positions of the two men during either meeting.[28]

After having established for the record that the cabin door stood open during Price's visits and that the two men always remained approximately one yard apart, at least when observed by witnesses, Angel launched a second attack against his accuser. The captain sought to establish that it was Price not he who infused familiarity into their relationship. When questioning Robert Barrels, his own steward, he asked whether Price was ever seen to "throw himself in my way in a remarkable manner to be taken notice of by me, as it were?" Barrels answered equivocally.[29] Then the captain's serving man offered stronger support for his master. The doors were open during the second visit, he said, when he and the two men were always about a yard apart. Price's only attempt to counter the servant's testimony came when he asked him if the captain liked model ships. Barrels answered affirmatively.[30] In his concluding statement, Angel fired a final shot of dubious effectiveness at his accuser. He claimed that the first man to whom Price related his tale of sexual advances was one Dempsey, who he previously had flogged for striking a sergeant. The captain claimed Dempsey would likely believe any evil of him.[31]

With the defense complete, time had come for the impaneled officers to render judgment. There is no indication of the length of their deliberations, but the verdict, when it came, was sharp and direct. "After examination of evidence in support of the charge, and likewise in behalf of the prisoner, [we] are of opinion that the charge is not proved against the said Captain Angel and the court does acquit him, the said Capt. Angel thereof, and he is hereby acquitted accordingly." The signatures of the nine officers who comprised the court martial and that of Judge Advocate William Pagett followed the verdict.[32]

The acquittal placed the Royal Navy in an awkward position. The officers of the *Stag* had by mutual and unanimous agreement mutinied against a captain accused only of indecency. A board of seasoned naval officers now certified his innocence. Had Angel been convicted, the mutineers would have been vindicated in their decision to arrest and incarcerate the captain, and the matter might have ended there. But that had not happened. For the navy at this stage, there was little room for maneuver. Despite what appeared to be extenuating circumstances, mutiny against an innocent captain could not be ignored. Only two decades earlier the first lieutenant of HMS *Ruby* confined the captain, Samuel Goodere, fearing he might escape justice for suborning two men to murder his brother in the purser's cabin while he stood guard outside the door, brandishing a sword to prevent interference. Although the captain was convicted and executed for his crime in 1742, the lieutenant was dismissed from the service. The ejected officer received a pardon in short order and returned to his previous post, but the case hardly served as a precedent for what Orde had done since his captain had been exonerated.[33] Naval justice and naval discipline required a court martial for Lieutenant John Orde, the chief mutineer. The proceedings against him began on board HMS *Vanguard* at Martinique on 1 February 1762. He was formally charged not with mutiny, but with "taking the command from and confining his captain."[34] Two of the nine men who acquitted Captain Angel were members of the group assembled to determine the guilt or innocence of the lieutenant.[35]

In his own defense, Orde relied simply on explaining what had happened. He claimed that if he had not acted, it would have been a dereliction of duty under the thirty-second of the *Articles of War*. He emphasized that he consulted with all the *Stag*'s officers and they unanimously urged him to act against the captain. And he argued that the captain's demeanor when notified of his being removed from command indicated he might well be guilty. Throughout, Orde emphasized that his actions and the actions of his officers only served to protect themselves, the crew, the ship, and the Royal Navy. Their intent was in no way mutinous, as proved by the facts that at first opportunity he notified Governor Dalrymple of Guadeloupe of what had transpired and shortly thereafter he sent the information to Admiral Rodney, the area naval commander. Orde put forward a persuasive case, but there remained the nagging truth that he had usurped the command of one of His Majesty's ships from a captain who, according to a court martial verdict, had done no wrong. In their decision the officers vacillated. "The court is of the opinion that the charge is proved," they said, "but upon consideration of many circumstances appearing in his favor in the course of the evidence, the court does adjudge him [only] to be dismissed from his present employment of lieutenant on board His Majesty's Ship, *Stag*."[36] Penalties far more severe could have been inflicted on Orde, but he retained his rank and commission. Removal from the ship, in fact, could hardly be considered a penalty. It is likely that after the episode on board her he would have been reassigned in any case. He remained in the navy, and eventually rose to the rank of commander. It is impossible to gauge what effect the court martial had on his career, whether or not it factored into his failure ever to attain the rank of captain. His name appeared on the superannuated list in 1805. He died fourteen years later.[37]

After his acquittal, Captain Angel wrote to Admiral Rodney complaining that ill health prevented him from doing his assigned duties and asking permission to return to England. He also asked the admiral not to report ill of him to naval authorities and not to send the record of his trial to the Admiralty.[38] There was little difficulty with the first request. Angel was paid off[39] and orders issued that he, his "servants, and equipage have a passage in the *Crown* store ship with the use of the great cabin."[40] Rodney assured him that he would "not represent things in an unfavorable light," but that no alternative existed to returning the court martial transcript to authorities in the homeland.[41] After the courts martial of both Angel and Orde were over, Rodney remained equivocal about the entire matter. In a letter to Secretary of the Admiralty John Clevland dated 10 February 1762, he explained that he had sent Angel back to England and made Lucius O'Bryan, who served on both courts martial, the captain of the *Stag*, but that he had done little else, waiting "till their lordships pleasure be known agreeable to their instructions to me on that head."[42] Nothing more is known of Angel after his return home, except that he died in 1777.

Of others involved in the matter, Rice Price disappeared from the historical record after his brief appearance as a self-proclaimed victim of a superior officer's lasciviousness. The *Stag*'s warrant officers, master, boatswain, purser, gunner, and carpenter probably continued on in their careers without difficulty, since as warrant officers they were as secure in the navy as it was possible to be. As for Lieutenant John Bazely, his involvement did not impede his advancement. Sixteen years after his participation in the Angel affair he received a captaincy, and when he died in 1809 he held the rank of Admiral of the Blue.[43]

The proceedings against Captain Henry Angel for indecent acts possibly leading to sodomy never became a precedent simply because no other case ever came to trial remotely similar to it. The entire affair is illustrative, however, of the power to inspire terror in the men of the Royal Navy. That on the word of a mere carpenter, a passenger on the ship rather than a warranted member of her crew, the officers of the *Stag* gathered together when their captain was ashore and discussed the possibility of removing him from his post, indicates the gravity of the charge. There may have been rumors of the man's homoerotic proclivities circulating on board the ship, but rumors and a single accusation of indecency rather than the capital crime of sodomy could not have led to Angel's arrest and confinement had not the seriousness of the situation, in the unanimous opinion of the *Stag*'s officers, exposed them all to the threat of courtmartial. Then, too, their testimony revealed that they thought themselves and their ship in danger of an unspecified sort by having Angel, whom they thought a failed seducer, in command.

The officers on the court martial that judged the entire episode also evinced the deep concern with which they regarded accusations of homoerotic behavior. Although they acquitted Angel, it was in all likelihood easy for them to do since no matter what his alleged crime, his only accuser was a civilian. Then, too, the captain mounted a vigorous and persuasive defense. The court martial of Lieutenant John Orde reveals even more of the thinking of the captains who passed judgment on him. They decided that this same carpenter's unsubstantiated accusations were sufficient grounds for a lieutenant and the rest of a ship's officers to rise up against their captain, remove him from his command and confine him to his quarters during time of war. Although the same captain was acquitted, they still regarded the information on which his officers had acted substantial enough, and the putative commission of indecency serious enough, so that they tried Orde only with removing his captain from command and incarcerating him.[44] There is no indication that they ever considered charging him with mutiny.

It was not until over thirty years after a court martial acquitted Henry Angel of indecency and attempted sodomy that another commissioned officer stood accused of committing a sex crime. In 1796, Charles Sawyer, captain of HMS *Blanche*, faced charges of indecent actions in violation of the articles of war. Sawyer's frequent pursuits of shipboard lads was well-known among all on board his thirty-two-gun fifth rate according to crewman Jacob Nagle. Officers in the Mediterranean squadron where the *Blanche* was stationed originally attempted to cover up his solicitations, but they eventually became too flagrant. He regularly summoned boys to his cabin late at night, ordered lights extinguished, then made small-talk with them while groping their private parts. He also tolerated a rare degree of insubordination from his favorites, enough to prejudice shipboard discipline and even suggest mutinous conduct. The specifics of his unacceptable conduct included being seen often in bed with his coxswain, Edward Mullins, engaging in mutual frigging or masturbation with a black seaman, and compelling two midshipmen, Thomas Rowe and Richard Pridham, to masturbate him. The mutinous act the captain was alleged to have tolerated was performed by the coxswain who denounced him on board his own ship as "a man-fucking bugger."[45]

The *Blanche*'s first lieutenant, Archibald Cowan, requested a court martial for the captain in a letter to the man who was then the area commodore, Horatio Nelson. Nelson responded favorably, although he did not order Sawyer arrested, as would have been done in the case of anyone without a commission. Still, he was chagrined by the entire matter. When he wrote to Sir Gilbert Elliot, the Viceroy of Corsica some weeks before Sawyer's court martial, he told him not to receive the disgraced captain until he rehabilitated his reputation. He also instructed Elliot to destroy the note he sent discussing the distasteful business. Nelson hoped, as he later explained, that Sawyer "would take himself off," perhaps as Captain Churchill had done four decades earlier, and save the navy and the officer corps considerable trouble and embarrassment.

It must have been a difficult decision for Cowan to set in motion a process that would bring his commanding officer to trial, particularly since he also knew Sawyer was well-connected, with "very respectable relatives of high rank and unblemished honor in the service." He fretted as well over the damage the public nature of a court martial might have for the careers of the two midshipmen who were ordered to frig their captain.[46] Considerable negotiation took place involving Sawyer, Cowan, and high ranking officers of the squadron, in which the accused commander of the *Blanche* at one point demanded that Lieutenant Cowan and others of his ship's officers be court martialed. He also offered to end the matter quietly by resigning and leaving the ship, literally "taking himself off" in Nelson's terminology. The apparent willingness of senior commanders even to discuss hushing up the episode indicated the navy's discomfort with the entire business, but in the end courts martial on board the squadron's flagship for both Sawyer and Cowan seemed the only proper course of action to straighten up the matter.

The testimony offered at the captain's trial on board HMS *Barfleur* on 18 October 1796 established his guilt, but the accused commander of the *Blanche* mounted a spirited defense which, in customary fashion, he had read to the court.[47] He stumbled trying to explain Edward Mullins's presence in his bed, and denied the coxswain ever called him "a man-fucking bugger," but his sense of indignation escalated to rage at the notion that testimony from a black crewmember was accepted by the court:

> I could wish to remark a little upon another part of the charge, but despair of being able for what language, gentlemen, can convey even a faint idea of what every man of liberality and honor must feel at finding the mere ipse dicit of a black man, who would possibly sell

> his father and mother for half a bit, erected at once into a charge of a most serious nature against a person in my situation in life ... . The very infamy of such a charge destroys it.[48]

In concluding, Sawyer cited his previous years of exemplary service. That line of argument was no more successful in this case than in any others. Sawyer was barred from ever again serving in the navy, and was replaced by Captain D'Arcy Preston. Lieutenant Cowan returned to his post on the *Blanche* when the matter was resolved, along with all of the other ship's officers. There is no way to judge whether the case would have affected Cowan's career; he died in 1800. The advancement of the two midshipmen was apparently unaffected by their having masturbated their captain. Richard Pridham was promoted to lieutenant two years after the court martial, and died a vice admiral in 1864. Thomas Rowe received his lieutenancy in 1804 and was a commander by 1810.[49] The day after Sawyer's conviction and cashiering, Horatio Nelson again expressed his aggravation, this time to Admiral Sir John Jervis. "A person who is impudent enough to do what has been proved on him," he wrote, "may fairly be supposed to have impudence enough for anything."[50]

The following year, a similar situation developed when Captain Henry Allen of H. M. Sloop *Rattler* heard charges levied against him by Lieutenant Edward Church, of his own ship. Captain Allen's court martial left little doubt that he not only committed sodomy, but did so with frequency and enthusiasm enough to seem possessed. Seaman Edward Woodger and a boy, James Bonny, both of the *Rattler* told stories of how they had been buggered in February, March, and April of 1797. First to denounce Allen was Seaman Woodger, who swore to having been twice victimized by the captain's lust. Hard usage of the sort he described inflamed his anus and stopped his urine, he told the court, and when the captain offered him money for his discomfort, he declined. The captain also ordered him to procure two other crew members for him "at the dead of night."[51] By revealing the two assignations, Woodger raised the question of his own willing participation. The court asked whether he knew sodomy violated the *Articles of War*, and implied that he should have reported the incidents. It is difficult to tell whether the sailor was sincere or simply crafty, but he managed to evade the question by responding that "he thought as the captain was so much his superior he would not have done him a damage." The court then told him that he must have known the captain was as much subject to the *Articles* as he was. No record survives of Woodger's answer, if he gave one, but members were evidently satisfied by his performance. Nothing indicates he was prosecuted for sodomy.[52]

The boy, James Bonny, when called to give testimony, was asked his age. He explained he was uncertain about it, but guessed he was fourteen or fifteen years old. The boy not only told how he had seen Allen and Woodger in bed together, but he spun out his own tale of victimization during his captain's sodomy marathon in the spring of 1797. Beginning on 26 March the captain buggered him seven successive nights, once behind the screens of the "necessary" in the cabin. Since the captain had private quarters on board the sloop, it is not certain why he hid his action behind the screens or confined them to the nighttime hours. Afternoons would have worked as well as evenings for the *Rattler*'s commander, although it might have been more difficult to guard against interruptions during the day. The use of "pomatum" did not lessen the boy's terror or protect him from pain, particularly "at stool." At a later point in the trial, the court, previously unsure whether Bonny understood the meaning of an oath, indicated a measure of hesitancy accepting his testimony against the captain. They asked him if he knew "what the act of sodomy consists in?" The response held no uncertainty. The boy may have been unsure of his age, unable to sign his name, and needed the substance of an oath explained to him, but on sexual matters he answered confidently. "He fucked me," Bonny answered, "He pulled down his trousers. He laid me on my belly on the locker. He put his prick into my fundament."[53]

It is unlikely that Allen's liaison with Bonny went unnoticed by the crew. On any vessel it would have been impossible that men of all ranks would not be aware of a man and a boy spending entire nights together in the great cabin, but such goings-on would have been even more difficult to mask on board a smallish, sixteen-gun sloop.[54] Over the course of March, April, and May, Woodger might have held his tongue for fear of doing the captain "a damage," as he put it, but Bonny had no similar reservation. His anus hurt, and he told Thomas Gains, the captain's servant, that Allen had sodomized him. Gains undoubtedly believed him, having been groped by his master at least once. Later, the pain drove Bonny to visit William F. Nye, the sloop's surgeon. When asked why he had an inflamed anus with the appearance that some substance had been forced into it, Bonny again told of his involuntary sexual service to the captain. Through whatever channel, via Gains, Nye, or some other crewmen of the *Rattler*, the accusation made its way to Lieutenant Stephen G. Church. He reported the matter to higher authorities, and in due course a court martial was authorized. The testimony against Captain Allen from Woodger, Bonny, Gains, Surgeon Nye, the master, the gunner, and others of the sloop's crew left little option for the court. While none but Woodger and Bonny actually witnessed or participated in Allen's buggeries, the remainder of the witnesses all provided circumstantial information indicating it took place.[55] One of the two seamen who testified that the captain tried to seduce them described his commander's technique. "He laid hold of my hand and put it to his privates," said Thomas Haines, "I immediately hauled it away. I went on the forecastle and almost fainted away."[56] James Burns, the *Rattler*'s cook, provided one of the trial's most graphic bits of evidence. Although hearsay, the court seemed unperturbed when he related how Bonny told him "that Captain Allen committed sodomy on him, then frigged him and sucked his yard and committed sodomy on him three times in a day."[57]

Throughout the court martial, the beleaguered captain defended himself as best he could. He regularly questioned prosecution witnesses, but gained little or nothing from it. When given the opportunity, he had a written statement read to the court. In it, he rambled on, first trying to impugn the testimony of several who testified against him. James Bonny was obviously too dull to give reliable evidence, he said. The boy did not even know how old he was, and he needed the nature of the oath explained to him. Allen also adopted several lines used without success in other sodomy trials. He cited his previous exemplary service and told of his family connections "which are of the first in England." He then concluded his efforts with another technique that had notably little success at courts martial over the years. He called a dozen character witnesses, then rested his defense.[58]

Officers charged with serious crimes sometimes surrendered their swords to naval authorities while being tried. After testimony ended and courts concluded their deliberations, the swords were then used to signify verdicts rendered. If placed on the tables at which the courts martial members sat with the hilts toward the defendants, they signaled innocence. When placed points toward the accused, they meant verdicts of guilty. If this practice were followed in Allen's case when he came before the court to learn its decision he saw his sword laid out on the table, point toward him. Despite the self-proclaimed social prominence of the defendant, he received a death sentence. On the appointed day, HMS *Queen* signaled for the squadron's boats to appear for the execution. By evening all preparations were complete. An officer intoned the *Articles or War*, and on 15 May 1797 "at 7 [the Royal Navy] hung Henry Allen, Esq., late commander of H. M. Sloop *Rattler*, at the starboard fore yard arm for the detestable crime of sodomy [and] committed his body to the deep with the usual ceremonies."[59]

Another shipboard uprising occurred in 1799, when Lieutenants Philip Brown and George Baker, both from the twenty-four-gun sixth rate HMS *Daphné*, along with the acting master, the purser, and the master's mate, charged the captain, Richard Matson with committing buggery numerous times on board the ship.[60] The members of the court did not mince words in pronouncing their conclusion. "The charges were groundless, vexatious, and malicious," they decided, "and therefore most honorably acquitted Captain Matson." The men who judged Matson not guilty also informed the local commander in chief of their opinion that the *Daphné*'s officers engaged in a conspiracy against their captain, and suggested the entire matter be investigated, "the conduct of those officers the same being highly dangerous to the public service."[61]

Before adjourning, the court ordered one witness to serve three months "solitary imprisonment" for perjury, but the ships' officers, apparently, never had to answer for their actions, which may have included forgery and perjury.[62] The man compiling the digest of the case suggested a reason for the failure to follow up Matson's court martial with an inquiry. In a marginal note, he wrote:

> This case is reported with fidelity from the records, but by information since received from one of the clerks belonging to the Admiralty (Mr. Dyer), the author of this digest, had learnt with astonishment that the surgeon of the *Daphné* by letter under his own hand sometime after the trial confesses that his own testimony in the prisoner's favor was totally false and that the other evidence on the same side was in like manner false and suborned by the captain. The surgeon, in consequence, found it necessary to resign his warrant and quit the service. His name was Robertson or Robinson. The captain also retired somewhere into the country, where he has since lived in obscurity but not without being repeatedly guilty of the crime for which he was tried by the court martial. This will sufficiently account for the investigation suggested by the court for the purpose of punishing the gentlemen who exhibited the charges against Matson never having been entered upon.[63]

Almost a decade after Matson's acquittal, in 1807, another naval officer, Lieutenant William Berry of His Majesty's Sloop *Hazard* stood accused of violating both the second and twenty-ninth articles of war. According to the court martial record he and one of the sloop's boys, Thomas Gibbs, masturbated one another on numerous occasions, and then Berry buggered Gibbs at least once. Their liaison followed the standard pattern, taking place in the privacy of the lieutenant's cabin, away from prying eyes, or so they assumed. The discovery of their activities also occurred in a familiar fashion. A tearful Gibbs reported what had occurred to the gunroom steward, John Hoskins, and asked him to tell the captain. Gibbs was not the only source for what was taking place in the privacy of the officer's quarters. Another witness, Elizabeth Bowden, serving on board the *Hazard* as third-class boy John Bowden, told the steward of peering through the keyhole of the cabin door and watching Gibbs fondling Berry's privates. Hoskins delayed moving the information upward for a time, but eventually told the purser who, presumably, passed the information on to a lower-ranking commissioned officer or directly to the captain.[64]

The testimony of a female shipping as a male attracted no particular notice at the trial other than a single mention of her sex in the transcript, and there was little reason it would. By the early nineteenth century, females masquerading as sailors or soldiers had become a cliché of popular culture both in Britain and in the Netherlands. Captain's clerk Thomas Collings wrote of one such girl who, when discovered, "was sent back to England an object of universal interest and commiseration."[65] Then, too, women in limited numbers regularly sailed on board warships without disguising their sex. Most accompanied their warrant officer husbands, and in battle worked as powder monkeys or in the cockpit assisting the surgeon. Bowden testified that she had often observed Gibbs entering Berry's cabin and the door closing after him. Wanting to know the nature of the visits, she peeked though the keyhole. When asked by a skeptical court how she could discern activities in a windowless cabin, she explained that a candle illuminated the scene she saw during her peeping.[66]

In addition to Hoskins and Bowden, the court called a host of witnesses seeking additional evidence on which to judge the charge of violating the twenty-ninth article. One of those summoned and sworn was the *Hazard*'s surgeon Charles Gregson. He testified to being present when Gibbs told the captain that, in the surgeon's words, Lieutenant Berry had put his "cock in his tail." He also explained that his examination showed Gibbs exhibited no outward sign of being violated, which, he hurriedly added, was no proof that sodomy had not taken place. A boy of his age could have been buggered without producing lacerations, the surgeon said, although he did not mention Gibbs's age nor is it mentioned elsewhere in the trial transcript. The use of the word "cock" by the surgeon provides a discordant note in the record. He is the only person involved in the trial employing crude sailor talk. The Berry court martial, in fact, is one of the most decorous in terms of nouns, employing for the most part only medical terminology and the most gentle euphemisms. Except for the surgeon's one reference to the lieutenant's "cock" in the boy's tail and the use several times of the same word in testimony by a ship's steward, only "fundament," "anus," "privates," "backside," and "making water" appear in the record. Masturbation in the testimony is "shaking."[67]

As might be expected when an officer's career and possibly his life rested in the balance, the court evidenced considerable skepticism about the word of a child. Surgeon Gregson was one of those questioned pointedly about the boy's character. When asked about whether Gibbs might be so vicious as to lodge false charges, he replied emphatically, "I think not." Captain Charles Dilkes of the *Hazard*, the commanding officer of Berry and Gibbs, spoke more guardedly. He told how the boy was once late for a ship's sailing and on another occasion stole a "seven-shilling piece" from a Lieutenant Hart, who was then his master. Still, the captain provided a positive assessment. Gibbs was "cleanly well-behaved," he said, adding that the boy was definitely not a liar. Gunroom steward Hoskins, who earlier reported Berry's relationship with Gibbs, seconded Dilkes' assessment. The boy had stolen small articles from time to time from officers of the sloop and occasionally lied, but in this case he was telling the truth.[68]

The court martial of Lieutenant William Berry is distinct in several respects from other Royal Navy trials for sodomy and indecency. It is one of the very few involving oral sex, and the only one containing detailed testimony on the subject:

Q [Court]: You [Gibbs] have stated to the court that at two different times the prisoner held down your head and put his privates in your mouth–did anything at either of these times come from him?
A [Gibbs]: Once–I don't know what it was, it was something white.
Q: How do you know it was white?
A: It runned out of my mouth.[69]

Even more unusual than reference to oral sex was the way Berry first attempted gain an acquittal by offering Gibbs £50 to desert the *Hazard*. The boy refused to flee, so the lieutenant tried to persuade him to change his testimony. Unfortunately for the defendant's efforts at witness tampering, he tried to secure the altered testimony through gunroom steward Hoskins, who later told the court Berry offered him £20 to persuade Gibbs to alter his story, "to say that he was not certain that Mr. Berry's cock was in him." Hoskins was either an honest fellow or had doubts about the lieutenant's ability to produce so substantial a sum. When it became obvious bribery would not set him free, or at least save his life, the defendant decided to escape. He turned to Warrant Officer Robert McCausland, the gunner of the *Hazard*. McCausland occupied the cabin next to Berry's, and so was essential to the planned escape. The accused proposed to the warrant officer that, when their sloop next came into port, he go ashore for at least one night. The defendant would then break through the common bulkhead separating their cabins, exit through McCausland's door, and flee. There is some indication that McCausland might have momentarily considered going along with the plot, but if he ever toyed with the idea of assisting Berry, he ultimately rejected it. He told the court of the solicitation, and none could doubt his words when at least twenty-five holes were found bored into the cabin partition on the lieutenant's side, close together in a line so a portion could be knocked out and the prisoner could flee.[70]

After failing at bribery, suborning perjury, and escape, Lieutenant Berry launched the most vigorous and multifaceted defense ever mounted by a commissioned officer to counter charges of sodomy, uncleanness, and indecency at a navy court martial. He first prepared a lengthy written statement which he had read aloud by the judge advocate. It contained provisions designed both to counter the charges and then mitigate their severity. He claimed, in a standard and invariably futile strategy, that he was an officer with eleven years of unblemished service, and had over the course of his career performed his duties in an active and enthusiastic manner. The captain of the *Hazard* supported his claims when called to testify. The defendant then called witnesses to impugn the character of his youthful accuser. Surgeon Charles Gregson returned to tell of how Gibbs usually did what he was told, but had once stolen some figs. Berry next called Robert North, mate of the *Hazard*, but his words provided little buoyancy for the defense. He testified that he had known Gibbs for two years and found his character much like that of the other boys on board the sloop. The accused lieutenant then called Gibbs to the stand once again, evidently trying to gain traction for his arguments by preying on the youth's naivete. He hoped to suggest the boy might be lying by challenging his understanding of the seriousness of the oath he took before giving testimony. If that had been his intent, it failed miserably. When asked by the defense if he knew the meaning of an oath, Gibbs responded with steely directness: "To tell the truth and nothing but the truth," he said, adding, "If I speak untrue I am sure I shall go to Hell."[71]

Berry next turned to the information provided early in the trial testimony in his attempt to secure an acquittal on the sodomy charge. Throughout the opening phases of the proceeding he had asked a variety of witnesses a question that seemed to have little relevance. Did Gibbs ever say, he inquired, that after the last encounter in the cabin his back was wet and he wiped it off with his shirt. Several witnesses replied that he had said that. Then, as Berry pursued his defense, the purpose of the question became clear. If the accused had ejaculated on the boy's back, penetration could never have occurred and the sodomy charge could not be sustained. This tactic proved no more successful than challenging Gibbs's understanding of an oath. Captain Dilkes put paid to the line of defense by explaining that when the boy spoke of his back being wet he actually meant it was his "fundament" that was wet and got wiped off with his shirt.[72]

Berry's defense in the end depended most heavily on male physiology, and he summoned an expert witness to come from London to speak in his behalf. The trial was adjourned for a short period to allow William Sandall, apothecary, "man midwife," and practitioner of surgery, although not "a regular bred surgeon" to make the journey to Plymouth. When called to testify, he explained to the court that the accused had been under his treatment for two years for "impotency and debility of muscular powers belonging to the penis so as to render the state of erection incomplete." His prescriptions did not work, according to Sandall, and he offered the opinion that buggery required a fully erect penis for successfully entering a boy of Gibbs's age. The court closely questioned the witness about the failure of his regimen over so long a period. He justified the course of treatment by claiming it might have worked if given more time. Berry also could have ejaculated without an erection he was forced to admit. Most damaging to Sandall's credibility, in all likelihood, was not his professional ineptitude but his admission that Berry was his nephew.[73]

It is unlikely that Sandall provided perjured testimony for his kinsman. Berry, too, had not been happy with the results obtained from his uncle's nostrums, and had over a period of time been in contact with three other medical men in London, none of who attended the court martial. Two of them, Dr. Edward C. Ford of Golden Square and Dr. J. C. Corpue of Dean Street in Soho, affirmed in writing that they also had provided medicines for his erectile dysfunction at various times.[74]

The members of the court martial refused to accept the expert medical testimony uncritically. They called on three of their own surgeons for professional opinions in the case, Charles Gregson of the *Hazard*, Richard Thomas of HMS *Resolve*, and Alexander Whyte of HMS *Salvador del Mundo*, a three-decker taken from the Spanish in 1797. The trio examined the defendant to discover if he were capable of producing an erection. Their report is included as appendix D of the trial record. They did not explain their method of discovery, but concluded that Berry was indeed able to generate an erect penis and ejaculate. Still, they inserted a cautionary message in their report. "We think it our duty to add," they explained, "that the subject, as it involves some [two words crossed out] nice and intricate points in physiology renders the criteria upon which we have grounded our opinion as not at all times absolutely conclusive."[75]

In the end, Berry's medical condition could not save his life. The court found him guilty of violating the second and twenty-ninth articles, and sentenced him to be hanged from the yardarm of a convenient ship. The condemned prisoner, conscious perhaps of the humiliation he had already undergone by claiming impotence in order to deny buggery, had had enough. He asked that he be allowed to "meet my fate at sea in the fleet and not before my friends in a populous part of the country." He was hanged on 19 October 1807, although it is not known if he got his dying wish. There is no record of where the execution took place.[76]

Two other officers were tried for sexual offenses in the eighteenth century, but in the absence of complete trial records and the availability of only the briefest summaries of their courts martial it is not possible to integrate their cases meaningfully with the proceedings against that of other officers for similar offenses. Lieutenant Samuel Blow was acquitted of attempted sodomy in 1780 at Hamoaze. The accusation against him made by Seaman Robert Boure was judged to be both malicious and baseless.[77] Nineteen years later, Lieutenant George Sargent was accused of having "frigged himself ... 'till he let fly all over" a cabin boy. On the boy's complaint, Sargent was tried, convicted, cashiered, mulcted of wages owed to him, and sentenced to two years in the Marshalsea prison.[78] Despite the vague and fragmentary nature of these cases, there are within them suggestions of the same patterns found in the courts martial of other officers. In the familiar paradigm, transcript summaries link both lieutenants with partners who were far below them in status. One officer stood accused of attempting sodomy with a seaman, and the other lost his career for uncleanness with a juvenile. There is no indication how the accusation lodged against Blow made its way into the chain of command and then upward to the point where a court martial was ordered, but in Sargent's case a boy first complained, and his complaint eventually reached a level high enough to authorize a prosecution. Were the records of the trials of Blow and Sargent more complete, it appears likely that they would reveal even more similarities to other proceedings conducted against commissioned officers for violating the second and twenty-ninth of the *Articles of War*.

5
Warrant Officers, Petty Officers, and their Boys

The largest number of naval courts martial for sodomy and sexual irregularity convened from the mid eighteenth century to the eve of the Victorian era involved warrant and petty officers accused of violating shipboard boys. Members of the two groups were defendants in one of every three such trials. There is no accurate estimate of the number of men who served in these uncommissioned but highly skilled posts during this span of almost one hundred years, but their ranks were relatively small, at least when compared to the number of ordinary sailors and commissioned officers active during the same period. Ships usually carried no more than one warrant officer for each maritime specialty – boatswain, carpenter, gunner, and master. The long years of service these men customarily served meant that turnover in their ranks was infrequent. Others who held posts as warrant officers, professionals in non-nautical specialties such as surgeons, chaplains, schoolmasters, and pursers, usually numbered no more than one per occupation in each ship, and smaller vessels ordinarily sailed without chaplains or schoolmasters. Similarly, the petty officer cadre on any ship was small, far smaller in number than the crewmen they superintended. The high rate with which men in these two categories were accused or formally charged with violations of the second and twenty-ninth articles of war hardly indicates a greater propensity for homoerotic connections within their ranks than among other classifications of men in naval service. The frequency with which they faced charges stems in part from the fact that warrant officers usually had cabins where they could conduct their liaisons, and petty officers on occasion also laid claim to semi-private or shielded areas where they could indulge their desires. Another factor in the relatively frequent prosecutions of these men was their vulnerability, at least when compared to lieutenants, commanders, or captains who could cloak themselves in the protections afforded by their commissioned status. The higher ranks who authorized courts martial boards indubitably had less inclination to hide the indiscretions of those immediately beneath them in the same manner that they had covered for captains Charles Sawyer in 1795 and Richard Matson in 1799.[1] When boatswains, carpenters, gunners, quartermasters, and the like were accused of sex crimes, they were far more likely to face courts martial than their commissioned superiors.

Before the Seven Years War, Admiralty records of sodomy and indecency courts martial survived only in isolated notations or severely abbreviated accounts lacking witness testimony, cross-examination, and defense arguments. Records of the proceedings against Quartermaster James Ball in 1706 and Boatswain John Coise three years later provide almost no detailed information. The same is true in the trial of William Slade, carpenter of HMS *Sheerness*, held at Hamoaze fifty years later in November of 1756. The documents from his court martial indicate hardly more than that he was tried and acquitted of sodomy, thereby escaping hanging at the starboard main yardarm, as was the manner of executing warrant officers.[2] The abbreviated documentation of Slade's case in mid century was atypical. By that time, careful record keeping was gradually becoming standard naval practice, and proceedings against warrant officers for sexual transgressions reflected this. The first such trial for which surviving materials are relatively informative dates from 1762, when Judge Advocate James Bruce made a copy of the minutes from the court martial of Boatswain Robert Garbut, of HM Sloop *Spy*, and sent it on the Admiralty. The judge advocate's purpose in making sure the document was received by higher authority had little to do with the increasing emphasis in the navy on careful record keeping. He hoped the transcript would aid in securing payment of his fee for service at the trial. It is not recorded whether Bruce received compensation, but as a result of his request considerable detail survives about Garbut's travails. In October of 1762, the *Spy*'s boatswain faced charges of attempting to commit sodomy with a boy, John Pyle, belonging to the sloop.[3] The trial transcript indicates that the most striking feature of his conduct with the youngster was its flagrant character. The several reports of his actions suggest widespread knowledge of his sexual advances among the *Spy*'s crew. Gunner Thomas Robertson learned of the pair's activities when five ratings came to him with the information that "a young lad belonging to the fore top ... had been guilty of sodomy with Mr. Garbut." This news did not startle the gunner, who knew that the boatswain had previously been confined on board the sloop for three or four months on similar charges. Still, on being presented with an accusation from five men, he had to react. Robertson went to the forecastle and questioned the boy, who explained that the boatswain had tried to bugger him on half-a-dozen occasions, but had never succeeded. When asked why he failed to report the incidents, Pyle answered that he feared reprisal if he did. The gunner then reported the matter to the officer of the watch.[4] Another member of the crew who knew or at least had heard the rumor that Garbut and Pyle were sodomists was the surgeon's mate, James Butler Broadbill. On the night of the twenty-sixth of September he was called to the forecastle and informed by a group of crewmen that Garbut and Pyle were committing sodomy in the boatswain's cabin. He decided to investigate. When he reached the cabin, he peeped through the keyhole and saw a penis being held in a hand. It is unlikely he observed more. The small size of warrant officers' cabins – scarcely big enough to accommodate a sleeping cot, some writing space, and a chest – provided little depth to broaden the arc visible through a keyhole-sized aperture. After completing his observation, Broadbill then turned around to the group that accompanied him to the cabin door and said he thought it was only "Mr. Garbut ... creating of pleasure to himself." He then added, "The people ... told me that Pyle was actually in with the boatswain ... and desired I would look again." He peered a second time through a crevice located above the keyhole. From the new vantage point he again saw a penis held in a hand and could discern motion, but he saw nothing of Pyle. He then instructed "the people" to report their suspicions to the officer of the watch, which was done. On hearing what the crewmen had to say, the officer of the watch, James Sheerer, went down and peeped through the crevice himself, but saw only someone urinating in a basin. Pyle then came out of the cabin, and Sheerer interrogated him. At first the boy admitted nothing, but finally confessed he and Garbut had been fondling each others' penises. The officer of the watch had no choice but to do his duty. He went to Lieutenant George Insell and told him what he had learned. The next morning Insell relayed the information to the *Spy*'s captain, Thomas Hayward, who ordered Garbut arrested and then wrote to the commander in chief at the Nore requesting a court martial be authorized.[5]

Garbut's trial at the Nore was a modest affair. It was held on board H M Fireship *Strombollo*, a small vessel of 268 tons that carried only eight guns. William Gordon, the presiding officer, had been promoted from captain to admiral only three days after Garbut was charged and two days before the court convened, and he was assisted by four captains, a smaller compliment than would be the case in later proceedings against accused sex offenders.[6] The reduced number of commissioned officers in attendance and the selection of so small a ship for the affair in no way indicates a lack of seriousness in the prosecution. It resulted most probably from the tactical needs of the moment. The Seven Years War required large numbers of warships to be at sea rather than riding at anchor at any given time, and a larger vessel or additional officers may not have been available for the trial.

John Pyle's court testimony agreed with what he had earlier revealed to Gunner Robertson. He told of numerous visits to Garbut's cabin, and explained how the boatswain attempted to ply him with alcohol and force him to commit sodomy. Although Garbut lowered the boy's trousers more than once, he never penetrated his anus. He managed only to engage Pyle in one or two bouts of mutual fondling.[7]

Garbut defended himself throughout by cross-examining witnesses and with a statement at the end of the trial which he hoped would exonerate him. His efforts were at best inadequate, at worst counterproductive. Garbut's cause was hardly improved by asking one of his own witnesses, "Did you ever see or hear of my being guilty in an affair of this nature?" The man replied, "I never saw you guilty of any practice of the kind, but I have heard of it."[8] When he had the opportunity to question John Pyle, he asked brief and specific questions. The answers resulted in disaster for him:

Q [Garbut]: When you came into my cabin did I pull down your breeches?
A [Pyle]: Yes.
Q: Where was I then?
A: Sitting on your bedside.
Q: Did I ever ask to bugger you?
A: Yes.[9]

After testimony ended, the presiding officer then put the question to the court, "Is the charge of an attempt to commit the detestable crime of sodomy proved?" The answer was yes, that Garbut was guilty under the second article. He was dismissed from His Majesty's service and "publicly drummed on shore with the usual marks of ignominy."[10]

The later trials of two petty officers in 1805 and 1806 provide additional examples of the increasing sophistication of admiralty record keeping. The cases detail not only the ways men in positions of authority obtained sexual service from boys on board their ships but how naval authorities reacted when the mens' violations of the *Articles of War* came to light. Both Bartlett Ambler and Hepburn Graham served as master's mates, the former belonged to HM Sloop *Tisiphone*, the latter to the *St. George*. As master's mates (usually called "mates" for convenience), Ambler and Graham belonged to an ill-defined class of inferior officers. Although officially classed as petty officers, mates were petty officers of a superior sort. Their educational levels and social position, coupled with the likelihood that they would someday receive commissions or serve as masters set them above other petty officers. They had the right to be present on the quarter deck, and they were expected always to conduct themselves as gentlemen.[11] By 1805, the year of Ambler's trial, the navy no longer produced skimpy, two- or three-page records of courts martial as they had done a hundred years earlier in the cases of James Ball and John Coise. The transcript of Ambler's case fills eighteen handwritten pages and the summary runs two-thirds that length. The location of the trial at the Hamoaze estuary, adjacent to the giant naval facility at Plymouth, only added to the administrative circumstance surrounding the affair. Rear Admiral William Carnegie, Earl of Northesk, who was second in command of all ships and vessels at Plymouth, presided over the trial. The nine members of the court martial included another rear admiral and eight captains, one of whom rated the prefix "lord" before his name. The small *Tisiphone* could not host so grand an assemblage. Instead, the trial took place on board a first-rate, the huge, 112-gun, 191-foot *Salvador del Mundo*.[12]

The first witness in the trial, thirteen-year-old John Davy of the *Tisiphone*, provided dramatic, detailed testimony of his encounters with Mate Ambler:

> About 3 months ago, one night after the gunroom had done tea, about 7 o'clock, the prisoner [Ambler] called me as he was sitting alone in his cabin and said to me are you in a great hurry? Not knowing what he meant, I said I was in no great hurry. He then put out his light that was in his cabin and drew the curtain of his cabin door. He sat down. I stood before him. He unbuttoned his breeches. He took my hand and put it into his breeches and told me to turn round. He then unbuttoned my breaches. He took me round the middle. I refused it and wanted to go out. He said don't be frightened. I shant hurt you. After I was turned round he took his cock and put it in my arse. He tried to put it in so far as he could. He put it in so hard that [it] made me cry out. I thought they heard it in the gunroom. After he had done that, he found I would not let him put it in my backside, he

> began putting it between my thighs and the water ran down my thighs. And then he told me to button up my breeches, and I had scarce buttoned up my breeches when he said be sure don't tell no person. I'll be very good to you, but if you tell any person of it I'll get you flogged. I did not make him any answer but went out of the cabin.
>
> About a month after, I was going by the gunroom door about the same time in the evening as when the prisoner first called me into his cabin. The prisoner called me to his cabin door and said he wanted me. I thought he was going to do as he did the first time so I refused to go in. O says he, come along in and he took me by the coat and hauled me in. After I was in I refused to bide in. I said I did not like no such works. He then blew out the light and drew the curtain. He unbuttoned his breeches and took my hand and put it in his breeches and put his cock in my hand and told me to draw it to and fro. Then he unbuttoned my breeches. I told him I did not like to bide there. Says he, don't be afraid, I shant hurt you. He told me to turn round. I wanted to go out, but he held me round the middle and I could not. Then he took his cock and put it in my backside again. He made me bend down, then he put it in so hard that I stood upright as I could, and would not let him put it in my backside. Then he began putting it between my thighs again. The water ran down my thighs. Then I wiped my thighs and buttoned up my breeches and went out. I went into the gunroom and told the gunroom servant, James Ford, of it.[13]

A month later, Ambler again managed to get Davy into his cabin. Ensuing events differed little from the first two encounters, only this time the mate gave him "three pence half penny." The prosecution called four more of the *Tisiphone*'s boys after the first witness withdrew. Three of them, only one of whom had passed his thirteenth birthday, provided accounts similar to that offered by Davy. They told of being lured to Ambler's cabin and being painfully buggered much against their wills. Their tales hardly differed from Davy's except they explained that Ambler clapped his hand over their mouths to prevent them from shouting out. Only one of them received compensation for the forced favors. John Wilcott, a volunteer of the third class, received three pence along with an injunction to silence. The court dismissed a final boy witness, eleven-year-old Thomas Hooper, a volunteer of the second class.[14] "Being examined by the judge advocate as to the nature of an oath and not giving any answers that could satisfy the minds of the members of the court as to his being a competent and [illegible] subject for taking an oath, he was dismissed."[15]

The members of the court regarded the stories told by the boys with considerable skepticism. They asked each of them a series of questions designed to impugn their testimony. A particular concern was whether the youthful coterie had conspired among themselves to have the mate hanged. "Have you ever consulted with the other boys who are witnesses in this case as to what you should say in evidence against the prisoner," they asked John Willcott.[16] He answered in the negative. Similar questions posed to other boy witnesses elicited similarly negative responses. Another concern of the court was to ascertain whether sodomy had actually taken place. The exchange with Richard Hopkins, a third-class volunteer followed the usual pattern:

Q [Court]:	Did you feel the prisoner's prick within your body?
A [Hopkins]:	I did and I singed out.
Q:	How long did the prisoner's prick remain in your body?
A:	Not above a minute.
Q:	What did you feel in consequence of his prick being in your body?
A:	I could not hold my water at that time.[17]

Another concern of the court's members was the manner in which Ambler's sodomy became public knowledge. They learned it could hardly have remained secret with so many boys involved. Davy told the gunroom steward immediately after Ambler's third attempt. Wilcott testified that another boy, identified only as Oliver, heard the story from someone and spread it among several boys in the squadron. The boatswain of the *Tisiphone* eventually heard the tale, pressed Wilcott about it, and he confessed. Young Richard Hopkins put the accusation more directly into the command chain by telling a lieutenant. Joseph Gammicliff, the last lad to testify, also informed the court of how widely accounts of Ambler's sodomy had circulated:

Q [Court]:	To what boy did you first tell that this had happened to you or who did you hear speak of it before you mentioned it?
A [Gammicliff]:	The boy, Hopkins, told me it had happened to him, and three other boys said they had been treated so, and I told them that I had been so treated.[18]

The court not only wrestled with the truthfulness of the boys, but they also considered what motives the lads might have for leveling false accusations against Mate Ambler, whether from anger against him personally, because they were disgruntled with navy life, or for other reasons. Each was asked how many times he had been flogged. Wilcott had borne the lash several times, once for not having his master's kettle boiled, other times for "skylarking or playing about at marbles." Hopkins had been twice flogged for breaking things of his master, and Gammicliff admitted to several floggings. Following a more dark and ominous track, the court asked one of the witnesses called by Ambler if he knew of any quarrel between the prisoner and anyone else on board the ship that might have caused them to bear witness against the prisoner. "I have heard the boatswain, gunner, and carpenter quarrel with the prisoner," he replied, "but I have not taken particular notice what it was about." This intriguing line of questioning went no further, but the menacing implication that the boys had lied at the instigation of their superiors remained with the those who later judged Ambler.[19]

After the youngsters completed their testimony, the court offered the beleaguered mate the opportunity to defend himself. He requested half an hour to prepare, and he received it. When the court reconvened, he presented a written document to the judge advocate, who read it aloud. It consisted of one sentence only proclaiming his innocence. He then asked to call witnesses to speak on his behalf. Joseph Dowman, the ship's corporal and the first to speak in support of the defendant, testified not only to Mate Ambler's exemplary character (he never heard of his committing sodomy and had no occasion to believe he did), but he also attacked the accusers. Hopkins and Wilcott had been twice punished for lying, he said, and Davy "bears a very bad character by the whole ship's company." The corporal also claimed never to have heard any boy cry out from the mate's cabin. Ambler next called to defend him Seaman Samuel Peter, his own servant. Peter was obviously a potential receptor for Ambler's sexual proclivities, particularly since his subordinate position made him vulnerable to his master. As a seaman, however, it was very likely he was an adult, which gave him some currency for resisting sexual advances, if ever they were made. Then, too, as an adult he may not have caught the fancy of the mate, whose purported sexual correspondents were all at most thirteen years old. Whatever Peter's relationship with the boatswain, he provided testimony useful to the defense. He claimed his master eschewed "that vice," and added that he had never seen any of the accusers within his master's cabin. When questioned about the possibility of a conspiracy of officers on board the *Tisiphone* to induce the boys to testify against the defendant, he replied he knew nothing of it. Midshipman Robert Baker echoed Peter's testimony, but added that he had heard some of the ship's officers speak disrespectfully of the defendant and that they also disparaged the character of the youngsters who testified against him. The boys were all liars, according to Baker, and he pronounced John Davy, the principle accuser, "a very wicked boy indeed as ever lived ... he would even hang his own father."[20]

Mate Ambler continued his defense calling a string of witnesses and asking them much the same questions posed to Dowman, Peter, and Baker. Their responses echoed those who testified earlier, although they seemed less severe in the judgments they offered about the character of the young accusers.

Ambler made only one departure from his first lines of defense, securing testimony of his good character and impugning the veracity of the boys who testified against him. He inquired of two of his own witnesses whether they thought him "inclined" or possessing a "tendency" toward "the vice with which [he was] charged." Nowhere in any other Royal Navy trial transcript for sodomy, attempted sodomy, or homoerotic indecency is there an indication that any officer or sailor harbored an inclination or a tendency to engage in sexual relations with other men or boys. Sodomy and other shipboard sexual offenses were always considered discrete activities, unconnected to taste, preference, pervasive inclinations, or to any inherent character trait. Both witnesses responded negatively to Ambler's questioning on the subject, and in any case the line of inquiry formed only a minor aspect of his defense. Still, the fact that the mate thought it useful to establish for the court that he had no inclinations toward homoerotic engagements indicates that there might be some submerged notion among the navy's personnel about the nature of sodomites that simply does not appear in courts martial testimony. The use of the adjective "unmanly" in the trial of John Ware and John Douglas, the two seamen found in a hammock together in 1800, provides the only other instance suggestive of a linkage between accused violators of the twenty-ninth article of war and the familiarity of eighteenth-century Britons with the flagrant and effeminate molly culture that flourished in London and possibly in other urban centers across the nation.[21] Again, there is no way to be certain whether or not notions of innate homoerotic preferences informed the attitudes of naval personnel generally or of officers in particular, but Bartlett Ambler's attempt to persuade members of the court that he had no such orientation hints that some in the navy may have believed that there existed men innately or temperamentally inclined to sex with other men or boys.

Ambler closed his defense in the usual but not particularly effective fashion by calling on William Foote, captain of the *Tisiphone* to testify that he performed his duty well. Foote provided the information that Ambler desired, added a negative comment about two of the youthful accusers, and withdrew. With the captain's testimony complete, the defense rested. The court then decided that the case had been proved against the prisoner and sentenced him to death. Still, there was considerable hesitancy in their pronouncement, and they took the unusual step of attaching a letter to their verdict. Addressed to William Marsden, a secretary at the Admiralty, it read:

HMS *Salvador del Mundo*
Hamoaze, 22 April 1805

Sir:

By desire of the members of a court martial assembled by me this day to try Mr. Bartlett Ambler, I have to request you will call their Lordships' consideration to the hardship the court have labored under in being obliged to condemn a man to death upon the evidence of four boys, the eldest not more than thirteen years of age, and therefore beg to recommend him to mercy.

I am, Sir, your obedient servant
(Signed) Northesk[22]

By the time a digest of the trial was completed for Admiralty records, an endorsement had been added on a corner of Northesk's letter. Dated 8 May, it reads "His Majesty is graciously pleased to pardon him – warrant accordingly."[23]

The next year, in 1806, Master's Mate Hepburn Graham faced charges both for importuning and committing sex with juveniles on board the ninety-eight-gun *St. George*. The navy accused him of engaging in sodomy with his servant, fourteen-year-old George Parr, and "making repeated attempts on John Sky, another boy." He was tried at Portsmouth, and as was the case in Ambler's prosecution at the sprawling Hamoaze facility, the large number of high-ranking officers on hand and the availability of the largest ships made possible the staging of a trial in a grand manner impossible to duplicate at smaller naval stations around the globe. The Commander in Chief at Portsmouth appointed Sir Isaac Coffin, a rear admiral and baronet, as president of the proceeding. The dozen members of the court, all captains, included a knight and one member who rated an "Honorable" before his name.

Although HMS *Gladiator*, where the trial took place, only carried a designation as a fifth rate, her 140-foot length made her one of the largest fifth rates in the navy. She served as a vessel dedicated solely to administrative functions. Although afloat from 1783 to 1817, the *Gladiator* never once went to sea.[24]

Graham had private quarters on board the *St. George*, although they were inferior to Bartlett Ambler's cabin on the *Tisiphone*. His privacy was protected only by sheets of loose canvas that screened off his hammock. After dark on 21 November 1806, according to the accusation, Graham grabbed hold of his young servant by the hair and pulled him into his hammock. Then, as young Parr explained, his master "pulled his yard out, and put it into my backside. He kept doing backwards and forwards, and made my arse wet." When the encounter ended, the mate told the boy he could return to his hammock, but admonished him to keep silent or he would get him three dozen lashes. Some days later Graham renewed his injunction to silence after seeing Parr chatting with two of his comrades. He put a spoon handle to the boy's neck, and suggested that if they were found out he might cut his throat and then himself jump over the side of the ship and into the sea. Repeated threats of murder and suicide followed over the next several days. A week after first buggering Parr, Graham buggered him again, and again threatened three dozen lashes if word of what took place were revealed.[25] With his own canvas-shrouded niche on board the *St George*, Graham had no need to confine his assaults to hours of darkness. A third occasion described by Parr occurred:

> Before breakfast, before the hammocks were up. He pulled a hole in my trouser's behind with his fingers and told me he would get them mended. He then pulled his yard out and put it through the hole of my trousers to my backside, but did not enter it, but kept moving backwards and forwards and made my arse wet.[26]

In all, Graham attempted to bugger Parr on five separate occasions, but was successful in penetrating his anus only twice.

John Sky, the second of the *St. George*'s boys who caught Graham's eye, proved more adroit at dodging the mate than servant Parr. The fifteen-year-old Sky threatened to "sing out" if the older man did not stop kissing him and attempting to get him to fondle his penis. When Graham realized his seduction tactics would not succeed, he tried another tack. Sky had apparently lost his hammock, and so his potential seducer attempted to curry favor by securing a replacement for him from the boatswain's storeroom. His attempt at bribery failed since no extras were available. In all, the best the mate managed to get from Sky was a single opportunity to slip his penis between the boy's thighs.[27]

Graham should have known that despite injunctions to silence and threats of flogging, murder, and suicide, small boys are not trustworthy keepers of secrets. The morning after the mate first buggered Parr the lad told Syms, a waister, and Williams, a mizzentopman, neither of whom believed the story. Somewhere during the weeks Graham chased after the boys, Parr told Sky of his encounter with him, and Sky told him that if he did not complain, he, Sky, would do so. Parr then went to the first lieutenant with both his own and Sky's accounts. The lieutenant reported all to Captain Thomas Bertie, who wrote to Admiral George Montague, the commander in chief at Spithead asking him to apply for permission to try Hepburn Graham under the twenty-ninth article of war.[28] Two of those questioned at the trial were expert witnesses, the surgeon of the *St. George*, Mr. Hugh Hughes, and his assistant, George Geilbraith. Hughes explained that he was called to the quarter deck and ordered to examine the boys as soon as the captain learned of the accusations so that a record of their injuries could be made while they were still visible. Sky's anus exhibited no symptoms of buggery, hardly surprising since Graham only managed to put his penis between the boy's thighs. The shipboard medicos agreed that Parr's anus was inflamed, but it had no excoriations. Hughes's testimony indicated Graham might have committed sodomy with Parr, but he added that the inflamation did not prove it. His assistant surgeon, George Geilbraith was only slightly more definite. Although the condition of boy's anus might have resulted from a number of causes, he explained, the boy's complaints of soreness resulting from what the assistant delicately styled "an improper connection," indicated that sodomy had probably been attempted. Whether it had been completed, he could not ascertain.[29]

The court wanted to make sure that Parr had not leveled a charge of sodomy against Graham as an act of revenge. As in the trial of Bartlett Ambler the previous year, officers sought to discover if Graham had ever ordered Parr punished, and if so how much time elapsed between the punishment and the accusation. In response to a question, the boy told of receiving "six strokes on the hand with a rope" at the mate's order, but could not remember for what offense or when it had happened. Members of the court also wanted to make certain that sodomy had actually taken place. Parr testified unequivocally that Graham had entered him and emitted, but the court pressed him on both matters. They asked him about the position of his thighs during Graham's assault and had him explain how he lay in the hammock with the mate. They wanted to know if he experienced pain when entered, whether the emissions were hot or cold, and if he actually felt the defendant's "yard in [his] fundament." The boy explained that he was too frightened to know if the emissions were hot or cold, but his responses to the other questions all indicated he had been buggered in the strict legal definition of the term which specified both penetration and emission.[30]

Throughout the court martial, Master's Mate Graham defended himself by cross-examining the prosecution witnesses. His questions and the answers they elicited probably did more harm to his case than good. It appears he had earlier coached George Parr on what to say if ever they were interrogated about their activities, and when Graham posed the questions in court to which he had previously told the boy how to answer, Parr responded by explaining that the mate had told him what to say:

> *Q [Graham]:* Did you then inform me that you had a complaint in your head which you did not know what you said at any time?
>
> *A [Parr]:* No. He [Graham] said to me if anyone asked me I should say I had [illegible] my senses, that I was trying a set of pantaloons that he had given and he was seeing if ever I had been flogged.[31]

Later in the same cross-examination the defendant tried to elicit an admission from Parr that he had punished him several times shortly before the boy reported him, the implication being that revenge motivated the charge. He did manage to get the subject of punishments into the record again with his questions, but the responses to questions designed to make him appear a caring master could only have had the opposite effect:

> *Q [Graham]:* Did I severely punish you several times before the twenty-first of November for not obeying my orders in not reading your book?
>
> *A [Parr]:* He beat me for not getting his victuals in time and made my nose bleed once. He never punished me for not reading my book that I know of. He told me to read it. It was a spelling book he borrowed.
>
> Q: Did I keep you up several times over past hours as long as my light was permitted, which was until half past nine on purpose to learn your lesson?

A: Yes, when the gentlemen have been in, he has told me he would keep me up to read my book, and when the gentlemen were gone out, he wanted me to come into his hammock.[32]

Graham also cross-examined John Sky and Surgeon Hughes perfunctorily, receiving replies to his questions that only strengthened George Parr's credibility. When given the opportunity to speak on his own behalf, Graham replied that "he had little to state in his defense," except that he had been in the service over a dozen years, sailed under Admiral Thomas Pringle, Sir Thomas Graves, and a Captain Prine, and had discovered and reported a mutiny on HM Sloop *Hope*.[33] He then called Parr as a defense witness, and again asked him questions to which he had previously instructed the boy how to answer:

Q [Graham]: Did you inform me before I was made prisoner on the twenty-ninth of November that a certain gentleman gave you a guinea to have connections with him, and then offered his watch?

A [Parr]: No, he [Graham] told me if any asked me, to say that a gentleman promised me a guinea to do as he did. He did not mention a watch.

Q: Did you inform me in coming from your work that a gentleman met you about a mile from your own house?

A: He told me to say that a gentleman met me in a field.

Q: Did you inform me that he gave you a guinea?

A: No.[34]

With George Parr's final "No" the testimony ended, the court was cleared and the members began their deliberations. Their could be little suspense about the verdict. None could doubt the sodomy charge, and the defense proved worse than useless. It served to condemn the accused almost as explicitly as the testimony elicited by the prosecution. Moses Greetham, the Deputy Judge Advocate of the Fleet certified the verdict. The court sentenced Hepburn Graham to hang. The members evidently were persuaded that neither Sky nor Parr conspired against the defendant, and so no request for a pardon followed the sentence as it had in Bartlett Ambler's case.[35]

Two years after Graham's hanging at Portsmouth, the Royal Navy was again vexed by charges of homoerotic sexual activity by one of its warrant officers. Master John McCasky of HM Sloop *Spitfire* was charged in 1808 with "unwarrantable indecencies with and forcibly attempting to commit an unnatural crime on Robert Walker (his servant), a boy of 13 years of age." Dealing with a master was a more serious matter than handling accusations against mere master's mates like Bartlett Ambler and Hepburn Graham. Masters were some of the best-educated standing officers in the navy. They came from status levels roughly comparable to those that produced midshipmen, drew pay almost equaling that of some captains and more than many lieutenants, and were well situated to obtain commissions if desired. Masters navigated ships, plotting day-to-day courses using their own instruments and their own charts, and in constricted waters they often served as ships' pilots.[36] Jack Aubrey, the Royal Navy's most famous fictional captain, knew masters, and he knew a good master's worth. When informed that one of them, who was the consummately able navigator of his sloop, had a taste for boys, he replied, "Don't tell *me* about rears and vices; I have been in the Navy all my life."[37] That ended the matter. The man was not investigated, arrested, or clapped in irons, nor was any other action taken. Aubrey, like his brother officers in real life, well understood that proficient warrant officers made successful captains, and the use of young backsides by some of them was best ignored unless it grew too conspicuous or troublesome, as had happened with McCasky. In his case, the navy launched the full ceremonial panoply for his court martial even though his was not a capital offense. The location contributed in some measure toward a willingness to produce a major legal pageant. The trial took place at Sheerness, one of the country's largest naval installations. The order setting the proceeding in motion was issued by the distinguished captain, Sir Edward Codrington, who had received a gold medal for his performance as one of Nelson's subordinates at Trafalgar and was, in 1808, captain of a powerful 74, HMS *Blake*, and second in command of the navy's ships at the Medway and the Nore. When the order came down, an ample supply of captains stood ready to participate. Unlike other trials, where the primary accuser or accusers testified first, in this case a string of half a dozen officers offered their sworn testimony before the boy who initially complained of McCasky's actions. This anomaly in no way provided cover for the accused. The higher-ranking witnesses detailed all the sordid events preceding McCasky's being charged with violating the second article.

The master's mate of the *Spitfire* testified that he earlier told the sloop's purser, Thomas Davis, that he once saw McCasky sitting on his bed sans trousers and "his boy stark naked holding his shirt in his hand before his face, apparently ashamed of being seen in that situation."

Davis himself told of hearing a shrill crying coming from the master's cabin on one occasion, but when he put his ear to the bulkhead shared by his cabin and the master's, the noise of the ship working made it impossible to hear anymore cries. Davis also knew from his own observation that Walker spent nights with McCasky, and testified to having seen the boy come out of the cabin carrying a blanket. The *Spitfire*'s lads customarily slept on the deck. Only one of them had indulgence to spend nights in an officer's cabin, a nine- or ten-year-old, too small to "carry his hammock up and down." Another witness told of having seen the young Walker, naked with shirt in hand in the darkened cabin of the master, whose trousers were down at his heels.[38]

Quartermaster James Honor told of observing McCasky and his servant in bed together, and added that of the two, only the master seemed drunk:

> I went down to the prisoner betwixt 12 and 1 o'clock on the 18th November at sea. I call him five different times. The first time I went to call him, he was laying with the boy, Walker. The 2nd time the same. I asked if I should put a light in his cabin. He said no. The third time I went down to call him, he said he would be up immediately. The fourth time, he also said he would be up immediately. On the fifth time, he told me to go out of the gunroom and tell Captain Ellis there were no slaves in this part of the world.[39]

Lieutenant Thomas Doorne testified to having observed young Walker emerge from McCasky's darkened cabin in the early morning hours and mentioned his suspicions to the purser. Later the purser revealed to Doorne that Walker once complained to him about the improper advances. The lieutenant, on receiving the new information, ordered the surgeon to inspect the boy and advance his complaint to captain. It was Captain John Ellis who then had the accused placed in irons, and wrote a letter asking a court martial be convened.[40]

When the string of officers had completed their testimony, young Robert Walker took the oath and began his story. He poured out a familiar tale, explaining how McCasky both courted him and used force, first to fondle him and ultimately to compel him to submit to intercrural intercourse when he failed to enter him anally even after lubricating his penis with spittle and trying to expand the boy's orifice by inserting a finger.[41]

McCasky made little attempt to cross-examine those who testified against him. He managed to work a small amount of vague information into the minutes from the prosecution witnesses, who responded to his few questions only by agreeing that he had once commanded the *Spitfire* when the lieutenant fell ill and that he never locked his cabin door.[42] When given the opportunity to speak in his own defense, he told of his eleven years of faithful service under Nelson at Copenhagen, Hood in the West Indies, and under George Cadogan when he helped quell a mutiny on board HM Sloop *Ferret*. McCasky also employed a tactic that in the past had proved no more effective than reciting a litany of previous honorable service. He claimed that his servant's accusations resulted from a conspiracy against him hatched not by a covey of ships' boys but by Purser Davis, with whom he had had disagreements in the past. Young Walker could never have put together so persuasive a confession, the master argued. Someone else must have conjured it into being, and given the bad blood between him and Davis, it must have been the purser who concocted the fabricated accusation. Having concluded his statement to the court, the accused then called a short string of character witnesses, the first of whom gave no indication of the incendiary revelations in the testimony that would follow. Surgeon Connell said that he had no knowledge of any liberties McCasky had taken with his boy, and added that the master treated him like a son, buying him clothing and proffering paternal advice.[43] It was John Redding, the second defense witness, who provided the startling testimony in support of the accused. He indicated that young Walker had a motive for denouncing McCasky wholly unrelated to his sexual aggression:

Q [Court]: Relate to the court the conversation which passed betwixt you and the boy, Walker, at the time you was sentry over the boat.

A [Redding]: The boy, Walker said to me I shall soon be home now along with my friends. What makes you think so? He would not tell me for some minutes. I asked him if it was through this job of your master. He answered yes. I asked him what was the reason. He said his master was sure to be hung and he should be dismissed from His Majesty's Service and get clear of a man of war.[44]

McCasky then tried to get Redding to say directly that the boy willingly lied about being violated to obtain his exit from the Royal Navy.

Q [McCasky]: Did you tell me the boy said his intentions were to swear my life away on purpose to get clear of a man of war?[45]

Redding was not willing to go as far as the defendant hoped, explaining only that Walker had not quite said that. He only mentioned that he would be free of a man of war after McCasky's hanging. The defendant pressed the same point with another witness, and called several more men to testify in his behalf, but none provided adequate leverage for his defense. The court decided he was guilty of indecent behavior, cashiered him, prohibited him ever again from holding office in the navy, and sentenced him to two years solitary confinement in the Marshalsea.[46]

The two-year prison sentence, the maximum allowed under law, cannot be considered light, but a man of McCasky's standing as a master placed him in a class not subject to the cat. The penalty was similar but less severe than to that meted out to another warrant officer almost a decade earlier for sex offenses less serious than sodomy. Boatswain Robert Patton made a practice of:

> Getting ... boys successively into corners, handling their private parts, and taking them into his mouth, thrusting his fingers up their fundaments, blowing into them, and with a wonderfully capricious and brutal depravity, making them ease themselves into his hands, and asking them to do it in his mouth.[47]

Patton's appetites obviously went beyond the usual fondling and mutual masturbation and into the realm of what the disgusted Admiralty penman classified as "wonderfully capricious and brutal depravity," but despite the colorful adjectives used to characterize the boatswain's deeds, the evidence contained no suggestion that the capital crime of sodomy ever took place. McCasky's conduct, too, could be described as capricious and depraved, at least that portion of it where he defied Captain Ellis's orders to report on deck and instead remained in bed with his lad. Still, despite explicit and repeated rejection of orders, no officer filed charges of insubordination against him. Courts martial cashiered both McCasky and Patton, but the boatswain, slightly lower in the naval hierarchy than the master, received two hundred lashes instead of two years in solitary confinement as had been ordered for McCasky.[48]

The final Royal Navy prosecution for violating the twenty-ninth article of war took place in 1829, long after the final defeat of Napoleon, and after Britain and the Empire had enjoyed over a decade of peace. The trial of William Maxwell, boatswain of HMS *Tweed* was a small thing compared to other proceedings for sexual infractions. The fact that it took place in Simon's Bay at the Cape of Good Hope dictated that it be a limited affair. The naval base there, acquired by Britain only in 1814, was a small station when compared to the expansive facilities almost half a world away at Plymouth, Portsmouth, or Sheerness. The president of the court, who also commanded the ships and vessels at the Cape station, carried only the title of commodore. The membership of the panel appointed to render judgment consisted of two captains and two commanders, indicating a dearth of senior officers available to serve. The designations of their vessels confirm that no major, line of battle ships were moored at Simon's Bay in early 1829. The commands of the four court martial members consisted of one sloop, two sixth rates, and HMS *Maidstone*, a fifth rate on which the court martial took place. Despite the distant location and the smallish size of the court, Maxwell's trial is one of the most carefully documented in Admiralty archives, and is distinguished by both abundant legal complexity and arguments far more learned and convoluted than those found in any other court martial for sexual offences.[49] The sophistication of the trial and the elaborate record it produced had little to do with the importance of Maxwell's court martial, but was the product of the increasing bureaucratization of the navy in the nineteenth century and the commensurate requirements for documentation it generated.

In the familiar pattern of warrant officers charged with sexual offenses, Boatswain Maxwell's chief accuser was a boy, William Pack, also a crewmember of the *Tweed*. Not only did the youngster press a charge of sodomy against him, but four other boys also came forward, charging the boatswain with "uncleanness and other scandalous actions in corruption of good manners" in breach of the second of the *Articles*. Once the president and members were assembled, the required oaths administered, and the charges read, the defendant addressed the court.[50] In well-constructed prose, he argued that the officers at Simon's Bay had no authority to try him since he had already:

> By a former court martial held in May last on the present station been once tried, convicted and sentenced to death, and in the meantime kept in prison until His Majesty or His Royal Highness the Lord High Admiral's pleasure should be known for my execution.
>
> That such judgment of death having been passed on me, I thereby instantly became dead in law, my blood corrupted, and I forfeited to the Crown all I had.
>
> That the sentence against me was in part executed by my being immediately thereafter closely confined a prisoner and taken to England on board His Majesty's Ship *Owen Glendower* until the

> 29th July last, when I was brought on the quarter deck of that ship and informed by the first lieutenant that I was reprieved from the sentence of death by the extension so far of the Royal Mercy and Clemency to me.
>
> That according to the universal maxim of the common law of England no man is to brought into jeopardy of his life more than once for the same offence.[51]

Maxwell elaborated at greater length on his claim of immunity, and the members took his arguments very seriously. The court ordered spectators to leave so they could debate the question in private. Commodore Robert Skipsey, the president then revealed, if it had not been known to the members earlier, that Maxwell's move had been expected. He produced a letter earlier solicited from the Admiralty that pronounced "the former trial and all proceedings under it ... null and void" and assured the court "that the prisoner may be now legally tried for the offenses charged against him." The author of the letter, one of the secretaries of the Admiralty, also anticipated and headed off another line of defense that Maxwell might have used. He assured Skipsey that "the law officers are also of the opinion that any officer having sitten on the former court martial is no objection to his also sitting on that now ordered." The prisoner then asked for a lawyer to assist him directly, but the court denied the request. Despite the failure to secure counsel, Maxwell was not without guidance. He had had the help of an able attorney at his first trial and he brought forward what he had learned when he faced charges a second time.[52]

With questions of double jeopardy, eligibility to serve on the court martial, and legal representation cleared, William Pack began his testimony. It revealed that Maxwell was not a man to dawdle when it came to satisfying his sexual needs. On the third day after he joined the *Tweed*, he summoned Pack to his cabin on the larboard side of the lower deck, and, as the boy explained, "he then throwed me down on the deck. He then hauled my trousers down .... He then turned to put his pintle into my backside. I felt him do all this. He hurt me very much." Later in his testimony, the boy affirmed seeing a white fluid come from Maxwell's penis. The court asked the usual questions of the witness: Why did you not cry out? Did he give you anything? Pack explained that the boatswain clapped his hand over his mouth to keep him quiet, and assured his questioners that he had received no monetary compensation or other favors for being buggered. The boy continued his testimony by detailing four additional instances when he had been sodomized by Maxwell. The occurrences were all much the same. Pack added only that the boatswain neither used alcohol nor offered him money after he forced his attentions on him. He also informed the court that after the third encounter, Maxwell bought some duck and had smocks and trousers made of it for him.[53]

Four other boys also recounted their experiences with the *Tweed*'s new boatswain. They did not accuse him of sodomy, but they provided ample evidence of repeated indecency. As had been the case in his initial approach to William Pack, Maxwell wasted no time in his search for other companionable lads on board his new ship. He made his first advances toward John Romney within a month after joining the *Tweed*. Romney and the three other boys who received the boatswain's attentions rebuffed them in every case, but the boys, nevertheless, exhibited a decided reticence about directly describing their encounters with Maxwell in the language commonly used in prosecutions a quarter of a century before. One required gentle prodding to induce him to reveal what took place. "What did you think he [Maxwell] wanted to do," the court asked William Dickson, and sensing the boy's embarrassment at the question, admonished him, "don't be ashamed." The boy only then replied that in his opinion the boatswain wanted to bugger him.[54] Dickinson's hesitancy and discomfort with the central subject matter at the trial is also evident in the testimony of other boy witnesses who constantly relied on euphemisms to explain what they thought Maxwell had in mind. Several described his intent with the phrase, he wanted to "do a dirty trick with me."[55] Another young witness told one of his comrades that the boatswain had been "poking him about." There was no need to elaborate on the phrase's meaning either to the boy to whom it was said or to the members of the court. It meant buggery, but by the 1820s, such unalterably crude terminology no longer dominated courts martial minutes. By then, the more circumspect "pintle" and "tool" had replaced the words "prick" and "cock" that appeared regularly in testimony from previous decades. "Arse" was another noun that fell into disfavor and disappeared from the records in the new, post-Nelsonian age of more refined judicial speech.[56]

The same hesitancy and sense of propriety that affected the language of all-male sexual encounters in 1829 also diminished to some extent the willingness of men to report such activities to the authorities. William Pack explained his initial failure to tell of Maxwell's sexual assaults for fear he would be flogged, but two other boys, neither of whom feared retaliation, offered more tentative explanations for their reluctance to inform higher authority of the boatswain's importunities.

John Ryner said, "I thought I should see further into it and find something more out." John Romney apparently considered reporting it a waste of time. "I thought if I had said anything to anyone," he explained, "no one would have taken any notice of it." Adolphus Waterworth, one of the first of the boys to testify at the trial, denied Maxwell ever touched him improperly, although he did admit to cleaning out his cabin on a regular basis and receiving grog from time to time when he did so. Carpenter James Sutton's testimony, offered immediately after that of Waterworth, indicated that the boy lied. Sutton told of entering Maxwell's cabin unannounced and finding him with his arm about the boy. "The instant I opened the door the prisoner sprung up and appeared confused ... The boy, Waterworth, remained on the chest playing with his fingers."[57] When questioned about why he failed to report his observations, Carpenter Sutton evinced the same hesitation as the boy witnesses. "I did not report it immediately," he explained, "but waited to see if anything more improper was going on." He admitted he thought the entire episode suspicious, but shared his thoughts with the *Tweed*'s gunner only when tales of Maxwell's profligacy and lack of discretion were already circulating widely about the ship. And there can be no doubt that a sizeable proportion of the two hundred crewmen on board the twenty-eight-gun *Tweed* suspected Maxwell was up to no good. He had solicited at least five boys, and a sixth boy who heard about the warrant officer's importuning had actually seen Maxwell in his cabin with trousers at his ankles standing near William Pack, who was draped over a chest with bottom bared. The quartermaster, the gunner, and the carpenter also knew or suspected what was afoot, and the quartermaster mentioned overhearing two mizzentopmen, John Perricks and George Isaacs, discussing it.[58] How many others beyond these nine may have been informed cannot be known, but it is certain that the information did not percolate upward as far as the *Tweed*'s captain, Lord Henry John Spencer Churchill, who testified that Maxwell "was never reported at all for being familiar with the boys of the ship."[59] No official action occurred, in fact, until Quartermaster Sandecombe informed the ship's lieutenant, Richard Peace, of the boatswain's actions. It was not until then that the matter went up from the quarterdeck of the *Tweed* to the Lord High Admiral, whose orders then moved back downward to Commodore Skipsey at the Cape of Good Hope station. Only then did Skipsey convene the court martial.[60]

Unlike most defenses offered up by accused sodomites, William Maxwell not only made his case ably and well, but he did so at considerable length. The opportunity to do so was of course a concomitant feature of the gradually increasing administrative complexity found at all levels of the government as the nineteenth century moved toward its midpoint and the Admiralty centralized its power. Almost half of the sixty-two pages of manuscript minutes from his court martial contain the intricacies of the legal points he disputed and the arguments he offered to establish that he was being twice tried for the same offense in contravention of British law. The defendant provided the officiating judge advocate with a twenty-page document rebutting the prosecution and offering material in proof of his innocence. The clear hand of counsel from the first trial is evident at every turn in Maxwell's presentation. Although defeated at his opening line of defense early on in the trial – the contention that trying him twice constituted double jeopardy – the boatswain did not lose heart. He offered the argument again near the end of the proceeding as part of his defense statement, then moved on to cite familiar admonitions by leading legal authorities on the dark nature of sodomy, how difficult it was to prove, and how those sitting in judgment should be wary of false accusations. References to the pronouncements of Hale and Blackstone were later followed by complaints on procedural matters drawn from McArthur's treatise on courts martial.[61]

As defendants in earlier sodomy trials had done, Maxwell charged that a cabal of evil-intentioned boys bent on revenge for floggings and other affronts stood at the heart of the accusations directed against him.[62] He offered no proof of the claim, but he made a "lawyerly" point about the inadmissibility of their testimony against him, explaining:

> I do most particularly beg humbly to impress on the minds of the court that you will not allow the evidence of the boys Waterworth, Romney, and Ryner to weigh in your minds with regard to the capital charge. It is totally irrelevant, as for instance if a man is tried for murdering another it cannot be brought in evidence that he has several times attempted to murder several other persons.[63]

The defendant tallied as many different arguments as possible to enlist the sympathy of the court, or at least to get the members to view his case more favorably. He told of his loyal service in HMS *La Loire*, HMS *Liverpool*, HMS *Impregnable*, HM Sloop *Icarus*, and HM Sloop *Sparrowhawk* before joining the *Tweed*, and explained how in 1804 his ship capsized while chasing pirates and he survived seven hours in the water clinging to flotsam and "swimming for [his] life." In that incident, he lost all of his possessions, including the certificates provided by previous captains affirming his good character and sterling service.

Maxwell also wrote eloquently in his statement of the torment he had undergone following his first condemnation.[64] He spent months as a

> Close and solitary prisoner on board the *Owen Glendower*, expecting every day the order for my execution that I have in its torment and the doubtful suspense of my fate already suffered as it were a hundred deaths, and such a miserable and wretched doom cannot fail of its consideration with the humane and compassionate feelings of the court."[65]

Boatswain Maxwell explained further how in his first trial the surgeons who examined William Pack shortly after the initial accusations failed to find any evidence of sodomy. Then he launched into an attack on the boy's credibility. The boatswain not only provided examples of variations in Pack's testimony between the first and second trials, he attempted to undermine his chief accuser's claim that he had recorded each of Maxwell's assaults with a piece of chalk on one of the iron mainmast hoops. The statements, testimony, and cross-examination on the subject ranged widely, but ultimately focused on a number of forensic issues: how often the mast was whitewashed, did the whitewash cover the hoop, was the hoop blackened after whitewashing, the width and circumference of the hoop, the number of syllables in each of the entries, the size of the writing, whether the specified number of entries could even be written on the hoop, and who might have passed by the mast and read what Pack had written. None of the dozen witnesses in the case testified to seeing the chalked records on the rusty hoop, but the boy proved unflappable when questioned by the defendant. He insisted that he kept the record of his abuse on the hoop, provided a believable roster of details on his record keeping – how he made his entries, when he made them, where he kept his chalk when not in use, etc.[66] The minutes of the trial provide no clear indication of the truth or falsity of the matter, and there is no way to judge the effect of the issue on the court martial board. Other than the argument over double jeopardy and the controversy over the alleged inscriptions on the mast hoop, Maxwell's defense followed the patterns used by mariners accused of sodomy over the preceding one hundred and twenty-five years. It relied on impugning witnesses, summoning friends and acquaintances to attest to the accused's good character, and repeated references to years of exemplary service. The result of the common threads previously employed produced a familiar result. No feature of the boatswain's multifaceted defense had any discernible effect. On 5 January 1829 the court found William Maxwell guilty and sentenced him to death. He was the last British mariner to be hanged for sodomy.

Although the twenty-ninth article of war prohibited sodomy and denominated it a capital crime, it contained no description of its constituent elements. Over the decades, naval courts consistently concluded that the essence of sodomy consisted at the very least of anal penetration. Decisions on whether the crime required emission during insertion came on an *ad hoc* basis, depending on the inclinations of the men hearing the cases, the quality of the defenses, and an assortment of additional factors. Modern historians, legal scholars, and theologians have suggested the term is broad enough to include fellatio and intercrural copulation in some contexts,[67] but such was not the case in the Royal Navy. This first of these activities created little ambiguity for courts martial. No men were ever condemned to death for fellation. Robert Patton's penis clearly entered the mouths of numerous ship's boys and emission followed entry, but he was not charged with sodomy. After his conviction for indecency he was only ejected from the navy and given 200 lashes. In 1807, Lieutenant William Berry was accused of indecency and sodomy, but the essential arguments at his court martial had nothing to do wih his indecent oral copulations. The court wanted to know only if he penetrated his partner's anus and emitted during penetration. Berry's actions met both standards, and he was hanged.

If courts martial paid little heed to oral sex, the same was not true with intercrural intercourse, a subject of continuous vexation. Officers on numerous occasions needed to decide whether penile insertion between the thighs or buttocks constituted sodomy, attempted sodomy, or merely indecency. There was discussion on the matter in almost every pertinent case. The conclusions were that it was only an indecent act. While intercrural intercourse was similar to sodomy, it never rose to the level of a capital crime.

The most conspicuous and constant feature in trials of warrant and petty officers is that the objects they chose for sexual gratification in every case were youngsters, usually thirteen or fourteen years of age. There is little surprise in this. Smaller boys were undoubtedly weaker and more tractable than sixteen or seventeen-year-olds or adult crewmen would have been. It is also possible that a portion of those prosecuted found them more attractive sexually, although there is no suggestion by the courts that this was the case. Neither did the act of an adult engaging in sex with a lad did particularly exercise officers judging guilt or innocence in sodomy trials. No notion surfaces in the proceedings indicating officers saw anything unusually pernicious in transgenerational connections.

Neither was there a sense that in such sexual engagements boys were victims or might suffer lasting harm of any sort. Such would be the concerns of centuries yet to come. The special efforts employed by courts martial when in dealing with juveniles most often was to ascertain whether they testified honestly. Again and again officers demonstrated their concern that boys or combinations of boys employed accusations of sodomy or other sex offenses to avenge themselves against adults who had angered or disciplined them. Lads were closely questioned about who had inflicted corporal punishment, and when and how often it was done. They were frequently asked to name those with whom they had discussed being sodomized, and adult witnesses were repeatedly requested to provide assessments of the characters and trustworthiness of boys setting out allegations of sodomy or indecency. Another common factor in the courts martial was that warrant and petty officers raped their boys, sometimes by direct force but more often by threatening them with flogging or other punishments. This was a language understood by commissioned officers who judged the cases, and it was the use of force or threats of force rather than youth or inexperience that provided the mitigating factors that saved the lives of boys old enough to be prosecuted for sodomy. They escaped the noose because their smaller size, subservient position, and lack of experience made them easier to rape than full-grown members of the crew.

Another constant feature of the sexual activities indulged in by warrant and petty officers who faced courts martial was the flagrant nature of their behavior. Although they usually had secure areas, most often private cabins, where they could indulge passions in secret, in every case prosecuted they exercised little caution, and their activities were widely known among the ratings. Under such circumstances it could only be a matter of time before commissioned officers learned of the situations and inexorable processes were set in motion to deal with them on an official level. Courts martial were authorized and convened. Surgeons, assistant surgeons, and surgeons' mates provided expert testimony to assist the courts in determining guilt or innocence, witnesses were called, questioned, and cross-examined, verdicts handed down and the guilty warrant or petty officers then cashiered, humiliated, flogged with the cat, imprisoned, or hanged from yardarms of Royal Navy ships.

6
Sodomy, Indecency, and HMS *Africaine*

Captain Edward Rodney of HMS *Africaine*, three of his lieutenants, and the ships purser assembled on 9 October 1815 for a particularly disagreeable task. They came together on the homeward leg of a four-year cruise in the East Indies to hear depositions from several crewmembers about events they had witnessed on board the ship that troubled them deeply. The men, marines William Dane and James Cooper and seaman Emanuel Cross (or Cruz), a Spanish-speaking Santo Domingan of African ancestry, all testified to the officers about seeing numerous of their shipmates engaging in anal intercourse and an assortment of other homoerotic activities.[1]

Their stories could not have taken the officers entirely by surprise. The captain and his lieutenants had known of problems with "uncleanness" on board the *Africaine* for over two years, and in fact it had been going on longer than that, at least since 1812 and probably even earlier. The first complaint actually made to Rodney came when the ship was in the "China Seas" in May of 1813. At that time, five of the crew reported that a pair of midshipmen and the captain's servant were observed engaging in uncleanness. The witnesses all claimed to have seen Midshipman William Crutchley and the servant boy, John Westerman, under the half-deck violating the second article of war. Another midshipman, identified only as Mr. Garroway, was in an unspecified way involved in the same offense. Rodney and the first lieutenant held a private inquiry in the ship's great cabin at that time. All three accused were punished for their actions, although precisely what they did cannot now be recovered. Garroway was turned out of the ship permanently. Crutchley was put ashore for six weeks, and Westerman lost his comfortable job as the captain's servant, a post he had probably secured through family influence. He was made an ordinary member of the crew, assigned to the mizzentop, and required to stand watches, a duty he very likely avoided in his previous assignment. At approximately the same time, the spring of 1813, Emanuel Cross spent eight weeks in irons for attempting an unspecified sexual act with marine William Dane.[2] The captain obviously found nothing in the conduct of the men to warrant requesting a court martial. There is no indication that any of the four, Garroway, Crutchley, Westerman, or Cross engaged in sodomy.

The following year, in 1814, a Mr. Downe, the *Africaine*'s third lieutenant, received a complaint about crewmembers identified only as Brown and Wardell committing unclean acts in the forechains. He reported it to Rodney who conducted an inquiry in public this time on the quarterdeck. Since there was no proof, nothing was done. At about the time of the inquiry, word reached another of the ship's officers that Robert Silvers, a boatswain's mate, and one Johnson, of the carpenter's crew, were lying on deck together clad only in their shirts. The lieutenant, who received the report in the early morning darkness of the middle watch, ordered two midshipmen who were nearby, the master at arms, and the quartermaster to surprise the pair in whatever evil acts they were performing, but the small task force was not quick enough. They found nothing. Silvers was also reported to have been seen with his arm around Johnson's neck, calling him "My Dear." When the matter came to Rodney's attention, he threatened to turn Silvers and Johnson ashore at the next port, but once more due to lack of evidence, nothing was done.[3]

In early 1815 there was another incident, a case of attempted sodomy. A black man identified only as Marbona tried to bugger the captain of the foretop, whom he found asleep on a chest. Moreland, the sleeping captain, hauled Marbona aft and related details of the attempted assault to the officers. The attacker was put ashore in Manila, ending the only incident in Admiralty records where a crewman tried to force sexual advances on a man of superior rank or status. Later in the year, on the ship's June visit to the Cape of Good Hope on the way home, John Westerman once more ran afoul of the *Articles of War*. A man identified only as Bowser reported seeing him engaged in "unnatural practices" with one Wilson. Again, nothing was adduced to substantiate the story, but the accused pair was punished for lying together on the same chest. The captain ordered Wilson never to go on the lower deck. Westerman received a second demotion. He was made a scavenger and forced to mess on the main deck. He was also "taken out of the mizzen top to prevent his corrupting the boys there."[4]

In October of 1815 another story of sexual irregularity came to Captain Rodney's notice. The bearer of the tale was James Green, a persistent fellow who had been investigating sexual activity on his own to discover exactly what was going on among the ship's company. Eventually his worst suspicions were confirmed when, on entering the galley, he observed the "Morisco," Frank (or Francisco) Jean groping marine James Cooper's private parts. Jean, actually a native of the island of Madeira, said something to Green which the latter took to be indecent. At that point Green, probably angered by Jean's comment, decided that he had heard and seen enough, and reported his observations to the captain. Although the evidence supplied to Rodney contained little information about sodomy let alone any indication of widespread homoeroticism among the crew, he decided to follow up on the report.[5]

If the captain assumed that Green's complaint could be handled neatly in the manner that he had dealt with similar matters over the preceding years, he was very much mistaken. This time, what was intended to be another small inquiry blundered into a thicket of evidence revealing widespread sexual activity throughout the ship that included dandling and groping, prostitution, boy rape, voyeurism, rampant mutual masturbation, and public, semi-public, and covert buggery. The investigation led to a raft of charges and counter-charges, and it quickly became clear that the problem was far to large to be handled on the quarterdeck or in the privacy of the great cabin. When it was all over three months later, the series of inquiries held at various administrative levels and the string of courts martial that followed destroyed the careers of several promising midshipmen, prescribed flogging and imprisonment for a good number of the crew, and left an assortment of the *Africaine*'s mariners hanging dead from her yardarms. The ship was disgraced in the aftermath of the prosecutions, and the admiral commanding the great naval installation at Portsmouth ordered an investigation of Captain Rodney.

A substantial portion of the *Africaine*'s crew were named in one capacity or another in the documentary record of the scandal. As a thirty-eight-gun fifth rate, the ship carried approximately two-hundred-and-forty persons when fully manned. That number included officers, warrant officers, petty officers, midshipmen, ratings, and idlers (men with occupational specialties such as stewards, servants, musicians, cooks, and others exempt from standing watch). The number of sailors – able seamen, ordinary seamen, and landsmen – authorized for a fifth rate would have been slightly less than half the total of men making up the ship's full complement. On her voyage home from the East Indies in 1815 there were probably fewer crewmembers than the total authorized due to deaths, those left behind when the ship sailed from various ports, and desertions. The ship was also returning home and most crewmen were owed considerable amounts of pay, which meant that the number of desertions, at least in the year immediately passed, might have been low. The navy's persistent difficulties in filling vacancies with qualified personnel or even unqualified personnel at foreign stations probably did not severely affect crew strength. Purser John Tapson wrote that deserters from East Indiamen were widely available and willing to join the navy in the ports visited by the *Africaine*. An estimate of the number on board Rodney's ship during the investigations of sodomy and uncleanness, made after taking these factors into consideration, would put the number between 210 and 220 men. Somewhat less than half of these were ratings.[6]

The one of every four of the *Africaine*'s men named in the investigative sessions and the subsequent trials represent a cross section of the crew. Appearing before the inquiries and courts martial in various capacities were as many as six commissioned and warrant officers, five midshipmen, one cook, one cooper, one quartermaster, one boatswain's mate, a carpenter's yeoman, seven boys from the first to the third class, and almost a dozen of the thirty or thirty-five marine privates who served on the ship. Eighteen of the *Africaine*'s crewmembers who participated in the proceedings were able seamen, ordinary seamen, or landsmen. Most of the men in the documentation were not accused of sodomy or indecency. Seven of the crew whose names appear in the record, the cooper, the quartermaster, the cook, a boy, two sailors, and a marine, were only deposed. Over twenty men included in the records were merely called as witnesses. About two dozen men and boys, approximately 10–12 percent of the crew, actually faced accusations of sexual impropriety. The violations of the second and twenty-ninth articles of war for which they were charged all occurred between late 1811, when the ship was on her passage to India, and October of 1815, when she was homeward bound.[7] The testimony provided at various inquiries and courts martial revealed a complex and enduring matrix of sexual relationships among the crew that included regular pairings, frequent changes of roles by men who alternated as insertors and receptors, a series of trysting places familiar to the participants, frequent solicitations, and the regular involvement of several boys – sometimes willing, sometimes not – who served as receptors but never as insertors. Another man, Boatswain's Mate William Brown, was reported to the *Africaine*'s officers merely for offering explicit and obscene commentary on the situation.[8]

Although Brown faced accusations for his frank speech from four of his shipmates – Thomas Wayman, a cook, quartermaster James Gibson,

William Aronston, the cooper, and Marine James Braun – during a second inquiry held on 13 October, he was neither charged nor tried for his comments. Still, the words that so agitated his fellows were included in the record, and they provide a rare flicker of light on the view of sodomy held by at least one crewman:

> He said that God must put it into men's hearts to commit the unnatural crime of buggery, and that therefore if God was to put it into his head to fuck a man he would as soon do it as fuck a woman and which expressions were by him several times repeated accompanied by horrid execrations.[9]

The irrepressible Brown continued on, railing that he would bugger not only the captain and the officers but would bugger "Jesus Christ if he was in his coffin."[10]

The nature and extent of the problems faced by Captain Rodney combined with potential difficulties of trying Brown for words rather than deeds under the second article of war meant that no action was taken against him for his commentary, but the incident indicates a division among the crewmen in their perceptions of sexual activity on board the *Africaine*. It was not ordinary ratings but three crewmen with occupational specialties requiring extensive training and skills that set them apart from those who actually sailed the ship who were sufficiently scandalized by his words to report them to authorities immediately after they were spoken. The fourth man who spoke out against Brown was a marine, whose terms of enlistment and duties also set him apart from seamen, although unlike cooks, coopers, and quartermasters, his fellow marines were as deeply involved in the ship's homoerotic life as ordinary sailors.

The man at the center of the sexual web of *Africaine* crewmen, Rafaelo Seraco, was in fact a member of the ship's marine contingent. When depositions were taken during the first investigations conducted by Captain Rodney, multiple accusations were leveled against him. Marine William Dane swore that on or about 1 July 1815 he happened onto Seraco "with his trousers ... loose and his arms hanging on the shoulders of R[afaelo] Treake [or Troyac], and his backside in quick motion, as if they were committing an unnatural crime," which Dane added he was certain they were doing. Dane clearly knew enough to have a good idea what they were about, even if he were not as certain as he claimed. He also admitted in a separate deposition to having been previously buggered by both Emanuel Cross and Dominico Gadize.[11] Another of Seraco's companions, marine James Cooper provided even more damning evidence against him. On 4 June during the second dog watch, he said he saw him "with his yard actually in the posterior of John Westerman ... they were committing an unnatural crime abaft the starboard roundhouse before the foremast gun in the main deck." The marine added that he had seen the pair engaged in the same act approximately three days later at the same time and at the same place. Cooper concluded describing his final observation of the two engaging in sex on 26 September, again at the same time of day and at the same location on the ship.[12] He also implicated himself in violations of the twenty-ninth article of war, confessing to having engaged in sodomy with a sailor, John Charles, four times between September and October of 1815. The acts were committed, he added, at the same location where he had committed sodomy with Able Seaman Rafaelo Treake, a man who it would be revealed was as deeply involved in the *Africaine*'s sexually active coterie as Seraco. Not only was Seraco a participant in buggery, but Seaman Emanuel Cross deposed during the opening day of the inquiries that six months earlier, on 4 April 1815, he observed Seraco watching while Treake buggered John Westerman. According to the deposition, neither Treake nor Westerman were wearing trousers when observed, and Cross, after stumbling onto the scene gave "Seraco a blow on his back, he ran away from him, and J. Westerman pretended to be making water." A boy, Thomas Bottomy, also testified to watching Treake bugger young Westerman on at least one occasion.[13]

Once the investigations began and it became clear that Rafaelo Seraco would be one of those most often accused of sodomy, he moved rapidly to protect himself. He became a star witness, denouncing others with a zeal comparable to that they demonstrated when denouncing him. There is no indication in Seraco's depositions that he thought he might receive leniency if he implicated others, but despite the absence of specific evidence, he well might have seen that as a possibility since Captain Rodney informed William Dane and James Cooper that it was certain that all iniquity would eventually be revealed and they might receive mercy from a court martial board if they told everything they knew. Alternatively, Seraco may simply have decided to retaliate against his accusers. Whatever his motives, in the several October inquiry sessions held on board the *Africaine* he spun out tales of unconstrained shipboard sodomy and provided his interrogators with the names of fourteen perpetrators. The first of them was William Copley, a seaman and a carpenter's yeoman who had deposed against Seraco. Copley had been involved with Westerman on at least four occasions, Seraco claimed. Another whom he denounced was Emanuel Cross, who had testified that Seraco had been present on 4 April when Treake buggered Westerman. Two more of the fourteen Seraco named were, of course, Rafaelo Treake and John Westerman, both of whom he himself had buggered, according to Dane and Cooper. None of the remaining ten accused by Seraco had any direct sexual connection with him that survives in the record. Eight of them were seamen, and the other two were boys. Among those Seraco denounced without any apparent cause for animus was fellow marine John Parsons, whom Seraco alleged had sodomized John Westerman a year earlier. Seamen William Brown (not the foulmouthed Boatswain's Mate William Brown) and Robert Smith were also accused of buggery by Seraco, as were five previously unmentioned mariners whose names were listed only in the margin of one Seraco's depositions, John Clarke, a crooked-eyed marine, Thomas Highton, Morgan Hughes, William Hunt, and the boy, Thomas Bottomy. Two other boys denounced were Christopher Jay and Joseph Hubbard, who at various times had served as a gunner's servant, a messenger, and at the time he was accused worked with the carpenter's crew. Seraco told of seeing in February of 1815 "Emanuel Cross, seaman, with his yard against the backside of the boy Christopher Jay and Cross's backside in quick motion as if he was committing the unnatural crime." Hubbard, according to Seraco, received Treake into his anus during the last week of February, 1815. Seraco also claimed that boy Hubbard told him of being buggered sometime over the summer by William Copley, a claim Hubbard would deny when interrogated later in England by Admiralty investigators.[14]

Seraco's testimony contained a good deal of truth, whatever his motives in confessing all. Joseph Hubbard substantiated some of the marine's assertions in his own testimony, admitting that he, himself, had been sodomized by Treake in the closing week of February, 1815. As the boy recounted the scene:

> Treake thereupon caught [me] by one arm round the waist let down [my] trousers and placing his naked yard against [my] bare backside shoved it partly into [me] and thus attempted to commit an unnatural crime ... , but [I] being much hurt sung out "Oh" ... . Treake got away to his hammock.[15]

Christopher Jay confirmed being penetrated by Emanuel Cross, as Seraco had claimed, and also explained that the first time he tried to bugger him, he was unsuccessful, and so settled for intercrural intercourse.

It was only during later attempts that the older man was able to enter his anus. Jay concluded his testimony with the information that Cross had also buggered an unnamed boy whose hammock was near to Jay's.[16]

Rafaelo Treake stood with Seraco at the epicenter of the *Africaine*'s storm over sodomy. One later witness, Frank Jean, put it directly and succinctly: "All the scandalous behavior in the *Africaine* has been owing to Treake and Seraco. They are the origin of the whole of it"[17] The two men not only buggered each other on a regular basis, but Seraco told of witnessing Treake commit anal intercourse with Joseph Hubbard.[18] Another boy, Rainbow Archer, claimed Treake once tried to get him to masturbate him, and had tried to bugger him on at least three occasions. Because the lad's orifice was too small to accept Treake's member and because the attempt put Archer in considerable pain, no penetration occurred. Instead the man satisfied himself by putting "his yard between his (Archer's) thighs, and in that position effected an emission ... between the second and third gun from forward on the larboard side of the main deck."[19] As the boy explained it when he later testified at one of Treake's three courts martial, "he heaved his dirt between my thighs."[20] The attempted buggery of Archer was confirmed by the testimony of Emanuel Cross, who also claimed that he once saw Treake bugger Westerman. There was even more to Treake's sexual exploits on board the *Africaine*. James Cooper admitted playing both active and passive roles while engaging in sodomy with him in the spring of 1815, and William Johnstone, a seaman, alleged that Treake stood before him in early May, 1815 with his "trousers unbuttoned and his yard exposed and in a state of erection" and importuned him to sodomy. Treake was momentarily distracted by a sailor "going forward to make water in the stair," and Johnstone made a hasty exit by crawling under the bowsprit.[21]

George Parsons, another of the *Africaine*'s boys provided additional information about the elaborate, confused, and overlapping constellation of sexual relationships on board the ship. He told of how seaman Frank Jean had twice tried to engage in sex with him in the early months of 1815. Jean had already been accused of groping a marine in the galley by James Green, and when he appeared before investigators on 3 November he made his own series of denunciations, hoping perhaps to earn leniency if ever brought to trial. He also claimed to have seen two midshipmen, Christopher Beauchamp and James Bruce engaging in sodomy, the pair trading positions as necessary. The act of mutual buggery, he said, took place about two months after the *Africaine* arrived at Simon's Bay, near Capetown on the homeward leg of her journey. His accusation carried a good measure of believability because William Dean had previously testified to Beauchamp's homoerotic activities, confessing that he had at least once allowed the midshipman to indulge in intercrural intercourse with him.[22]

Arthur N. Gilbert claimed that the *Africaine* had a reputation as a "man-fucking" ship in a 1974 article on the sodomy courts martial of members of her crew. The implication, of course, is that there was on board the *Africaine* a higher frequency of homoerotic activity than on other ships of the Royal Navy. The absence of data suitable for comparison with what is known about the *Africaine* situation and sexual activity on other naval vessels makes it impossible to draw any firm or meaningful comparisons let alone postulate for the entire Royal Navy, but the depositions give credence to Gilbert's suggestion that the *Africaine*'s widespread and frequent sexual activity was unique within the service. An extensive network of relationships that had endured for as long as three years existed on board the fifth rate according to numerous crewmen who corroborated each others' testimony over and again. In prosecutions for violations of the second and twenty-ninth *Articles of War* on other ships both before and after 1815 and 1816 those facing courts martial were involved almost exclusively in paired relationships, one man with another or one man with one boy. No courts martial other than those involving *Africaine* crewmen indicate the existence of anything remotely similar to the inclusive matrix of sexual relationships extant on Rodney's ship. Several warrant officers over the course of the eighteenth century stood accused of sodomy or indecency with more than one of the boys from their ships, but even in these cases there exists no widespread evidence of interconnected relationships. In such situations, boys talked among themselves of rapacious boatswains or masters, and sometimes warned other boys against them or teased boys who had been victimized, but nothing in any earlier trial testimony even hints at a situation as complex and interwoven as that uncovered by Captain Rodney and his officers as they sailed home to England in the autumn of 1815.

Another feature of the sex life on the *Africaine* that distinguishes it sharply from revelations at other sodomy and indecency trials throughout the eighteenth century and during the Napoleonic Wars is the nature of interactions between men and boys. The commissioned and warrant officers earlier prosecuted for engaging in sexual relations with shipboard boys in all cases held sway over the boys not only by virtue of their greater size and superior strength but because in almost every instance they exercised direct authority over them. Their status raised them far above their juvenile partners in rank, and most often when officers engaged with boys, the boys were their official servants or in some other ways directly beholden to them through the naval hierarchy. Officers also had their own cabins on board their ships, where nothing would be considered amiss if one of their youthful servants was present. The degree of privacy obtained allowed them to engage in kissing, fondling, groping, mutual masturbation, and buggery without fear of discovery. On board the *Africaine*, no officers faced charges for sodomy or indecency. All of those accused belonged to the lower levels of shipboard society, midshipmen, ratings, private marines, and boys. Only one of the accused, a carpenter's yeoman, possessed special training and skills, but his position was only slightly elevated above ordinary crewmen, and far below even the most insignificant holder of a warrant. When crewmen used boys as sexual partners they had no such luxury as private quarters. They had to make do with whatever darkened or semi-isolated corner or bay they could locate on board a ship where two hundred or more men inhabited a space no longer than 154 feet, only 40 feet across at the widest point, and with only a few habitable levels between the keel and the quarter deck.

Although *Africaine* crewmen who engaged with boys were in all likelihood larger and stronger than the boys of their choice and ranked above them in the navy's scheme of things, it remained far easier for any youngster to avoid sex with them than would have been the case had he caught the eye of a warrant officer with a private cabin or even a petty officer who might lay claim to a screened off nook or portion of a bay. The experience of George Parsons illustrates the latitude available to one boy intent on dodging the advances of a sailor. Parsons was sleeping on the main deck when he was awakened by Seaman Frank Jean putting "his yard against his backside." The boy fled immediately, and later informed other ship's boys of the attempt. Some months later Jean again attempted without success to bugger Parsons, climbing into his hammock and again trying to "put his yard against his backside." The record does not explain exactly how Parsons "obliged him to desist and leave his hammock," but it would have been easy enough to do by hallooing loudly across the closely tenanted deck.[23] When Rafaelo Treake attempted to bugger young Rainbow Archer between the second and third gun on the larboard side of the main deck, the boy faced a similar situation. "Treake put his yard against Archer's backside, but in consequence of its hurting him Archer obliged Treake to desist." Exactly what he said or did to avoid penetration is unknown, but the possibility of a pain-induced shriek on the darkened deck might well have been enough for Treake to lower his aim, as he did, and ejaculate between the lad's thighs.[24]

Rafaelo Treake was not to be discouraged by the failure of his attempt on Archer's anus. He could indulge his passions with several boys who were more willing and able than Archer. The ubiquitous observer and participant in the sexual life of the *Africaine*, Rafaelo Seraco, told of once seeing Seaman Treake and young Joseph Hubbard, in the galley. Hubbard had his pants down, and light from the stove made it obvious that Treake had his penis in the boy's fundament. Hubbard cried out in pain, but evidently the galley offered enough privacy, at least compared to the main deck, so that Treake continued. Later, according to the deposition, Hubbard had blood running from his backside down his thigh. In his later testimony before an Admiralty-authorized investigation held in December after the *Africaine*'s return to England, Hubbard made no mention of bleeding but told how "it hurt him very much" shortly afterward when he tried to defecate.

Seraco continued with his depositions, telling how on the passage from Penang to Madras in February of 1815 he saw Emanuel Cross with his penis inserted into the backside of the youth, Christopher Jay, and Cross making quick motions as if he were engaging in anal intercourse.[25] Hubbard confirmed Seraco's words, complaining in his own testimony of how the pain of Treake's large yard caused him to holler out. He also related how he, like Seraco, had seen Emanuel Cross attempt to bugger Christopher Jay, but was repelled when the latter "sang out 'Go to Hell you black b ____r.'"[26]

When Jay came before the 2 November session of Rodney's board of inquiry, he admitted to another encounter that occurred as the *Africaine* sailed between Penang and Madras. "Emanuel Cross, seaman, took him to the foremost gun on the larboard side of the main deck," he explained, "unbuttoned his trousers and put his yard between the thighs of his (Jay's) and there effected an emission, having previously attempted to commit the unnatural crime, in which he could not succeed." Jay further testified to watching Cross bugger another boy whom he did not name, and added that just weeks earlier, in September, Cross had taken him out of his hammock, placed him against the second gun forward, larboard side of the main deck, and buggered him.[27]

Most of the boys in the *Africaine*'s sexual fraternity participated with enthusiasm. Unlike the earlier courts martial of several warrant officers where testimony revealed that brute strength and threats of flogging were employed to bring youngsters into compliance, there are no indications that physical force played any role in the seductions of Archer,

Hubbard, and Jay, although Christopher Beauchamp later claimed at his trial that Frank Jean offered ship's boys "drink and other things such as dainties which as a cook he prepared for them to tempt them to consent to his having had practices with them."[28] The only man known for certain to have offered bribes was Rafaelo Treake. He provided assorted presents to adults Frank Jean, John Clark, and Joseph Tall in exchange for sex. His job as gunroom cook also facilitated his importuning. He gave food to Archer, whose anus was too small to penetrate, and offered cakes and other items to Thomas Bottomy because, as the boy told it, "He wanted me to go with him to fuck me."[29] Archer may have been quite willing to let Treake have his way with him, but the pain he experienced changed his mind. Hubbard apparently went willingly to the galley late in the evening with Treake, and although Cross initially could not force entry into Jay's backside, he eventually managed to bugger him, achieving both penetration and emission.

Commissioned and warrant officers summoned before courts marital in earlier years had confined their alleged "unnatural acts" to the privacy of their quarters. Ratings answering charges of violating the second and twenty-ninth articles had been discovered in darkened and secluded areas of their ships by men who happened to stumble upon them, quite literally in one case. The *Africaine*'s sodomites, too, sought out darkened and secluded locations but did not seem to trouble themselves unduly with wanting to be unobserved. Indeed, a salient feature of sodomy on the *Africaine*, setting it apart from sodomy as it occurred on board other ships, is the open commission of sexual acts and widespread knowledge that they occurred. There is no indication that participants ever posted lookouts to warn of approaching officers or unsympathetic crewmen. While some of the engagements took place in early morning, or late in the evening or at night when hammocks were piped down and lights put out, by far the greatest number of them occurred during the last dog watch, between 6:00 p.m. and 8:00 p.m., when most of the crew were awake and about. Then, too, multiple witnesses told of seeing couples engaged in the same acts of sodomy. Some of the testimony may have been exaggerated or even false, induced by fear once the investigations got under way, but given that much of it was confirmed by multiple observations it seems likely that there was considerable truth in the information provided to the investigators. The shipboard locations chosen by crewmen as well as the time of day in which they most often practiced sodomy indicate that they did not consider privacy a requirement. While accused sailor-sodomites or on board other ships often engaged between guns, presumably on the deck itself, the *Africaine*'s men buggered their partners against the guns, surely making them more conspicuous than couples copulating down low on the decks in the spaces between guns. Only one pair chose the comparative isolation of the starboard roundhouse, a fully enclosed toilet near the galley reserved for those on levels above "the people."

The places where sex acts occurred are frequently mentioned in the depositions. Of the acts connected with specific locations, a fourth of them took place in the galley, on guns in the galley, or on the flagstones of the galley. John Clarke, testified to its ordinariness. "It was known fore and aft the ship by everyone," he claimed, "that those in the galley were guilty of it."[30] It was not only the galley that attracted sodomites, but the entire fore portion of the ship. The bow, the manger, and the spaces between forward guns were all popular places for assignations on board the *Africaine*. Over half of the engagements for which shipboard locations are mentioned took place either on guns or between guns, near hatchways, by the bills, or three times "abaft the starboard roundhouse before the forward gun on the main deck." At one of the courts martial convened after the series of investigations, Emanuel Cross testified he had seen Westerman and Charles together wiggling about on the quarterdeck, although they had sufficient discretion to do their wiggling under a tarpaulin. William Dane also witnessed the event. Dominico Gadize and Dane once had the temerity to engage in buggery "between the two aftermost guns on the larboard side of the quarterdeck between six and eight o'clock in the evening," but there is no indication if they were similarly shielded from the gaze of the officers and men regularly tenanting the quarterdeck. If they made any effort to escape notice it was not successful, at least not successful enough to avoid being seen by one of the ship's company. In another case, when a witness at the second court martial of John Parsons was asked if, at the time the defendant took indecent liberties with him, there were others present who might have witnessed what occurred, he replied in the affirmative. "The sentry at the [illegible] was walking there," he testified, "and there were people passing along the main deck at the time." Emanuel Cross and Frank Jean were once observers while Treake buggered Hubbard, Jean first spotting the copulating pair and then pointing them out to Cross. Cross later reported that they were unperturbed by his watching. "They began and went on deliberately," he said, "without being the least affected by my presence." Cross had watched Treake engage in sex with four or five others over the course of the voyage, and cautioned him that he might be seen by Englishmen on the ship who might not approve. He warned that dire consequences could result when the ship reached Portsmouth.

Jean, in fact, told of watching Treake bugger Westerman on numerous occasions. Although he did not actually see penetration, he described them as copulating in plain view like dogs. Cross also observed Seraco bugger Charles early one morning at 4:00 by the first gun near the manger, and two or possibly more crewmen watched late one afternoon as John Charles bent over, placed his hands on a bow port sill and allowed Seraco to bugger him. One of the witnesses, Rafaelo Treake, puffed on a cigar as he observed the dogwatch event. There was it seems little need for discretion. The master at arms, Andrew Johnson, once passed by a buggering pair without comment or interference even though his lantern provided enough light to see them plainly.[31]

Occasionally, efforts were made to secure a modicum of privacy for sexual activities, but they were few and only half-hearted. Frank Jean once took a bowl of soup and some other unnamed gift from gunroom cook Treake to absent himself at an inconvenient moment. Emanuel Cross on another occasion discovered Treake and Hubbard engaged in sodomy by the billboard, immediately beneath the fore chains. They had gone outside the decks of the ship to be alone with one another, Cross speculated, because a number of people were at the time smoking in the galley. When he peered out of a port and saw them, they also saw him, but did not desist. The master at arms testified at one of the courts martial that he had observed Rafaelo Treake "on the billboard outside under the fore [illegible] waiting for [Thomas] Bottomy to go out to him." The two, he claimed, intended to commit sodomy.[32]

The large number of active participants in sexual activity on board the *Africaine*, their involvement with one another in fluid rather than dyadic relationships, the network that existed among them, the semi-public or public nature of some of their engagements, the stability of the group over an extended period of time, the existence of recognized meeting places where sexual acts took place, and the general awareness among the ship's crewmen, whether or not involved in sodomy and indecency, suggests that there existed on board a company of men bound together in a loose confraternity of some sort by their sexual activities. Further evidence that a measure of bonding existed among those involved in homoerotic activities on board the ship is provided by their reluctance to inform officers of such doings. Knowledge of widespread sexual activity did not receive official cognizance until the October 1815 investigation ordered by Captain Rodney, but it is unlikely that most of the crewmen involved would have volunteered the information they did without the pressure of a shipboard inquiry and after being told that all would eventually be found out. The draconian nature of the punishment prescribed for sodomy may well have been the reason that some or even many failed to report it, but there were other reasons as well.[33] When adults responded to questions about their unwillingness to report sodomy and indecency at the various inquiries and later at courts martial, the answers given by the *Africaine*'s men indicate that they had some sense of loyalty to their sex partners and no desire to inform on them. In his testimony, William Dane explained at one point why he allowed three years to pass before he reported an incident involving John Parsons to the commander of the *Africaine*'s marine detachment. That was all there was, he said, nothing else occurred, "and I took no more notice of it."[34] Emanuel Cross at one court martial first admitted it was an error to have kept silent, and later implausibly explained that he did not know whom to tell. At another court martial, black Caribbean native Cross justified keeping silent because there were "plenty of English that should take notice of it before me." At a third trial, he exhibited a similar reticence when questioned about why he had not reported an act of sodomy that he had witnessed until years later. He said only "I did not like to do it [report it]." A boy, William Johnson failed to report Treake's importuning because he "did not like to disgrace the ship's company, as no such thing had happened at that time to my knowledge." Only the boy, Thomas Bottomy, stated flatly that he was afraid of the consequences if he reported Rafaelo Treake.[35]

In December of 1815, the *Africaine* sailed into Portsmouth carrying almost two dozen men and boys accused of sodomy and indecency by their fellows. The problem of having so many putative criminals on board, one in every eight or nine of the crew, was neatly solved once the ship was at anchor. On 8 December, while most of the ratings scrubbed hammocks and washed clothes, twenty-one of the *Africaine*'s complement, all of them directly involved in the scandal were transferred in pairs to ten nearby warships, most of them smaller fifth and sixth rates. The odd boy, Thomas Bottomy, went alone to another vessel.[36]

It was only after the men had been removed and ensconced on other ships, that the Admiralty launched its own investigation to affirm and supplement what Captain Rodney and his officers had discovered in October and November. Such a procedure seemed necessary given the magnitude of the situation before any courts martial could be authorized. Captain George Jones directed the inquiry, which met at Portsmouth on board the *Queen Charlotte*, a recently built 104-gun first rate authorized to carry a crew of nine hundred men. Everything had to be done correctly, for the situation of the officers appointed to investigate the matter as well as the situation of the *Africaine*'s officers was precarious in 1815.

The difficulty of their position grew not only from the seriousness of the charges and the large number of men implicated but because all of their jobs were at risk. The Royal Navy had begun reducing its personnel in 1809 when it became clear that the French were no longer able to mount any serious challenge to Britain at sea or launch a cross-channel invasion. In the years after the British installed Napoleon at Elbe in 1814, the number of ships in commission dropped from 713 to 134. There was a similar contraction of the numbers of commissioned personnel. By early 1815, over half the navy's officers were ashore on half pay with no chance of ever returning to sea, and all knew the situation would only worsen. The final defeat and exile of Bonaparte to St. Helena insured that the constriction of the navy would accelerate even more rapidly over the next several years. Even though the navy sent out increasing numbers of exploratory and hydrographic expeditions, the total of the ships and men involved in such efforts was tiny compared to what had once been. Only 15 percent of the lieutenants retained shipboard assignments after the coming of peace, and all but those with exceptional influence in the loftiest reaches of the government or the Admiralty knew that their careers hung by the most fragile of threads. Removal from active service with pay reduced by half awaited as many as nine of every ten officers who led the Royal Navy to victory over the previous quarter century of war.[37]

Captain Jones conducted a meticulous investigation from the outset, taking care to resolve all details, large and small, that if ignored might return to bedevil him. Any undue embarrassment to the service, the appearance of incompetence, mere bumbling, or actions displeasing to the Admiralty on the part of any of the commissioned participants would hasten an end to careers that by this time were problematic at best.[38] When confessed sodomite James Cooper came down with a urethral infection, Jones summoned surgeon James McDonnell to testify whether or not buggery caused it. The surgeon made no definite pronouncement on Cooper's affliction, but he did not equivocate in his conclusion after being ordered to examine Frank Jean, who claimed to be incapable of committing sodomy due to his impotence. McDonnell found his generative organs in "perfect" condition.[39]

When the Admiralty investigation on board the *Queen Charlotte* concluded in mid December, it was unclear if anything more of substance had been discovered than Rodney had found in the questioning on board the *Africaine* over the previous two months. Midshipman William L. Crutchley confirmed again the open nature of some homoerotic encounters on board the ship when he told of five of the crew observing him engaged in "unclean practices" under the half deck with John Westerman, but this information and a few other newly uncovered bits of data had little effect since the navy was concerned with routing out sodomites, not persecuting boy masturbators.[40] Even though the Jones inquiry heard more testimony and provided additional depositions, the basic question for the navy remained not who did what, but what to do next? Hanging almost two dozen men for sodomy would be impossible to justify. In the aftermath of the Nore mutiny in 1797, an event far more destructive to naval discipline than an assortment of buggery cases on board an obscure fifth rate, only twenty-four of the ringleaders were executed. Some winnowing had to be done. How it would be done was yet to be determined.

In late December the courts martial began, with the same officers serving, for the most part, in every trial. Once the proceedings were under way, it became clear how the navy would confer mercy on some and exact retribution from others.

The first group whose members were spared the navy's wrath in varying degrees were the boys of the *Africaine*. This had to be an easy decision for the courts. Those under fourteen could not be charged with sodomy or any other felony. The ages of most of the lads accused during the preliminary investigations do not appear in the records, but even if all were over the age that afforded them statutory protection, it is unlikely that they would have been convicted of buggery. Throughout the entire course of prosecutions from the earliest during the reign of Queen Anne, officers appeared reluctant to court-martial or convict youngsters for violating the twenty-ninth article, and they were even more reluctant to hang them from the yardarms of the Royal Navy's ships. It must have been a relief when testimony revealed that the boy, Rainbow Archer, could not under any circumstances be accused of sodomy because his small anus prevented Rafaelo Treake from penetrating him. His participation with Treake in intercrural intercourse, even if it had been voluntary, was surely unenthusiastic. He proved his worth to the prosecution in the series of trials by providing a mass of evidence against his partners. No charges of indecency were ever filed against him, but the reason for the failure to do so is not preserved. His cooperation in incriminating others may have been a factor, but he might also have been under fourteen years old. The mention of his small anus at several points in the trial records indicates he was a diminutive lad, suggesting he was too young to be a felon. Another boy, Christopher Jay also escaped trial although he had been buggered by Emanuel Cross. It is unclear whether he avoided prosecution because of his age or because he denounced Cross to the investigators, but bringing him to trial would have been difficult for the navy. Although Jay admitted to having been buggered by Emanuel Cross, and Seraco confirmed it, Cross was a premier witness against several of the most notorious sodomites and would himself escape court martial in return for his cooperation. Thus, it seems Cross's testimony not only protected him, but it also conferred immunity on young Jay. It would have been unseemly at the very least to ignore the crime of a man who sodomized a boy and then try the boy for sodomy.[41]

Joseph Hubbard was one of the *Africaine*'s boys who actually faced a court martial. He had served as the "woman" multiple times for Rafaelo Treake as did Joseph Tall with whom Treake was also tried for sodomy.[42] After one of Treake's connections with Hubbard, Emanuel Cross explained that the boy "had no shame [and] deliberately buttoned [his] trousers up without being affected by my presence."[43] As a seventeen-year-old, Hubbard could have been convicted of sodomy and hanged, but it seems likely his willingness to denounce Treake persuaded a court to save his life. Although not convicted of sodomy, the youth did not escape naval justice. He stood trial for indecency with William Crutchley, the midshipman who had earlier admitted engaging in "unclean practices" with John Westerman under the half-deck. Both were convicted. Hubbard received his punishment with the cat o' nine tails, while Crutchley was ejected from the navy and sentenced to two years in the Marshalsea.[44] George Parsons, another boy who had masturbated Midshipman Crutchley, also received punishment. A court martial found both man and boy guilty of uncleanness. Parsons received six months in prison. The light sentence, only one-fourth as long as that given previously to his partner, Crutchley, might have been due to his youth.[45]

Of the four boys actually brought to trial, only one escaped punishment entirely. Thomas Bottomy, who faced a court martial for sodomy with Rafaelo Treake in what became Treake's third trial, went free. He testified against Treak, who had penetrated him and emitted "spendings" into his anus on multiple occasions and whom he had also seen buggering John Westerman.[46]

Westerman was the only one of the six boy crewmembers involved in sexual encounters on board the *Africaine* who was convicted of sodomy, and there seemed little alternative to returning a guilty verdict against him. He was almost as notorious and flagrant a sodomite as Seraco and Treak. Neither did he testify against any of his compatriots, although the records contain no hint of why he did not do so. A host of witnesses told how he willingly allowed half-a-dozen adult shipmates to sodomize him and how he regularly engaged in mutual masturbation with several others.[47]

Another group that avoided the full force of naval law, in addition to the boys, comprised some of the men who denounced their shipmates and testified against them at length and in detail. William Dane was one of the first to bear witness against his fellows. He provided a store of testimony at the initial inquiries and later at the courts martial. To make certain his words would not appear tainted he was asked whether anyone offered him a pardon for his own acts of sodomy with Emanuel Cross and Dominico Gadize if he gave evidence. He answered, "No, there was no pardon held out to me. I was desired to declare the truth against every one I knew."[48] That being done, he proceeded with his testimony. One of those whose crimes he recounted with precision was John Parsons, another marine. He told of an indecent encounter three years earlier, after their ship left Madeira on its voyage from England to India. According to Dane:

> Between the two guns abreast of the main hatchway, he [Parsons] thrust his hand into my trousers through the flap, and laid hold of my yard. I put my hand against his wrist, and shoved his hand back ... nothing more passed.[49]

When his testimony at several courts martial was complete, Dane had not only implicated Parsons in acts of indecency, but had denounced, Beauchamp, Charles, Seraco, Westerman, and Treak. Another reason why the prosecutors might have spared Dane in addition to his willingness to implicate others, might have been his youth. Although he was nineteen or twenty years old in 1816 when the *Africaine* courts martial took place, he had been one of the ship's marines for over three years. Some or perhaps all of the acts of buggery in which he engaged might well have been committed earlier, when he could have been considered a naive boy who was misled or coerced. James Cooper, who along with Dane, provided the first confessions in depositions before Captain Rodney and his officers in the autumn of 1815 also escaped court martial. He, too, proved himself an able witness, ultimately helping condemn four men to death.[50]

In like manner, Emmanuel Cross, a leading witness against several of the accused, stoutly proclaimed his innocence in the face of seemingly irrefutable accusations by Rafaelo Seraco, Joseph Hubbard, and Christopher Jay. It is unlikely that the court believed him, but his enthusiastic efforts on behalf of the prosecutors did in fact provide protection.

At least two of those accused by Cross, Midshipmen Christopher Beauchamp and William Crutchley, claimed that Cross provided evidence against them in exchange for a pardon, and other defendants in the courts martial regularly charged that those testifying against them had been promised leniency. The courts martial were deeply sensitive to such charges and throughout the series of trials asked witnesses if they had received promises of pardons or other favors. The answers, not surprisingly, were negative in every case, but the allegations of the defendants remained troubling. At one point a court martial summoned a Mr. John Knight to refute any notions that those leveling accusations against their fellow shipmates would receive special considerations. He swore that he had been present on board the *Queen Charlotte* during the Admiralty investigation and no promises of pardons were given and neither were threats made against any man. His testimony is supported by surviving "Law Officers' Reports." Still, both Cross and Jean quite likely expected some manner of reciprocity for their assistance in bearing witness against as many as a dozen of their shipmates, and they received it. Although both men could easily have been convicted of sodomy and hanged, the persuasive testimony they provided meant they would not be tried.[51]

James Bruce and Christopher Beauchamp were another pair who like Cross and Jean escaped hanging, though they stood accused of both indecency and sodomy.[52] Their trial, one of the last of the series that originated from events on board the *Africaine* differed dramatically from all of the others. It not only produced the most copious and complete record of all the courts martial in the series generated by events on their ship, but because the two defendants were midshipmen, young, educated, articulate gentlemen once destined to be commissioned officers, their defense differed in volume and substance from those offered by ordinary sailors and marines accused of violating articles two and twenty-nine.

Early on in their trial, their chief accuser, Frank Jean, provided damning evidence against the two. His graphic description of what he saw one night as he lay in his hammock in the galley watching them had the potential to hang them both:

> They [Bruce and Beauchamp] went to the starboard fore bits and they each unbuttoned their trousers .... I then saw one of them but which of them I cannot recollect, place himself with his trousers sufficiently low, I think, for the purpose they went there for, leaning his arms over the bits. I perfectly recollect having seen his backside naked, and his shirt turned up. The moment the one had placed himself over the

> bits as described the other placed himself on the back of the other. The flap only of the latter's trousers was opened. I can only swear to have seen a motion the same as a man to a woman, but nothing else, and after one had done, the one who was before leaning on the bits in his turn went behind the other and did precisely what the other had done.[53]

The court demonstrated considerable suspicion of Jean's account. Their unease was not because they believed that midshipmen were necessarily a chaste and morally unimpeachable group. The experienced officers well knew the midshipman's mess was what one naval historian called "the last stronghold ... of the pig-sty conditions of the Old Navy," where in the evenings the older members of the mess could be as bawdy as they liked and the conversation unimaginably gross.[54] What troubled the court was that they were allowing "Morisco" Frank Jean, a quondam cooper's helper and second cook, to bear witness against two gentlemen. They questioned him closely about how he had seen what he described. How much light was there below decks? The size of the lantern? The distance from his hammock to the bitts, and the like. When asked if he had been offered a pardon for his testimony, the witness replied ambiguously, "No promise."[55] Other accused sodomites, William Dane and Emanuel Cross also weighed in against the two midshipmen. They described no specific sex acts, but told how on several occasions they observed the accused pair go together into the single-seat roundhouse. On one visit they remained inside it "three-quarters of an hour by the glass at the cabin door" according to the trial transcript. The testimony offered by Dane and Cross, spread over two separate sessions, also received close scrutiny from the board of officers and from defendant Beauchamp. The cross-examination focused on details such as lighting conditions, the location of the roundhouse key, whether pardons were offered, and the amount of time the accused men spent together in the roundhouse.[56]

The most revealing aspect of the court martial of Bruce and Beauchamp is the lengthy, complex, and well-prepared defense offered by the latter. It is far more than a compendium of strategies used by defendants in previous sodomy and indecency prosecutions. The exculpatory materials prepared by Beauchamp, in consultation with someone obviously well-versed not only in naval law but in the laws of England, is perhaps the longest single document ever presented by the defense in any case involving violations of the second and twenty-ninth articles of war. It not only lays out the case for the defendant's acquittal in over sixty hand-written pages, but reveals much about the background, education, training, hopes, aspirations, attitudes, and fears of a young English gentleman who chose a career in the post-Nelson navy. In an obvious bid for sympathy, and well aware he faced a death sentence, the accused midshipman presented biography designed to persuade the officers judging him that he was one of them, of their own class and kind, that he could have been any one of them's son:

> I, your prisoner, Christopher Beauchamp, am but just in the bloom of opening youth, the second of a family of ten children all living, of whom seven are brothers and three sisters, having a widowed and respectable mother but for years past been deprived of the fostering care of their father who was an independent country gentleman–I am myself but just now emerging from childhood, little more than four years having elapsed since I quitted the tuition of the naval college at Portsmouth where as the best of naval seminaries my dear mother concluded a liberal education which she bestowed on me for a service it was the fond hope both of herself and my family and friends as it was my ambition that I should have done honor to … . I am one against whom until the present hour the breath of calumny dared not in any shape to approach. One whose character, whose manners, and habits have ever been interesting, amiable, and conciliatory of the esteem and affection of all around me and particularly gaining the highest approbation and confidence of my officers until the present accusation. Such, sir and gentlemen, is the individual now arraigned at your tribunal![57]

Beauchamp then turned to flattery, assuring the court that he believed they would reach "the most impartial judgment blessed with every liberal and merciful inclination … . And here, sir and gentlemen, am I cheered by the firmest assurance that all that is dear and sacred to me cannot be safer than with yourselves."[58] The narrative continued, page after page of garrulous prose, extolling the navy, denouncing sodomy, and regularly citing works of authorities from jurists Hale, Blackstone, and McArthur to the eighteenth century's preeminent literary figure, Samuel Johnson. Throughout the document Beauchamp made it clear he was defending both himself and his fellow midshipman, James Bruce. He could hardly do otherwise. If the court judged one of the pair guilty, the other could hardly be acquitted.

After his initial bid for sympathy, Beauchamp turned to race, ethnicity, class, and reputation to impugn those who testified against him and Bruce:

> That palpable infamy in the character of the witnesses (foreigners and men of color as to me are in the present case) the probable cause of their accusation and the doubtful credibility of their own testimony ought not for a moment to be lost sight of ... these witnesses are of such a stamp (of which from the miserable disgusting samples you have had in all the former trials as well as in this, there can be no doubt) you will I am sure look well whether to screen themselves and elude their own prosecution of their infernal guilt it is not evident that with a halter round their own necks, they have now maliciously and unjustly imputed the horrible crime to us and Satan-like involved as they are themselves in guilt and misery not only have been seducing poor unfortunate youths of their own class, and by previous intoxication brought themselves into their [illegible], as it has, I understand come out in evidence before you on the former trials but would seek also to bring railing accusations against youths respectable as we are, and in all these sparing neither distinction of age or rank! A reasonable doubt must therefore arise in your minds and hence that the testimony of such wretches ought not to be received but with the utmost possible caution.[59]

The parenthetical reference to foreigners and men of color, obviously Jean and Cross, was added later above the line of regular text. A caret below the line indicated the point of insertion. Beauchamp also claimed that Cross provided the testimony he did in revenge for the many times the defendant had beaten him with a bamboo cane.[60]

The close questioning of Cross and Jean when they testified indicates the members of the court martial were deeply suspicious of their testimony that Bruce and Beauchamp were sodomites, but there remained the charge of indecency, and it presented a particular problem for the defense. There was no need to trust two, sepia-toned, foreign sailors on that charge. The midshipmen had told of masturbating one another during the preliminary investigations. The only viable tactic was to get the confessions thrown out, and to do this Beauchamp argued they were inadmissable because they were obtained in a manner inconsistent with English law. The defendant offered no allegation that the authorities used physical force to extract admissions of guilt from him and Bruce, but he described the tremendous psychological pressure they were under. As Beauchamp told it, the navy's inquisitors had:

> All the accused parties brought before them, and ourselves [Beauchamp and Bruce] suddenly surprised as we were amongst the rest, are brought under escort of marines as prisoners from our own ship where we have been some time confined. Terrified as we were in the idea of being prosecuted for the horrible crime imputed to us, dismayed and alarmed we submitted to an examining of us separately made, and in the duress of our situation, our minds and feelings every moment distorted by hope and fear without a friend to counsel us, we trembled lest we should undergo our present prosecution, and in the hope amidst such a [illegible] of feelings that an acknowledgment of the minor offense of boyish indecent indiscretion would insure us compassion and avert the evil we feared.[61]

In short they confessed to violating the second article of war hoping to avoid prosecution and a mandatory death sentence if convicted under the twenty-ninth article of war.

The claim that the authorities obtained the confessions by unfairly or unlawfully pressuring the two young midshipmen carried little weight with Deputy Judge Advocate of the Fleet Moses Greetham. He dismissed the complaint as a "crotchet," forcing Beauchamp to experiment with several other strategies. The midshipman then explained that he and Bruce regularly retreated to the one-seat roundhouse together to smoke, since Captain Rodney had forbidden the practice at other locations on the ship. In any case, he added, two men going into a roundhouse together, "indelicate as it might be for us so to do, guilt is not thence to be presumed."[62] Sensing, perhaps, that such a line of argument carried little persuasive force, and having failed to have the confessions disallowed, Beauchamp tried another tack. He argued that mutual masturbation hardly constituted a serious matter, particularly when compared to the panorama of evils present everywhere on warships. Then, too, what they had done was what all boys do. Disgusting at it might be, he proclaimed:

> Its practice is too often imbibed at schools where boys feeling the rising passions of our sex, unhappily indulge a filthy gratification, and many become victims to it in early life. And it is yet a practice which has pervaded without exception almost every public and private seminary from all times, undoubtedly arising from a passion

> honorable when used lawfully with the other sex for the procreation of our species, but which from the infirmities of our nature particularly in early life when we have not the restraints of maturer age, youth is too apt improperly to indulge. With our nature and constitution, this may be checked, but with the weakness and infirmity attached to us it can never be always eradicated 'till manhood arrives and an acquaintance with the other sex passes it away.[63]

Beauchamp found his voice in the discourse on masturbation, and perhaps carried his defense past the point where it might have been persuasive. He did not stop after labeling it a natural, ordinary, and widespread youthful indiscretion, but in muddled syntax he may well have inadvertently persuaded members of the court martial board that he believed they should acquit him and Bruce because they, too, might have at one time been guilty of the same practice:

> I mean this observation to apply to men professing the generous and noble feelings of our nature were at best, I say, of such in a group now before this most honorable court with one voice charging the offenses on us it would we are sure, Sir and gentlemen, but afford every one of you the opportunity of compassionately saying (and we are as sure it would be the delight of your benevolent souls to do so as the great pattern of all virtue did on almost a similar occasion but with one of the other sex) which among you the prisoner's accusers is without sin cast ye the first stone.[64]

Beauchamp buttressed the defense with character witnesses. Several of the *Africaine's* officers testified to his exemplary performance on board ship, and John Broome, the incumbent at his home parish in Gloucester, provided written testimony to his good qualities. The accused midshipman then concluded with a pathetic entreaty of several pages, begging the court to preserve both his career and good name, promising in the future to be a credit to the Royal Navy, and assuring his judges that what he termed "youthful indiscretion" would not be repeated. James Bruce defended himself much more succinctly, explaining he could offer little more to what his co-defendant had already said. He added only that he, too, came from a respectable family where he gained the advantages of learning and developed "habits of virtue." They would be devastated by news of his conviction. The *Africaine* was his first and only ship. He joined her at fourteen, and at the time of the trial was "only in the 18th year of [his] age."[65]

Beauchamp and Bruce did what they could to sway the court by pleas based on the genteel backgrounds he and Bruce shared with the officers and the sympathy he hoped to evoke among them with the specter of humiliation that would be visited upon their families if the court returned a guilty verdict. It was a tactic that the two might reasonably have hoped would succeed. Most Royal Navy officers, by the early nineteenth century, came from middling backgrounds like their own. There were few other careers where men without independent income could be gentlemen. Admirals Samuel and Alexander Hood, as well as Horatio Nelson were the scions of country clerics. Officers who sprang from respectable but ordinary families had even become staples of fiction by the late Georgian era.[66]

The court martial acquitted both midshipmen of sodomy. The members might have found the testimony provided by Cross and Jean unpersuasive, they may have had doubts about their reliability as witnesses, or they could have been opposed to convicting midshipmen of a capital crime on the basis of testimony by foreign sailors. On the second charge, uncleanness and scandalous actions, William Dane and Emanuel Cross reported only that they had seen them enter the roundhouse together. Neither witness observed any crimes that might have been committed, but the thirteen captains who heard the case decided that the two midshipmen's confessions could not be ignored. They were found guilty of violations of the second article of war, and were "to be dismissed from His Majesty's Service, to be rendered incapable and unworthy of ever serving His Majesty, his Heirs or successors in any capacity again, to have their uniform coats publicly stripped from their backs on the quarter deck of His Majesty's said ship, *Africaine*, and to be imprisoned in His Majesty's prison called the Marshalsea in solitary confinement for the term of two years."[67] The prison sentence was the same as that handed out to their messmate, Midshipman William Crutchley.

While cooperation with prosecutors surely contributed to saving Jean and Cross from the noose, it did not help Rafaelo Seraco avoid a death sentence even though he accused almost two dozen men of sodomy. His frequent and enthusiastic participation in shipboard buggery undoubtedly made it difficult or impossible to grant him immunity from prosecution despite his denunciations of others. He was linked in multiple acts of sodomy to half-a-dozen shipmates. The fact that he was an Italian and most assuredly a Romanist guaranteed he would be hanged, since sodomy, Popery, and Italy were still an inseparable trinity in the minds of early nineteenth-century Englishmen. He was twice court martialed, once on 27 December 1815 for sodomy with John Westerman, and again in January, 1816 for sodomy and indecency with John Charles. Seraco received death sentences in both trials, along with his two partners. The others condemned to death at various courts martial in addition to Seraco, Westerman, and Charles were Joseph Tall and the Italian Rafaelo Treak.[68]

In the case of Joseph Tall, unspecified "circumstances" caused the court martial to ask that he be given clemency, and the request was granted. His death sentence was commuted, and he was instead ordered to spend three years in the Winchester county jail.[69]

On 1 February 1816, the judgments of the courts martial were carried out. The laconic prose of the officer who wrote the ship's deck log entry for that day preserved the grim events:

> A. M. Fresh breezes and cloudy ... employed getting ready for punishment. At 9 made signal [with] a gun. At ll executed Ralph Seraco, John Westerman, John Charles, and Raphael Treak for a breach of the 29th article of war, and punished alongside Jonathan Parsons ... with 200 lashes and Joseph Hubbard with 170 lashes for a breach of the 2nd article of war as sentenced by a court martial. P. M. ... sent the bodies of the executed to the hospital. Read the articles of war to the ship's company, etc. etc.[70]

Admiral Sir Edward Thornborough, the commander at Portsmouth, wrote promptly to the Lords Commissioners of the Admiralty informing them that the hangings and floggings had been done as ordered. He assured them that "The four men died truly penitent, acknowledging the justness of their sentences and admonishing their shipmates to take warning from their unhappy fate not to be guilty of such detestable practices."[71]

The executions did not end the matter of the *Africaine*. As captain, Edward Rodney had to answer for what had transpired on board. Admiral Thornborough moved quickly to investigate the state of discipline on the ship during her four-year cruise to the Pacific and the East Indies. On 1 February the same day as the executions, he appointed three captains to head the inquiry. The following day they were on board the ship questioning the four lieutenants, the commander of the marine detachment, and the master. The inquisitors were very much interested in how often the *Articles of War* were read and how often divine services were conducted. The navy lieutenants were in general agreement that neither took place very often. Once or twice a year was the consensus. The lieutenant of the marine detachment, agreed with them, but added disingenuously that the reason for the persistent neglect was the good conduct of the crew. No officer among those testifying condemned their captain. They were all adamant that discipline on the *Africaine* compared favorably with discipline on the many other ships with which they were familiar. Hearing no dissent, the investigators cleared the captain of all culpability, and in their report tendered on 3 February laid blame for the debacle on "the unfortunate introduction of men of these depraved habits into the ship."[72]

After the investigations, courts martial, and the executions the routine returned to normal on board the *Africaine*. By the middle of the month the ship was in the Thames being prepared for decommissioning. Stores and ballast came ashore and rigging and masts came down. On 27 February 1816 the log noted the pendant was lowered. Then followed the final item in the book, Captain Edward Rodney's signature.

Later in the year the infamous ship was broken up, ending the saga of the "man fucking" *Africaine*.[73]

7
The Last Sex Court Martial

With the conclusion of the *Africaine* courts martial, the hanging of the men convicted of sodomy, and the floggings and imprisonment of those guilty of less serious offenses, no more prosecutions for sexual irregularities perturbed the navy for a dozen years. Only an incident in the South American Squadron suggested homoeroticism still lurked in darkened bays, canvas cubbies, and private cabins of British warships. At Callao in 1820, a guilt-ridden Lieutenant Horatio Darby deserted his ship when his homoerotic liaisons became general knowledge among the crew.[1] It was not until almost a decade after Darby's precipitate departure that three naval courts martial dealt with sex offenses. The first was the 1829 case of Boatswain William Maxwell who was accused of buggering young William Pack. The court judged Maxwell guilty, thus providing him with the unsought distinctions of being both the last man convicted of sodomy in the sailing navy and the last to be executed for the crime. Of the two courts martial for sex offenses that followed, both dealt with minor breaches of regulations that did not fall under the twenty-ninth article of war. These last trials were far different in cast and composition than any that had been held in the previous one hundred and fifty years.

The first of these came several years after Maxwell's hanging, when marine privates John Peach and Edward McGee faced charges of indecent and immoral conduct after being discovered in bed together in their barracks. Their only actions were rooting about and giggling under the covers, but the Royal Marines were not amused by whatever humored the two men. Their indiscretion earned them each three hundred lashes and ejection from the service.[2]

The final case was that of Lieutenant Richard Morgan, who in 1838 appeared before the last court martial for sexual misconduct and obscenity convened during the period. A decade after the last execution for sodomy, his case made clear that accusations of homoerotic practices still retained their ability to agitate the service. The proceeding against Morgan, in fact, represents the most bizarre and opaque of all prosecutions for sexual irregularities in the history of the Royal Navy. The events leading up to it began on the first or second of January in 1838. On that day, Midshipman Frederick Edward Rose, of the seventy-four-gun, third rate HMS *Pembroke* presented a letter to Commander John W. Aldrich, one of the ship's officers. It contained a brief but inflammatory message.[3] Dated 31 December 1837, it read:

> Mr. [Robert] D'arcy [a *Pembroke* midshipman] having mentioned yesterday that some of the gentlemen were in the habit of taking indecent liberties with him, we deem it our duty to inform you of it. We also hope we have not deviated from the proper course in this mode of communication.[4]

It was signed by Rose, midshipmen John Frere, Owen P. Knott, and Charles Barker, and the clerk of the ship, Thomas R. Hallett, who also penned the letter.

The letter originated as a result of actions by Mr. D'arcy, who some days earlier had told Rose of indiscretions Lieutenant Morgan had taken with him. Rose then took it upon himself to drive the matter forward. He first conferred with some of his peers, the younger midshipmen in the gunroom mess, some of whom decided they were dealing with a serious matter. They initially sought advice from senior members of the mess, trying to discover the proper course of action, and it was only after due deliberation that they decided a letter was in order. After it was written there was still considerable hesitation. It took Rose's urging to get Hallett and Frere to attach their signatures. Frere and Rose then persuaded Barker to sign. Barker and Rose then pressured Knott, and he signed as well.[5] There is no indication of how many members of the gunroom mess, probably comprising as many as ten or a dozen men, were asked to sign and refused to do so.

It was only then, after deliberation and a fair amount of arm twisting to obtain signatures, that Commander Aldrich received the letter. He exhibited the same sense of unease with the information as did the midshipmen. Despite his misgivings, there were no alternatives for him. He forwarded the letter to Captain Fairfax Moresby, who had commanded the *Pembroke* over the past year.[6] Moresby seemed little more certain of what to do than Aldrich, but decided not to pass the problem upward.

He called a conference to deal with the matter the next day, 2 January 1838. The attendees included almost all of the ship's wardroom and gunroom officers, a number approaching two dozen on a third rate. Only two lieutenants and the chaplain were not present.[7]

At the meeting, held in the captain's cabin, Moresby sat at a table on the larboard side with his officers circled around him. The central participant in the saga that unfolded was Midshipman D'arcy, who explained to those assembled that several of the ship's crew had taken indecent liberties with him. He did not reveal the identities of all whom he accused, and it is not possible to discover who they were. In neither the documentation ultimately generated by his charges nor in subsequent revelations did the complete list of names ever appear. The only person identified was Lieutenant Richard Morgan of the *Pembroke*. The precise details of what he is supposed to have done cannot be retrieved from surviving records. The only certainty is that D'arcy told his story to Frederick Rose in the last weeks of 1837, Rose told others, and the story spread through the ship's crew. The telling varied over time, and memories of Midshipman D'arcy's tale, heard second and third hand, surely mutated to some extent in the minds of the hearers by the time they were eventually called to testify to what they thought he had said or what they had learned from others. The testimony on what happened to D'arcy ranged from accounts claiming Morgan only touched his thigh to others asserting he reached into his trousers and fondled his privates while commenting on how he had "grown."[8] Despite the varying descriptions, the general nature of D'arcy's accusations emerge from the investigation Moresby held in his cabin. The midshipman claimed Morgan had touched his private parts in some manner, perhaps on two separate occasions, the first time when the two men were together during the dog watch in the starboard surgery on the voyage from Gibralter to Malta in 1837. The second incident occurred on the starboard gangway or the quarterdeck when the *Pembroke* was anchored at Salamis Bay in Cyprus later in the year.[9]

At the inquiry Captain Moresby convened after reading the letter signed by the five men, one of the signatories, Midshipman Charles Barker, explained why he had affixed his signature. He thought D'arcy's statement had an "air of truth" about it, he said, but explained that while Lieutenant Morgan's "indelicate" conduct was not "strictly proper ... it had no tendency to anything further." Barker concluded by adding that he thought D'arcy was not "sensible of the gravity of the charge."[10] There is no record of the discussions that followed, but at the conclusion of the inquiry, the captain asked anyone with additional information to come forward. None did, and it was generally agreed that the investigation had gone as far as possible.[11]

Shortly after the meeting in the captain's cabin, D'arcy admitted the charges he leveled against Morgan were inaccurate or false, claiming he now could not recall if the lieutenant took indecent liberties with him or not, and suggesting that he might have misunderstood his intentions. As might be expected, D'arcy drew some measure of disapprobation for his indiscreet charges. His associates expelled him from the gunroom mess, and Captain Moresby wrote a letter to his father explaining what the son had done. There is no copy of the letter or record of its disposition in Admiralty archives. The only indication it ever existed is a petition from a number of midshipmen asking *Pembroke* lieutenant James Charles Prevost to intercede with Moresby and ask him not to post it. In due course, a method was devised to reinstate D'arcy in the mess, but only on the condition that he write a letter of apology to the maligned lieutenant. This was done at a meeting in the captain's cabin attended by Moresby, Morgan, and several other officers.[12] With their assistance, D'arcy wrote:

H. M. Ship *Pembroke*
March 24, 1838

Sir:

It is with deep regret that I misunderstood any action or motion of yours that induced me to make a false accusation against you, and I think you will give me your pardon for the same.

I am, Sir, your obedient servant,
(Signed) Robert D'arcy

To: Lieutenant Richard Morgan, R. N.
HMS *Pembroke*, Malta[13]

With the apology made, Captain Moresby ordered Midshipman D'arcy readmitted to the gunroom mess.[14]

The affair with D'arcy ended after his recantation and return to the mess, but Lieutenant Morgan's difficulties which began with Rose and his comrades presenting their letter to Commander Aldrige in late December continued without abatement. Throughout the first months of 1838, Rose spread another set of stories about Morgan. He explained that though D'arcy's accusations were unfounded, the lieutenant had behaved in an unseemly fashion with several other crewmen. He told this to a number of his gunroom friends, and from that point onward

Morgan's actions became conversational fodder for the entire mess. The table talk in due course spilled over to all on board the ship, officers, sailors, and marines.[15]

Rose also provided specific information on the lieutenant's alleged indelicate conduct, telling Lieutenant James Prevost who, upon receiving the information, decided that he needed cover. He summoned his fellow lieutenant, Edward Bevan, who had reported for duty on board the ship only a short time before the alleged indecent events were supposed to have occurred. Prevost had Rose repeat his accusations before the two of them. Commander John Aldrich also became privy to the stories during this period, and they soon reached Captain Moresby who questioned Rose to discover precisely what had occurred. "When you made that statement to Lieutenant Prevost," he asked, "did he request you to repeat it before Lieutenant Bevan?" Rose replied, "Not the first time, but the 2nd time I did."[16] Rose, as might be suspected, was not a disinterested reporter of events. He disliked Morgan intensely for reasons that are not revealed in the trial transcripts. On one occasion, he referred to the lieutenant as a "blackguard," and later when he had the opportunity, he bore brutal witness against him.[17]

The substance of Rose's allegations fell into three separate categories. He accused Morgan, first, of using obscene language in an exchange in December when he and Midshipman John Boyd made a visit to the lieutenant's cabin. He also accused the lieutenant of placing his hand on Midshipman Boyd's thigh in an unseemly manner and later putting his arm around Signalman William Chapman. Rose did not voice accusations only to Prevost and Bevan. He told others about the incidents, and they retold the story to any willing to listen. As a result, when witnesses later testified under oath, they offered various incarnations of what they heard had transpired.[18] The basic version, offered up by Rose himself in answer to a question from Captain Moresby, contained little extraneous material:

> I was in Mr. Morgan's cabin leaning over the after part of the gun reading *Jack Bray* … . [Boyd] was sitting at the foot of the bed and Mr. Morgan was lying at full length on the couch. He, the prisoner [Morgan] said to Mr. Boyd, "Lay up here and lay upon my belly and keep my cock warm." I immediately went up to Mr. Boyd, laid hold of him by the collar, and said it was high time he was out of the cabin. When Mr. Boyd was gone, I remonstrated with Mr. Morgan on the impropriety of speaking in that way at all to anyone.[19]

Midshipman Rose was equally direct in responding to Moresby when asked about the lieutenant placing his hand on Boyd's thigh:

> On Saturday evening the 29 December last, I was smoking on the main deck. Mr. Boyd was sitting on the after bitts abaft the main mast, athwart ships. I saw Mr. Morgan come up and place his hand on what I conceived to be a very indelicate position upon Mr. Boyd's thigh. I saw Mr. Boyd make some motion–what I could not tell as it was dark. But I went up to him and asked him what Mr. Morgan had said or done to him. Mr. Boyd answered, "He put his hand upon my thigh. I shoved it off and told him that I did not wish him to take those liberties with me." Before which he said Mr. Morgan replied, "If you don't hold your jaw you young rascal," or words to that effect, "I'll haul your cock off." I then repeated my former advice to him not to have anything to do with him.[20]

The third and final story involved Signalman William Chapman, who Rose claimed approached him on the poop deck and complained that Morgan had taken "indecent liberties" with him. At the time, Rose advised him to do nothing, but some months later, after witnessing Morgan's conduct in the cabin and observing him place his hand on Boyd's thigh, he decided he had better find out the details of what had happened with Chapman since he decided an inquiry might be held.[21] When the investigation was at last convened, he explained to Moresby:

> I think it was the night before St. Patrick's night and [I] asked him if he recollected having on a former occasion reported Mr. Morgan to me for indecent conduct. He said he did, but hoped that I would not bring him forward as a witness as he said most likely Mr. Morgan being an officer of the ship would get him four dozen for so doing. I told him that I was not aware if he would be required or not. He said, "If I am brought forward I must tell the truth, and then I shall be able to tell a great deal more" or [words] to that effect. I asked him what he meant. He said that whilst hoisting up the quarantine light lantern, Mr. Morgan came to him, shoved up against him, and put his arms round his waist and tickled him and said to him, "Would you like to be on shore in the rope walk, old boy, to have an upright or with a standing cock." That was the purport of it. I turned round immediately and told Mr. Boyd of it and Mr. Frere shortly afterwards, and Mr. Barker the next morning.[22]

With three such tales circulating among the crewmen of the *Pembroke* about one of the commissioned officers, it was clear by the final days of March something had to be done. Action came from two directions. Captain Moresby commenced a second investigation and Mr. Morgan demanded a court martial be held to clear his name. He then withdrew from the wardroom mess until the entire matter could be resolved. The lieutenant had no other options. As a gentlemen he had to respond to the slanders against his reputation, and only by requesting a full-scale court martial could he preserve his reputation. It was also possible that he would have been ejected from the mess had he not voluntarily departed.[23]

No record survives of the second investigation conducted by the captain in late March, but much of the testimony given on that occasion would be repeated subsequently when Morgan was brought to trial.

Moresby wrote to the commander in chief of the Mediterranean on 26 March, requesting authorization for a court martial. Admiral Sir Richard Stopford answered directly, demanding to know the precise nature of the charges, details which Moresby had omitted from his letter.[24] In his response, Moresby evaluated the allegations. "These statements made by Mr. Rose, mate, and by Mr. Boyd, midshipman, *if proved* [emphasis mine]," he said, "will show that Lieutenant Morgan has been guilty of conduct highly unbecoming the character of an officer and a corruption of good manners." In his opinion, though, a conviction seemed unlikely. He assured the admiral that Morgan would probably be acquitted.[25]

Moresby's letter to Stopford indicated that at this early stage in the events preparatory to a court martial no determination had been made on how to charge Morgan, but in due course the decision was to bring him to trial for violating the thirty-third of the *Articles of War* rather than number two, as was usual in earlier cases of indecency. The choice of the latter article restricted the severity of the sentence Morgan would receive if convicted. Under article two, guilty mariners incurred "such punishment as a court-martial shall think fit to impose, and the nature and degree of their offense shall deserve." Courts martial could impose sentences of imprisonment, forfeiture of pay, or death, whatever they deemed appropriate. The thirty-third article applied only to commissioned officers, and no latitude existed in pronouncing sentence on admirals, captains, commanders, and lieutenants who fell afoul of its provisions. They could only be "dismissed from His Majesty's service." A conviction would not subject Morgan to any manner of public humiliation, fines, or the possibility of time in jail. The only stipulation would be that he leave the Royal Navy.

Once Admiral Stopford authorized a court martial, the provost marshal took Morgan into custody. He had been relieved of duty some time earlier. The documentary record of the court martial of Lieutenant Richard Morgan is the most extensive in Admiralty archives for the prosecution of a sexual or at least a semi-sexual misadventure. It contains over one hundred hand-written pages, and unfortunately raises many questions that cannot be answered. The trial began on 2 April. All eligible officers at Malta were appointed to the board, which numbered five including the president. Captain Moresby could not serve since he had presided over the previous investigations. Instead, he was named as prosecutor. Morgan asked for and received permission to be assisted in court by a "professional friend," presumably a lawyer or someone conversant with naval regulations.[26] The prosecution called almost a dozen witnesses, most of whom provided hearsay evidence since they had only learned of the events in question either second-hand from Rose or third- or fourth-hand from others. Only three who testified were actually involved in the events they described. Rose and Boyd told the court of the incident in Morgan's cabin where the lieutenant allegedly made an indecent suggestion and used an obscene term. The pair also told of how he placed his hand on Boyd's thigh and indulged his proclivity for obscenities when Boyd asked him to desist. The single witness to provide direct evidence that did not corroborate the shipboard gossip was William Chapman, the signalman. While he told the court that Morgan had put his arm around him, he denied that the lieutenant had ever said anything about "a standing prick" as Rose had maintained, and he also denied Rose's claim that he had asked him to intercede with Morgan and persuade him to stop rubbing against him.[27] Morgan carefully cross-examined the parade of witnesses, almost always asking whether they had ever heard him use obscene language. Although Lieutenant Prevost repeatedly characterized some of the expressions Morgan allegedly used as "beastly language," and Moresby, too, called such terminology "beastly," neither officer testified to having ever heard Morgan utter the words, and no one other than Rose and Boyd provided direct testimony to his having used obscenities between October of 1837 and March of 1838, the period during which his alleged offenses took place. D'arcy, Rose, and Boyd additionally claimed they had had improper conversations about women with Morgan, but the accusations had no relevance to the proceeding then under way, and were ignored by the court.[28]

Lieutenant Morgan began his defense by authorizing the judge advocate to read an opening statement. In it he maintained that his high sense of honor prevented him from committing acts of the sort he stood accused, and summoned almost a dozen witness to vouch for his character. Among them were the *Pembroke*'s chaplain, brother officers, past commanders, and his captain. All agreed that Morgan was an honorable gentleman who eschewed bad language.[29] Only one witness seemed to equivocate. Morgan's commanding officer, Fairfax Moresby, undermined his own testimony in support of Morgan by adding the unsolicited comment that he never doubted his character until 1 or 2 January, the time he first heard of what turned out to be D'arcy's spurious charges. Moresby also added without being asked that he had the highest opinion of Frederick Rose and that John Boyd came to the *Pembroke* with good certificates.[30]

Morgan explained in his own testimony that he had only pinched Boyd above the knee firmly enough to "make him sing out very hard 'Oh.'" There was no more to his action than that. On the matter of Chapman, who had denied under oath as a prosecution witness the portions of Rose's testimony claiming that he asked the midshipman to persuade Morgan to stop rubbing against him and that Morgan had used crude language, the defendant claimed that putting his arm around the signalman was a case of mistaken identity. In the dark, he explained, he thought he had come up behind Mr. Stoker, the second master, and put his arm round him, the implication being that he would never indulge in such familiarity with a mere rating, even one who had competence in signaling.[31] Several character witnesses lent credence to the explanations, testifying to Morgan's gregarious, uninhibited ways. Sir Francis Fellowes, captain of the *Pembroke* in 1836 and 1837, spoke of the lieutenant's playful manner and familiar habits with messmates. Commander John Aldrich told of his spontaneity, relating how he sang, danced, and once waltzed around the wardroom with a surprised ship's surgeon who was "not at all prepared for it." Another captain, John Ashmore, told how Morgan frequently put his hands on people to whom he spoke. I do not see anything evil, he said, in "an act which I believe proceeded from habit."[32]

Morgan countered Rose's description of the scene in the cabin where, the midshipman claimed, the lieutenant asked Boyd to lay upon my his stomach and "keep my cock warm." "I deny it in toto," Morgan proclaimed in his statement to the court, "on my word of honour as an officer and a gentleman." The phrase "in toto" was underlined in the text of his statement that formed part of the trial record. He then attacked his accusers, pointing out that at the 2 January inquiry when Moresby asked if any one present had any more information, both Rose and Boyd remained silent. If they had this information, he said, they should have made it public at that time. The charges against him were formulated entirely by Rose, Morgan claimed, as had been the case with the discredited D'arcy letter. "Of their motives for conduct such as this I know nothing," he said, then speculated that perhaps their youth and intimacy were to blame.[33]

Morgan's use of the term "intimacy" did not appear in his musing by chance. It would be central to his defense strategy. As Morgan explained, even though the length and width of the couch in his cabin were so small that it was obvious Rose and Boyd's accusations were false, in the conflicting accounts of what transpired in his cabin he was outvoted two to one. He then went on to argue that in fact the two midshipmen were so closely connected, so intimately involved with one another that they must be considered one in their testimony. He called six witnesses to testify that the nicknames of the two men on board the *Pembroke* were "Substance" and "Shadow," Rose being the former and Boyd the latter. One of the witnesses also testified that the pair were, in some quarters, called "the inseparables." Another said that in addition to being Substance and Shadow, they were also known as the "Seamice Twins."[34]

Morgan did not develop his effort to bind Rose and Boyd figuratively into a single witness beyond the attempt to make the conflict between his own testimony and theirs a one-on-one contest. If he were able to do so, presumably his version of events in the cabin would prevail with the court's five officers, he being a lieutenant and the two of them counting as only one midshipman. There was no possibility the defendant could go further. In first days of the Victorian era there existed no context for a psychosexual interpretation of a nexus between the defendant and his detractors. Even if Morgan's lawyer had been one of the most creative at the bar he could hardly have made a credible argument for a conspiracy of young men bent on destroying an adult who inadvertently intruded into their relationship. Such a defense, which would have anticipated the work of the leading German sexual theorists of the closing decades of the century or relied on now well-recognized and normal patterns of youthful male bonding, could only have seemed bizarre beyond belief to naval officers in 1838.

Still, at least one commentator on the case broached the theory of an untoward combination among Rose and Boyd to destroy Lieutenant Morgan. Throughout the trial transcript there are inserted regular marginal entries denouncing the frequent presentations of hearsay evidence to the court with comments such as "inadmissible" or "not evidence." The contrarian commentary appears on as many as 40 of the manuscript's 102 pages. The handwriting is not that of either of the two scribes who produced the court record, nor is there any indication of when the comments were written. The only clue to the mysterious scribe's identity are the initials "C. J." at the end of one of the marginal notations. In addition to the marginalia, C. J. laid a small sheet of paper between pages two and three of the transcript. One of the comments on it reads "I do think this poor fellow [Morgan] has been the victim of a foul conspiracy between two mates." He did not elaborate on the theory.

Morgan's trial concluded on 4 April 1838, and the verdict presented in time-honored fashion and with the standard phraseology:

> And having carefully and deliberately weighed and considered the evidence in support of the charges as well as what the prisoner had to offer in his defense, as also the evidence adduced in his behalf, and very maturely weighed and considered the whole, the court is of opinion that the charges are proved, and that he falls under a breach of part of the 33rd article of war. In consequence whereof it doth adjudge the said Lieutenant Richard Morgan to be dismissed from Her Majesty's service.[35]

The record of Morgan's 1838 trial and conviction is a disconcerting document, particularly the portions dealing with his use of foul or obscene language. Oaths, execrations, crude language, and scatology occurred as a matter of course on board ships over the early eighteenth century, throughout the age of Nelson, and afterward. Courts martial transcripts are seasoned with basic terms. "Cocks," "arses," "buggery," "pricks," "fucks," and "frigs" abound. Even the common euphemisms that from time to time soften the trial records would hardly have been welcomed in polite company. Conversational references to "pintles," "yards," "privates," "backsides," "bottoms," or "hinder parts" would have earned any who spoke of them a substantial measure of opprobrium in a wide variety of social situations on shore.

Understanding the pervasiveness of off-color language in the navy is an easy matter. Although the depraved character of sailors is probably exaggerated, the service nonetheless provided refuge to companies of:

> Highwaymen, burglars, pickpockets, debauchees, adulterers, gamesters, lampooners, bastard-getters, imposters, panderers, parasites, ruffians, hypocrites, threadworn beaux, jack-a-dandies [and] those with their roses faded and their lilies soiled.[36]

Seagoing cleric Edward Mangin explained the gruff nature of shipboard talk he encountered on board HMS *Gloucester* where he served in 1812:

> As for the chaplain's constant efforts to rebuke the seamen, etc. for profane swearing and intemperate language of every kind, the injunction sounds plausible: but when the after-guard is called, and the people are lazy in turning up; or at the coming of a gale, when the order is given to strike top-gallant masts, and this is clumsily done; the chaplain had better spare both his lungs and his ears and retreat as fast as he can to his own deck or to the ward room.[37]

Mangin's complaint might be considered the exaggeration of a disgruntled soul. He had only joined the navy, after all, because he could secure no clerical employment ashore, but his testimony is borne out by others. Experienced seafarers John Nicol, Samuel Leech, Robert Wilson, and most others who wrote of life in the Royal Navy in the eighteenth and early nineteenth centuries attested to the ubiquitous profanity before the mast. Even during battle or the most severe storms when the danger of shipwreck and death was the greatest and the power of the Almighty most visible, to the consternation of clerics, sailors often shouted out torrents of blasphemy rather than offering up the prayers that would have been appropriate in such situations. When the chaplain of HMS *Glory* commented on the paradox, he found his wardroom dinner partners offended by his observation.[38]

More pertinent to the accusations leveled against Morgan, it is evident that ratings had no exclusive claim on the use of profanity. One warrant officer, Purser Walter Sands of HMS *Camilla*, was actually court martialed for bad language in 1807. He directed his disparaging characterizations at a lieutenant in the Royal Marines, and it is likely that besmirching the honor of a commissioned officer rather than the pejoratives he used, "blackguard" and "low-life vagabond," provided the impetus for holding the trial. While Sands received only a reprimand for his words and his challenge to the integrity of a lieutenant, there is no doubt that the intemperate speech common to ordinary crewmen intruded into the gunroom mess and informed the vocabulary of the quarterdeck as well. Ramblin' Jack Cremer wrote of a captain who was always "damning and sinking," and Admiral Sir Richard Strachan was famous for his profanity. Crewmen awarded him the sobriquet of "Mad Dick," and claimed, "that when he swore he meant no harm, and when he prayed he meant no good." Captain Robert Cavendish Spencer, a prodigious swearer, tried to curb his language, but without much success. The 1757 edition of *Regulations and Instructions Relating to His Majesty's Service at Sea* prescribed a one shilling fine for officers cursing or blaspheming in the name of God, but the pronouncement, included in editions throughout the eighteenth century and into the nineteenth, evidently had little effect. In 1766, officer Edward Thompson claimed that during the previous war "a chaw of tobacco, a rattan, and a rope of oaths were sufficient qualifications to constitute a lieutenant," but he seemed to think the situation was improving. Whether his optimism was justified is unclear. James Morrison, HMS *Bounty*'s boatswain, commented repeatedly in his memoirs on Captain William Bligh's foul language, but neither the infamous captain's setback on the *Bounty* nor his frequently abusive tongue scuttled his career.[39]

Chaplain Mangin, who lamented the cursing of ordinary sailors, judged the language and morals of those holding higher rank to be only slightly improved over those of the men they commanded. He characterized the behavior of midshipmen as "riotous," and with considerable circumspection he noted that the manners of the officers with whom he messed occasionally exceeded "the limits of decorum."[40]

Foul-mouthed officers had by the early nineteenth century even intruded into fiction. Although Jane Austen generally depicted naval officers favorably, in *Mansfield Park* she offered up the character of Lieutenant Price, a filthy man who swore, drank to excess, embarrassed his daughter with his uncouth ways, and read only the newspapers and the navy list. Admiral Crawford in the same book was a lecher of some renown whose niece fled his house to salvage her reputation. Another of Austen's officers, Captain Wentworth, exhibited a scarcely less lusty demeanor in *Persuasion*.[41] One officer with literary pretensions wrote light-heartedly of a post-captain, presumably fictional, who made a note to himself that when speaking to ladies "An occasional 'Damme' may not be amiss – oaths indicate manliness, and carry weight with women."[42] Gilbert and Sullivan continued the tradition into the later half of the century. In their 1878 musical comedy on the decline of manliness and character in the Royal Navy, the captain they created for HMS *Pinafore* was known to swear with enthusiasm like officers of earlier generations, although his fault was mitigated because he only gave voice to oaths on rare occasions.[43]

Regulations prohibiting swearing on board warships date from the Commonwealth or even earlier, and attempts by commanders suffused with moral zeal attempting to reduce or eliminate sailors' execrations can be found as early as the first decades of the eighteenth century.

None of the efforts were notably successful. Indeed, there seemed to be little that could inhibit foul language among sailors. Rear Admiral of the Red Jeffrey Raigersfeld not only recorded that as a boy of twelve, newly-gone-to-sea, he was once made "quite afraid" by the curses of a man brought on board HMS *Mediator* after having been flogged around the fleet. Later in his career Raigersfeld objected so strongly to a lieutenant's foul language that he obtained a discharge from his ship. Captain William P. Cumby tried to prohibit swearing by proscribing oaths in the "Orders and Regulations" he drafted for his ship, HMS *Hyperion* in 1811. In the document, Cumby clearly had the interests of his men at heart. He prohibited "starting," the summary flogging of sailors by petty officers, and he provided a lengthy and detailed set of instructions for the surgeon and assistant surgeon to insure the health of the crew. Cumby's method of reducing profanity did not involve fines or the cat. He proposed to do it by having all his officers avoid foul language and thus by "setting an example of that correctness, regularity and rigid attention to duty so essential to the character of an officer, impress on the minds of the inferior officers and ship's company the necessity of similar deportment." Nothing in the archives indicates whether or not his approach succeeded, but other recorded efforts to improve mariners' language in the closing decade of the eighteenth century and the first years of the nineteenth did not. James Gambier, captain of HMS *Defense* and a man of Methodist principles, tried to stamp out foul language both on the quarterdeck and before the mast in 1793. Swearing officers were fined one shilling. Ordinary mariners paid for their oaths by being forced to wear a heavy wooden collar with a thirty-two pound shot affixed to each shoulder. They then walked the poop for several hours while wearing this apparatus. One seaman, according to William Dillon, fell into a stupor from the punishment. William Richardson wrote of a captain who ordered seven or eight lashes administered to the bare backs of sailors mouthing obscenities. While not a particularly severe punishment, according to Richardson it almost ignited mutiny on board the ship, and the captain quickly abandoned the policy.[44]

Courts martial for men in positions of authority for swearing occurred only on the rarest of occasions. Two officers from HMS *Confounder*, "Sub-Lieutenant" John Richardson and Assistant Surgeon Ralph Willoughby Cleghorn, were tried at Malta in 1810 and dismissed from the navy. The charges against them included drunkenness along with unsuitable language. Significantly, their oaths and execrations were directed against their captain, which surely made the matter more serious than random or undirected swearing. Nothing is known of

Richardson, his family, or his connections, but it is almost certain that as a mere ship's surgeon, Cleghorn had scant influence with the Admiralty or among highly placed political figures.

Lieutenant Richard Morgan's service record, like that of the cashiered Cleghorn, indicates he had no influential friends. He was what was known as "an old officer," a man lacking sufficient wealth and connections to obtain promotion or shield him from his indiscretions. Any officer who had spent almost three decades in the Royal Navy with only eight years of commissioned service did not rely on social position or birth for advancement or protection. Such men regularly fell between the planks after 1815. Morgan's lack of "interest," as "influence" was known, did not bring down the wrath of the navy upon him, but once it descended there were none to assist him in having it lifted. Morgan could count on no immunity like that enjoyed by Robert C. Spencer, a captain known for his quarterdeck oaths, who was also the son of a former First Lord of the Admiralty and the brother of a leading Whig politician.[45]

The lack of influence alone, however, can hardly be blamed for the destruction of Richard Morgan's career. He was the victim, too, of changes that took place in the Royal Navy beginning in the late eighteenth century and continuing on for the next one hundred years. His prosecution for offenses that surely would have earlier gone unnoticed is explained in part by the alterations slowly induced into the navy by British evangelicals and later by the Church of England.[46] Near the turn of the century, men and women concerned with what they saw as the deficient moral climate in the navy organized The Religious Tract Society expressly to bring salvation to the nation's mariners. The objectives of the Society, and of similar groups begun later on, were four, to end prostitution, promote temperance, halt Sabbath breaking, and eliminate swearing. Throughout the country there was considerable organizational, emotional, and financial support for their efforts. During the wars of the French Revolution and the long struggle against Napoleon, Britain underwent an evangelical revival, kindled in part by fears of the social leveling taking place across the Channel. The Baptists, Methodists, and other dissenters at the forefront of the newly emergent religious enthusiasm expended a generous measure of their efforts on the seafaring population. William Wilberforce, of the anti-slavery crusade, assisted in the efforts to transmit the Gospel to mariners, as did several other men of ability and commitment such as Zebedee Rogers and George C. "Boatswain" Smith. Many naval officers with abiding religious beliefs supported the movement wholeheartedly, believing that there were spiritual benefits that would accrue to ships with crews committed to serving both God and country. Other officers, less touched by religious enthusiasm, supported it as well, understanding as they did its value for maintaining discipline.[47]

The London Bible Society, founded in 1813, was another of the organizations dedicated to bringing spiritual improvement to seamen, and over the years many similar local societies took root in seaports along the coasts of Britain. The most powerful of these evangelical organizations, the Bethel Union Societies, developed after the end of the Napoleonic wars. In due course, they established prayer meetings on shore and afloat almost everywhere in the British Empire. Their flag, with its white lettering on a blue field that was sometimes decked with Christian iconography, grew to be a familiar sight wherever ships flying the Union Jack dropped anchor. George Smith became a pivotal figure in the movement that historian Roald Kverndal rightly characterized as a British naval awakening. Richard C. Blake seconded his assessment, calling the period from 1775 to 1875 a "missionizing century for the navy." Smith's series of tracts, published under the title *The Boatswain's Mate*, became immensely popular, as did the works of Anglican Richard Marks, another writer-preacher. Marks, a veteran of Trafalgar, resigned his lieutenancy in 1814 to devote himself to the spiritual well-being of navy men. His many pamphlets, with titles like *Nautical Essays; or a Spiritual View of the Ocean and Maritime Affairs* (1818) and *The Ocean, Spiritually Reviewed* (1826), sometimes required dozens of editions to satisfy the demand for them.[48] The Church of England, having ignored mariners throughout the eighteenth century, decided at some point that their navy was being shanghaied by dissenters. In the 1820s they, too, began making efforts to bring religion to the King's ships, although not with the enthusiasm exhibited by other groups. They soon trumped the tract distributors by requiring that every seaman be furnished a Bible as part of his kit. The attempts of Anglicans to secure a larger role in shipboard religion also benefitted from British worldwide missionary activity and by the movement to stamp out the slave trade. Both efforts were profoundly Christian in character, and both depended in some measure on the Royal Navy to insure their success.[49]

The "Naval Awakening" described by Kverndal did much more than advance the spiritual welfare of individual sailors and officers. Although it might not have ushered in a "new age" as he claimed, it had its effects. The Royal Navy gradually changed under the divinely inspired onslaught of Baptists, Methodists, and others of like mind. In this it reflected British society both at home and throughout the Empire. The early nineteenth century was an age of religious revival across the English-speaking world, and it would only be remarkable if the swelling currents of Christian enthusiasm passed the navy by. After 1815, newly established nautical Bible societies, Christian sailors' hostels, churches, and chapels directed toward the spiritual improvement of Britain's mariners flourished as never before. Evangelical officers, while never a majority, exerted influence far beyond their numbers, and when Charles Middleton, Lord Barham of the evangelical Clapham Sect became First Lord of the Admiralty, the cause of religion advanced dramatically. In the 1820s, Admiral C. V. Penrose commented on the enhanced discipline, order, and morals found in the fleet, and he was not alone in his judgment. A wide range of observers wrote on the elevated moral standard of the British tar since the establishment of the Bethel movement. Religious services on board ships, sorely neglected and frequently ignored in Nelson's day, now proliferated. On some ships elaborate preparations preceded religious exercises. John Bechervaise told of how on a Sunday officers ordered a regular church to be set up.[50] An awning was rigged, a bell was rung as on shore, and a church flag was hoisted to a gaff end to signal all ships nearby that a religious service was underway. It was not only the devout who commented on the new religious fervor. William Glascock, a captain of doubtful spiritual commitment, saw it as well, although his comments lacked the joy contained in reports by evangelicals. He wrote disparagingly of converts singing psalms in the storerooms during the week and on deck on Sundays. Religious crewmen were a lazy lot, in his opinion.

In the case of Richard Morgan it was the changes of attitude among the middling and upper classes that contributed to his downfall. Cultural transformations influenced naval officers just as they influenced landsmen of similar social origins and station. As notions of romantic love were insinuated into relationships between men and women, the explicit language of earlier decades became too shocking and socially disruptive, according to Randolph Trumbach, for members of middling and upper classes to accept.[51] This was reflected ashore in a reduction in the defamation cases brought to the courts and at sea in the euphemisms that replaced cruder terms commonly used in courts martial throughout the eighteenth century. The new hesitancy is nowhere more apparent than in the 1809 trial of Midshipman Roderick Colquhoun and Surgeon's Assistant Robert Fleming. The mens' alleged violation was referred to almost a dozen times in the trial transcript as either an "unnatural crime," an "unnatural situation," or an "unnatural position." Although "sodomy" and "buggery" remained unmodified and unmitigated in the

Articles of War, such base terminology crossed the lips of no one at this court martial in the newly evangelized navy.[52] The same was true twenty years later at the trial of William Maxwell, the boatswain convicted of sodomy. The young subjects of Maxwell's advances abjured the vulgar but specific nomenclature once associated with shipboard life and only reluctantly admitted that the defendant had ever made sexual advances toward them. One denied that the boatswain even put his arm around him, but his testimony was contradicted by the ship's carpenter. Young William Dickinson, reticent over revealing what occurred, required gentle prodding by an officer before saying that he thought boatswain wanted to bugger him.[53] The boy's hesitancy and discomfort with the central subject matter at the trial is also evident in the testimony of his comrades who constantly relied on euphemisms to explain what Maxwell had in mind. The standard way they described his intent again and again was to say he wanted to "commit dirty tricks with me."[54] One young witness told another shipboard boy that the boatswain had been "poking him about." There was no need to elaborate on the phrase's meaning either to the boy to whom it was said or to the members of the court when a witness used it in his testimony. It meant buggery, but well into the nineteenth century, such unalterably base terminology no longer appeared in courts martial transcripts. The more circumspect "pintle" and "tool" also replaced the "pricks" and "cocks" that commonly appeared in testimony from previous decades.[55]

The combination of religious enthusiasm, developing notions of romantic love, and the sentimentalization of women had an effect on the navy's officer corps and on those who aspired to the quarterdeck. Young men in the navy like *Pembroke* midshipmen Frederick Rose, John Boyd, and their cohorts, may have been closely attuned to the new ways, but in such a shifting social context an old officer with three decades of faithful service may have been unaware of the changes taking place about him. The propriety of cursing and what he considered friendly or avuncular physical gestures no longer had a place in the navy of the 1830s. Mired in the patterns of the past, oblivious to changing times, and with no friends in government or the Admiralty, Lieutenant Richard Morgan fell victim to a reordered world which he little understood. In consequence, his reputation, his career, and possibly his life were destroyed. After his conviction, the disgraced officer left the *Pembroke* and disappeared from the historical record, his only claim to distinction being that at the dawn of the Victorian era he was the last officer of the Georgian navy to be convicted of a sexual offense.[56]

Notes

Introduction

1. On rare occasions women served in the navy disguised as men. The number who did so is not known, but it is unlikely it could have been statistically significant. Wives of commissioned officers and warrant officers also sailed on board warships from time to time, but were not counted as naval personnel (see Chapter 4).
2. Philip Jenkins, *Moral Panic: Changing Concepts of the Child Molester in Modern America* (New Haven: Yale University Press, 1998), xi–xii. See also David M. Halperin, *How to Do the History of Homosexuality* (Chicago: University of Chicago Press, 2002), 63, 71–2, 106, *et passim*.
3. N. A. M. Rodger, *The Wooden World: An Anatomy of the Georgian Navy* (London: Collins, 1986), 16, 26.
4. David Cressy, *Travesties and Transgressions in Tudor and Stuart England* (New York: Oxford University Press, 2000), 26; G. R. Elton, *Star Chamber Stories* (London: Methuen, 1958), 10.
5. G. S. Rousseau, "The Pursuit of Homosexuality in the Eighteenth Century: 'Utterly Confused Category' and/or Rich Repository?" *Eighteenth–Century Life* 9 (May 1985): 132.

1 Law, Literature, Sodomy, and Royal Navy Officers

1. ADM 1/5376 (Graham court martial, 9 December 1806).
2. The court martial record, ADM 1/5376, mentions *An Act of Parliament made and passed in the twenty-second year of the reign of His Majesty King George the Second entitled An Act for Amending, Explaining and Reducing into Act of Parliament the Laws Relating to the Government of His Majesty's Ships, Vessels, and Forces by Sea* (22 Geo. II c. 33). Graham was actually tried under a later, amended version of the *Articles* adopted in 1779 (19 Geo. III c. 17). The alterations under George III in any case would not have affected Graham's court martial or sentence. They left untouched articles two and twenty-nine dealing with sex offenses. For a complete text of the *Articles of War* enacted under George II and the amendments added under George III see *Anno Regni Georgii II … At the Parliament Begun and Holden at Westminster the Tenth Day of November, Anno Dom. 1747 in the Twenty-first Year of the Reign of Our Sovereign Lord George the Second … An Act for Amending, Explaining, and Reducing into One Act of Parliament, the Laws Relating to the Government of His Majesty's Ships, Vessels, and Forces by Sea. Also an Act Made in 19 Geo. III to Explain and Amend the Said Act* (London: Charles Eyre, 1794). There were at least six measures dealing with naval discipline passed during the reigns of Charles II, William and Mary, Anne, George I, and George II that were consolidated into 22 Geo. II. c. 33, 3–4; John D. Byrn, *Crime and Punishment in the Royal Navy: Discipline on*

the Leeward Islands Station, 1784–1812 (Aldershot, UK: Scholar, 1989), 66–7; Old Quartermaster [John Bechervaise] *Thirty-six Years of a Seafaring Life* (Portsea, U. K.: Woodward, 1839), 125–7; John Harvey Boteler, *Recollections of My Sea Life from 1808–1830*, ed. David Bonner-Smith, vol. 82, *Publications of the Navy Records Society*, (London: Navy Records Society, 1942), 115; William P. Cumby, "Orders and Regulations for the Government and Discipline of His Majesty's Ship *Hyperion*, William Pryce Cumby, Captain," in H. G. Thursfield, ed., *Five Naval Journals, 1789–1817*, vol. 91, *Publications of the Navy Records Society* (London: Navy Records Society, 1951), 89; Jacob Nagle, *The Nagle Journal: A Diary of the Life of Jacob Nagle, Sailor, from the Year 1775–1741*, ed., John C. Dann (New York: Weidenfield and Nicolson, 1988), 211; G[eorge] Thompson, Torbay, to Mrs. Thompson, London, 9 September 1797, in Thursfield, *Five Naval Journals*, 357.

3. Ed Cohen, "Legislating the Norm: From Sodomy to Gross Indecency," *South Atlantic Quarterly* 88 (Winter 1989): 185; Michael Goodich, *The Unmentionable Vice: Homosexuality in the Later Medieval Period* (Santa Barbara, CA: ABC Clio, 1979), xii, 7–9; Cynthia B. Herrup, *A House in Gross Disorder: Sex, Law, and the 2nd Earl of Castlehaven* (New York: Oxford University Press, 1999), 53. On the early fourteenth century trials of the Knights Templar, see Anne Gilmour-Bryson, "Sodomy and the Knights Templar," *Journal of the History of Sexuality* 7 (October 1996): 151–83. For the bill of accusations levied against the Templars see B. R. Burg, ed., *Gay Warriors: A Documentary History from the Ancient World to the Present* (New York: New York University Press, 2002), 89–102.
4. 25 Henry VIII, c. 6.
5. *Ibid.*; 28 Henry VIII, c. 6; 31 Henry VIII, c. 7; 33 Henry VIII, c. 7, 28–9.
6. A. D. Harvey, *Sex in Georgian England: Attitudes from the 1720s to the 1820s* (London: Duckworth 1994), 136. See also the anonymously written *Plain Reasons for the Growth of Sodomy in England: To Which Is Added the Petit Maitre, an Odd Sort of Unpoetical Poem in the Trolly-lolly Style* (London: A. Dodd and E. Nutt [1730?]). The last execution for sodomy in England was probably in 1835 (Nicholas C. Edsall, *Toward Stonewall: Homosexuality and Society in the Modern Western World* [Charlottesville, VA: University of Virginia Press, 2003], 62). In 1861, life sentences for sodomy were substituted for the death penalty, and a quarter of a century later, in the "Criminal Law Amendment Act," that the penalty was reduced to two years at hard labor for those convicted of what was relabeled "gross indecency with another male person." It was under this new act that Oscar Wilde was convicted in 1895 (Cohen, "Legislating the Norm," 183; H. Montgomery Hyde, The *Cleveland Street Scandal* [New York: Coward, McCann, 1976], 15–18; Roy Porter and Leslie Hall, *The Facts of Life: The Creation of Sexual Knowledge in Britain, 1650–1950* [New Haven: Yale University Press, 1995], 224–5).
7. Burg, "Ho Hum, Another Work of the Devil: Buggery and Sodomy in Early Stuart England," *Journal of Homosexuality* 6 (Fall/Winter 1980/81): 69–78; Cohen, "Legislating the Norm," 185–7; Edward Coke, *The Third Part of the Institutes of the Laws of England Concerning High Treason and other Pleas of the Crown, and Criminal Cases* (London: s. n., 1648), Chapter 10, 59; Coke, *Reports of Sir Edward Coke. Diverse Resolutions and Judgments Given upon Solemn Arguments, and with Great Deliberation and Conference with the Learned Judges in*

Cases of Law (London: Henry Twyford and Thomas Dring, 1658), 36–7; Netta Murray Goldsmith, *The Worst of Crimes: Homosexuality and the Law in Eighteenth-Century London* (Aldershot, U. K.: Ashgate, 1998), 36–7; Herrup, *House in Gross Disorder*, 27–8, 34–5; 25 Henry VIII c. 6; 2 and 3 Edward VI, c. 17; 5 Elizabeth I, c. 17; Harvey, *Sex in Georgian England*, 122–3; Rictor Norton, *Mother Clap's Molly House: The Gay Subculture in England, 1700–1830* (London: Gay Men's Press, 1992), 15–16; Leon Radzinowicz, *The Movement for Reform*, vol. 1, *A History of English Criminal Law and Its Administration from 1750* (London: Stevens and Sons, 1948), 632; Randolph Trumbach, *Sex and the Gender Revolution*, vol. 1, *Heterosexuality and the Third Gender in Enlightenment London* (Chicago: University of Chicago Press, 1998), 91. For discussion of the differences in the various pieces of Tudor anti-sodomy legislation, see Bruce R. Smith, *Homosexuality in Shakespeare's England* (Chicago: University of Chicago Press, 1991), 45–8, 51–2.

8. Coke, *Institutes*, Chapter 10, 59.
9. *Ibid., passim*; Coke, *Reports*, 36–7.
10. *Ibid.*, 36; Daniel Defoe, "The True-Born Englishman: A Satyr," in vol. 2, *Poems on Affairs of State: Augustan Satirical Verse, 1660–1714*, ed. Frank H. Ellis (New Haven: Yale University Press, 1970), 2: 268; Markus Eder, *Crime and Punishment in the Royal Navy of the Seven Years' War, 1755–1763* (Burlington, VT: Ashgate, 2004), 111–2; [Anon.], *Plain Reasons for the Growth of Sodomy*; Goodich, *The Unmentionable Vice*, 3. Not surprisingly, Spaniards saw other nations as nurseries of sodomy (Fredrico Garza Carvajal, *Butterflies Will Burn: Persecuting Sodomites in Early Modern Spain and Mexico* [Austin, TX: University of Texas Press, 2003], 9).
11. William Blackstone, *Ehrlich's Blackstone*, ed. J. W. Ehrlich (New York: Capricorn Books, 1959), 2: 408; William Eden, *Principles of Penal Law* (London: B. White and T. Cadell, 1771), 2: 242; Matthew Hale, *Historia Placitorum Coronae: The History of the Pleas of the Crown* (Dublin: E. Lynch, 1778), 1: 628.
12. *Ibid.*, 1: 635.
13. Blackstone, *Ehrlich's Blackstone*, 2: 408.
14. The book went through five editions in the nineteen years from its first publication in 1621 to Burton's death in 1640. Four more editions were published in the seventeenth century, the last appearing in 1676 (Holbrook Jackson, "Introduction to the 1932 Edition," [New York: New York Review of Books, 2001], xxv, pt. 1, 178, 197, 233–4, 300–29, 419, pt. 3, 39, 244).
15. William Pyrnne, *Histrio-Mastics: The Players Scourge* (London: Michael Sparks, 1633), 75–6, 546.
16. David Cressy, *Travesties and Transgressions in Tudor England* (New York: Oxford University Press,1996) 101, 213, 214.
17. The new phenomenon was not confined to London and smaller English cities. It appeared in Paris and Amsterdam at about the same time. By the 1780s, there was an established subculture in Berlin as well (Edsall, *Towards Stonewall*, 10, 11, 13, 14, 17, 33).
18. Scholars most prominent among those studying the emergence and expansion of London's molly subculture include Alan Bray, Rictor Norton, G. S. Rousseau, Antony Simpson, and Randolph Trumbach. Their works are too numerous to list here, but all subscribe in some measure to the position

that the creation or emergence of a conspicuous homoerotic sexual identity modified perceptions of heterosexuality, encouraged a level of insecurity and trepidation in the general male population, and generated a reaction against mollies. Transvestism and the caricaturing of female behavior created an "other" against which "normality" could be measured, and fostered the emergence of a new and sexually aggressive heterosexuality (Goldsmith, *Worst of Crimes*, 7; Tim Hitchcock, *English Sexualities, 1700–1800* [New York: St. Martin's, 1997], 70; Tim Hitchcock and Michèle Cohen, *English Masculinities, 1660–1800* [London: Longmans, 1999], 4–5, 11.

19. Goldsmith, *Worst of Crimes*, 3–4, 6, 17; Herrup, *House in Gross Disorder*, 133–4; Norton, *Mother Clap's Molly House*, 11, 54, 57–8, 71, 117.
20. Alan Bray, *Homosexuality in Renaissance England* (London: Gay Men's Press, 1982), *passim*; Cohen, "Legislating the Norm," 182–3; Goldsmith, *Worst of Crimes*, 6; Mary McIntosh, "The Homosexual Role," *Social Problems* 16 (Fall 1968): 182–192; Randolph Trumbach, "Sodomitical Subcultures, Sodomitical Rules, and the Gender Revolution in the Eighteenth Century," *Eighteenth-Century Life* 9 (May 1985): 113–16; Trumbach, *Sex and the Gender Revolution*, 4–5; Halperin, *How to Do the History of Homosexuality* (Chicago: University of Chicago Press, 2002), 130. Michel Foucault maintained, in a now famous quotation, that it was only in the nineteenth century that:

    > The ... homosexual became a personage, a past, a case history, and a childhood, in addition to being a type of life, a life form, and a morphology, with an indiscreet anatomy and possibly a mysterious physiology ... . Homosexuality appeared as one of the forms of sexuality when it was transposed from the practice of sodomy onto a kind of inter androgeny, a hermaphrodism of the soul. The sodomite had been a temporary aberration; the homosexual was now a species (*The History of Sexuality: Volume I, An Introduction*, trans. Robert Hurley [New York: Vintage, 1980], 43).

    Almost all historians of human sexuality, including those noted immediately above, would argue the transformation described by Foucault took place several hundred years earlier than the date he offers. Halperin argues that Foucault is not incorrect on this, but that he is simply misunderstood by many of those who interpret him Halperin, *How to Do the History of Homosexuality*, (Chicago: University of Chicago Press, 2002), 29–32.
21. Harvey, *Sex in Georgian England*, 133; Hitchcock and Cohen, *English Masculinities*, 4–5; McIntosh, "Homosexual Role," 187–9; Stephen O. Murray, "Homosexual Acts and Selves in Early Modern Europe," *Journal of Homosexuality* 16 (1988), 458–9; Norton, *Mother Clap's Molly House*, 9–11, 16–8, 20–5, 35, 96; G. S. Rousseau, "Pursuit of Homosexuality in the Eighteenth-Century: 'Utterly Confused Category' and/or Rich Repository?" *Eighteenth Century Life* 9 (May 1985), 151–2.
22. [Anon.], *The Trial and Condemnation of Mervin, Lord Audley Earl of Castle-Haven ... for Abetting a Rape upon his Countess, Committing Sodomy with His Servants, and Commanding and Countenancing the Debauching of His Daughter* (London: s. n., 1699); [Anon.], *The Case of Sodomy, in the Tryal of Mervin Lord Audley, Earl of Castlehaven, for Committing a Rape. And Sodomy with Two of His Servants* (London: John Morphew, 1708); [Anon.], *The Trial of Mervin Lord Audley, Earl of Castlehaven, for a Rape and Sodomy* (London: E. Curll, 1719);

[Anon.], *An Account of the Proceedings against Capt. Edward Rigby ... for intending to Commit the Abominable Sin of Sodomy on the Body of one William Minton* (London: F. Collins, 1698); Herrup, *House in Gross Disorder*, 134–6; Thomas A. King, *The Gendering of Men, 1600–1750*, vol. 1, *The English Phallus* (Madison, WI: University of Wisconsin Press, 2004), 104.

23. Hitchcock, *English Sexualities*, 16; Peter Wagner, *Eros Revived: Erotica of the Enlightenment in England and America* (London: Secker and Warburg, 1988), 128; [Anon.], *A Full and Genuine Narrative of the Confederacy Carried on By Cather, Cane, Alexander, Nixon, Patterson, Falconer, and Smith ... Against the Hon. Edward Walpole, Esq. Charging Him With ... Sodomy, ... Together with an Account of their Remarkable Trial and Conviction* (London: J. Fox and B. Tovey, 1751); [Anon.], *The Bloody Register ... A Select and Judicious Collection of the Most Remarkable Trials for Murder, Treason, Rape, Sodomy, Highway Robbery, Piracy ... From the Year 1700 to the Year 1764, Inclusive* (London: E. and M. Viney, 1764); [Anon.], *Select Trials at the Sessions-House in the Old-Bailey, for Murder, Robberies, Rapes, Sodomy, Coining ... . In Four Volumes From the Year 1720 to this Time* (London: J. Applebee, 1742). In addition to several four-volume printings of this work, a two-volume version also appeared. For a discussion of the various editions, supplements, and excursions into *Select Trials* published before the American Revolution, see Francis Hargrave, "Preface" to vol. 1, [Anon.], *A Complete Collection of State Trials and Proceedings for High Treason and Other Crimes and Misdemeanors; The Fourth Edition Commencing with the Eleventh Year of the Reign of King Richard II and Ending with the Sixteenth Year of the Reign of George III* (London: T. Wright, 1776–81). See also Thomas Cobbett and T. B. Howell, eds., *Cobbett's Complete Collection of State Trials and Proceedings for High Treason and other Crimes and Misdemeanors from the Earliest Period to the Present Time*, 33 vols. (London: R. Bagshaw, 1809–26); Herrup, *House in Gross Disorder*, 139–40, 151.
24. [Anon.], *A Faithful Narrative of the Proceeding in a Late Affair between the Rev. Mr. John Swinton, and Mr. George Baker, Both of Wadham College, Oxford: Wherein the Reasons That Induced Mr. Baker to Accuse Mr. Swinton of Sodomitical Practices ... Are Set Down ... . To Which Is Prefixed a Particular Account of the Proceedings Against Robert Thistlethwaite, Late Doctor of Divinity and Warden of Wadham College for a Sodomitical Attempt on Mr. W. French* (London: s. n., 1739), 1. See also [Anon.], *College Wit Sharpened on the Head of a House ... . Addressed to the Two Famous Universities of S-d-m and G-m-rr-h* (London: J. Wadham, 1739) and [Paul Whitehead?], *The State of Rome under Nero and Domitian: A Satire Containing a List of Nobles, Senators, High Priests, Great Ministers of State, Etc., Etc., Etc., Etc., by Messers Juvenal and Persius* (London: C. Corbett, 1739); Norton, *Mother Clap's Molly House*, 159–68.
25. [Anon.], *Faithful Narrative of the Proceeding*, 3.
26. *Ibid.*, 4, 5.
27. Herrup, *House in Gross Disorder*, 133–4; Nicholas Bernard, *The Case of John Atherton, Bishop of Waterford in Ireland: Who Was Convicted of the Sin of Uncleanness with a Cow, and Other Creatures; for which He Was Hanged at Dublin* (London: E. Curll, 1710); [John King] *Bishop Atherton's Case Discussed in a Letter to the Author of a Late Pamphlet, Entitled The Case of John Atherton, Bishop of Waterford in Ireland, Fairly Represented* (London: E. Curll, 1711); [Anon.], *The Political Balance, for 1754. The Mock-Patriot, for 1753. To Which Is Added,*

the Case of John Atherton, Bishop of Waterford in Ireland, Who was Convicted of Bestiality With a Cow and Other Creatures (Originally published, Dublin, 1661; reprint, London: Rodger Lapis and Judas Alcock, 1754). See also [Anon.], *The Life and Death of John Atherton, Lord Bishop of Waterford and Lysmore ... Who for Incest, Buggery and Many Other Enormous Crimes After Having Lived a Vicious Life Dyed a Shameful Death: And was on the Fifth of December Last Past Hanged on the Gallows Green at Dublin* (London: s. n., 1641). The pamphlet rebutting the sermon is John King's *The Case of John Atherton, Bishop of Waterford in Ireland: Fairly Represented. Against a Late Partial edition of Dr. Barnard's Relation, and Sermon at His Funeral* (London: Luke Stokoe, 1710).

28. Cohen, "Legislating the Norm," 193; Harvey, *Sex in Georgian England*, 139–40; Hitchcock, *English Sexualities*, 70–4; Hitchcock and Cohen, *English Masculinities*, 9; Norton, *Mother Clap's Molly House*, 184–5; Polly Morris, "Sodomy and Male Honor: The Case of Somerset, 1740–1850," *Journal of Homosexuality* 16 (1/2 1988): 384–5;Trumbach, *Sex and the Gender Revolution*, 6, 11, 44, 91, 116.
29. [Anon.], *The Whole Proceedings on the Wicked Conspiracy Carried on Against the Hon. Edward Walpole, Esquire by John Cather, Adam Nixon, Daniel Alexander, Patrick Cane alias Kane and Others* was printed by H. Gifford in 1751 and sold at shops in London and Westminster. The anonymously written *Full and Genuine Narrative of the Confederacy Carried on by Cather, Cane, Alexander, Nixon, Patterson, Falconer, and Smith ... Against the Hon. Edward Walpole, Esq.* was printed the same year, perhaps in two editions. The title page noted it was "printed for the author, and sold by J. Fox, B. Tovey, and the other booksellers in Westminster-Hall and at the Royal-Exchange"; Goldsmith, *Worst of Crimes*, ix–x, 36, 37, 43, 44, 55–7, 69, 72, 80, 89, 97, 169, 195; Herrup, *House in Gross Disorder*, 141; Norton, *Mother Clap's Molly House*, 139–40; Adam Sissman, *Boswell's Presumptuous Task: The Making of the Life of Dr. Johnson* (New York: Farrar, Straus, and Giroux, 2000), 107.
30. Ian McCormick, ed., *Secret Sexualities: A Sourcebook of Seventeenth- and Eighteenth-Century Writing* (New York: Routledge, 1997), 49–51. See also the anonymous 1739 satire, *College Wit Sharpened*. For several limericks on the case, see Norton, *Mother Clap's Molly House*, 159–60.
31. Defenses of sodomy were published in Britain during the eighteenth century, to be sure, but they could not compare in number or weight of argument with works by those opposed to homoerotic sexuality. One of these defenses, not surprising to Anglo-Saxons, was written by an Italian, Alberto Radicante, the Count of Passerano. His ninety-four-page treatise, entitled *A Philiosophical [sic] Dissertation upon Death* appeared in 1732. The work was not intended solely as a defense of sodomy. Instead, the author argued among several other things that social norms defined good and evil. There were no universal proscriptions against murder, theft, fornication, sodomy, rebellion, treachery, sodomy, adultery, and the like. "And in fine," he wrote, "many nations greatly venerate, or at least willingly tolerate every one of those things which, by the Christians and by sundry other people, are utterly condemned" (Alberto Radicante, *A Philiosophical [sic] Dissertation upon Death. Composed for the Consolation of the Unhappy. By a Friend to Truth* [London: W. Mears, 1732]. Page citations are to the reprint edition, entitled *An Account of the Troubles Contained in This Pamphlet, the Author (Who Wrote It in Italian) Was Obliged to*

Fly the Kingdom; the Translator Was Sent to Newgate, and the Publisher Confined to the Fleet. A Philiosophical [*sic*] *Dissertation on Death. Composed for the Consolation of the Unhappy. By a Friend to Truth* [London: s. n., (1732)], 39. British authorities found little of merit in the English version of the book and much that was outrageous. The title page of the 1732 reprint of Radicante's work succinctly chronicled several results of the first edition: "On account of the bold truths contained in this pamphlet, the author (who wrote it in Italian) was obliged to fly the kingdom [Britain]; the translator was sent to Newgate, and the publisher confined in the Fleet [another prison]." Seventeen years later another writer, an Englishman on this occasion, published what appears to have been a full-scale defense of male-male sex. Since no copy of the 1749 book survives, the arguments Thomas Cannon advanced in *Ancient and Modern Pederasty Investigated and Exemplified* are lost. The only certainty is that he failed to persuade the authorities of the merit of his logic. He was arrested, but after posting bond for good behavior went free (Goldsmith, *Worst of Crimes*, 17; Harvey, *Sex in Georgian England*, 125).

32. Byrn, *Crime and Punishment ... Leeward Islands*, 148–9; Eder, *Crime and Punishment ... 1755–1763*, 150; [William Nugent Glascock], *Naval Sketchbook: or the Service Afloat and Ashore: with Characteristic Reminiscences, Fragments, and Opinions, by an Officer*, new ed. (London: Colburn and Bently, 1831), 1: 223.
33. Wagner, *Eros Revived*, 37; McCormack, *Secret Sexualities*, 49–51.
34. [Thomas Newcomb], *The Manners of the Age: In Thirteen Moral Satires. Written with a Design to Expose the Vicious and Irregular Conduct of Both Sexes, in the Various Pursuits of Life* (London: Jer. Batley, 1733), 415–16.
35. Smollett, *The Adventures of Roderick Random*, ed. Paul Gabriel Boucé (New York: Oxford University Press, 1979), 310, 316; Norton, *Mother Clap's Molly House*, 119–20.
36. Smollett, *Advice: A Satire* in *The Works of Tobias Smollett, Poems, Plays, and* The Briton, intro. and notes by Byron Gassman (Athens, GA: University of Georgia Press, 1993), 32, 442 n. 28. Smollett, of course wrote novels rather than history, and the information he provides must be considered with that in mind. The caution offered by N. A. M. Rodger about relying too heavily on him as a source is well taken (N. A. M. Rodger, *The Wooden World: An Anatomy of the Georgian Navy* [London: Collins, 1986], 14).
37. Smollett, *Roderick Random*, 194–5, 309–10, 316; Smollett, *Advice*, 30, 32, 33, 441 n. 12, 443 n. 30; Smollett, *The Adventures of Peregrine Pickle in which Are Included Memoirs of a Lady of Quality*, ed. and intro., James L. Clifford (New York: Oxford University Press, 1964), 242–3, 366. Although Smollett had been to sea and wrote extensively of his experiences afloat, at least one knowledgeable critic found his depictions shipboard life wanting ([Glascock], *Naval Sketchbook*, 1: 121–40). See also Rousseau, "Pursuit of Homosexuality," 132–68.
38. David Garrick, *Miss in Her Teens: Or, The Medley of Lovers* (London: s. n., 1747; later edition, London: Alexander Cleugh, 1789. Page citations are to the 1789 edition). For a discussion of effeminate stereotypes and post-Restoration drama, see Lawrence Senelick, "Mollies or Men of Mode? Sodomy and the Eighteenth-Century London Stage," *Journal of the History of Sexuality* 1 (July 1990), 33–67.
39. Garrick, *Miss in Her Teens*, 12, 15, 16.
40. *Ibid.*, 23.

41. The full title of Lancaster's 1747 piece was *The Pretty Gentleman: or, Softness, of Manners Vindicated from the False Ridicule Exhibited under the Character of William Fribble, Esq.* (London: M. Cooper). The following year, Lancaster published a seventy-seven-page exposition entitled *The Plan of an Essay upon Delicacy: With a Specimen of the Work in Two Dialogues* (London: R. Dodsley, 1748). It is an apparently serious defense of delicacy in the male character, devoid of the sarcasm and satire in his previous work. In it he makes a sharp distinction between "the tears of manly affection and ... the meltings of weak effeminacy" (32).
42. Harvey, *Sex in Georgian England*, 136–7; Wagner, *Eros Revived*, 37–9.
43. Boteler, *Recollections of My Sea Life* 26, 175; Peter Cullen, "Memoirs of Peter Cullen, Esq.," in Thursfield, *Five Naval Journals*, 94; William Henry Dillon, *Narrative of My Professional Adventures (1790–1839)*, ed. Michael. A. Lewis in vol. 93, *Publications of the Navy Records Society* (London: Navy Records Society, 1953), 2: 24, 40, 205, 286, 401, 406, 430; Terrance M. Freeman, *Dramatic Representations of British Soldiers and Sailors on the London Stage, 1660–1800: Britons Strike Home* (Lewiston, NY: E. Mellen, 1995), 28–41; M. D. Hay, *The Memoirs of Robert Hay, 1789–1847* (London: Rupert Hart-Davis, 1953), 128; Roald Kverndal, *Seamens' Missions: Their Origin and Early Growth: A Contribution to the Church Maritime* (Pasadena, CA: William Carey Library, 1986), 116, 119; Margarette Lincoln, *Representing the Royal Navy: British Sea Power, 1750–1815* (Burlington, VT: Ashgate, 2002), 29, 39, 66; Isaac E. Land, "Domesticating the Maritime: Culture, Masculinity, and Empire in Britain, 1770–1820," Ph. D. diss., University of Michigan, 1999, 17; Nagle, *Nagle Journal*, 151–3; Harry William Pedicord, *The Theatrical Public in the Time of Garrick* (New York: King's Crown, 1954), 28–9, 35–6; William Richardson, *A Mariner of England: An Account of the Career of William Richardson from Cabin Boy to the Merchant Service to Warrant Officer in the Royal Navy as Told by Himself*, ed. Spencer Childers (London: John Murray, 1908), 298. Royal Navy sailor Samuel Leech witnessed with approval a drunken pilgrimage to a New York theater by the crew of an American warship in the early nineteenth century after a naval victory in the War of 1812 (*A Voice from the Main Deck: Being a Record of the Thirty Years' Adventures of Samuel Leech*, intro. Michael Crawford [Annapolis, MD: Naval Institute Press, 1999], 104).
44. [Newcomb], *Manners of the Age*, 548.
45. See Burg, "Another Work of the Devil," 69–78.
46. Reed Browning, *Political and Constitutional Ideas of the Court Whigs* (Baton Rouge, LA: Louisiana State University Press, 1982), 35–6, 175–6; Caleb D'Anvers [William Pulteney], *A Proper Reply to a Late Scurrilous Libel: Entitled Sedition and Defamation Displayed, In a Letter to the Author* (London: s. n., 1731). It is not certain that Hervey actually wrote the pamphlet that drove Pulteney to respond. He denied authorship on at least one occasion. William Younge may have been the author (John Hervey, *Lord Hervey and His Friends (1726–38): Based on Letters from Holland House, Melbury, and Ickworth*, ed. Earl of Ilchester [London: John Murray, 1950], 68).
47. [Pulteney], *Proper Reply*, 5–6.
48. [Anon.], *The Trial and Conviction of Several Reputed Sodomites Before the Right Honorable, the Lord Mayor, and Recorder of London, at Guildhall, the 20th Day of*

October 1707 ([London]: J. Morphew, 1707); [Henry Dutton Colt], *A Full and True Account of the Discovery and Apprehending of a Notorious Gang of Sodomites in St. James's: With the Examination and Commitment of Two of them to Newgate, by Sir Henry Dutton Colt* (London: T. Bland, 1709); [Anon.], *Hell Upon Earth; Or the Town in an Uproar. Occasioned by the Late Horrible Scenes of Forgery, Perjury, Street-Robbery, Murder, Sodomy, and Other Shocking Impieties* (London: J. Roberts and A. Dodd, 1729); [Robert Holloway], *The Phoenix of Sodom, or the Vere Street Coterie, Being an Expedition of the Gambols Practiced by the Ancient Lechers of Sodom and Gomorrah Embellished and Improved with the Modern Refreshments in Sodom* (London: J. Cook, 1813); [Anon.], *Faithful Narrative of the Proceeding*; [Anon.], *Some Particulars Relating to the Life of William Dillon Sheppard, Who Was Executed ... for Sodomy on Monday the 1st of June, 1761* (Bristol: E. Ward, [1761]); [Anon.], *The Trial of Charles Bradbury, for the Detestable Crime of Sodomy Said to Be Committed on the Body of James Hearne at Justice Hall on the Old Bailey on Thursday the 11th of September, 1755* (London: M. Cooper, 1755).

49. *The Original Weekly Journal* (London), 20 June 1719, 1460; 4 July 1719, 1472; 25 July 1719, 1490–1.
50. [Anon.], *The Woman-Hater's Lamentation: or, A New Copy of Verses on the Fatal End of Mr. Grant, a Woollen-Draper, and Two Others that Cut Their Throats or Hanged Themselves in the Counter; With the Discovery of Near Hundred More that Are Accused of Unnatural Despising the Fair Sex, and Intriguing With One Another* (London: s. n., 1707).
51. The 1708 edition is entitled *The Modern World Disrobed* and carries the subtitle *Adam and Eve Stript of their Furbelows: or, the Fashionable Virtues and Vices of Both Sexes Exposed to Public View* (London: J. Baker, J. Woodward, and J. Morphew). The later version carries only the subtitle, which becomes the title: *Adam and Eve Stript of their Furbelows: or, the Fashionable Virtues and Vices of Both Sexes Exposed to Public View* (London: A. Bettlesworth, [1715?]).
52. [Ward], *Adam and Eve*, 213.
53. [Ward], *A Complete and Humorous Account of all the Remarkable Clubs and Societies in the Cities of London and Westminster from the R_____l-S_____y down to the Lumber-Troop*, 7th ed. (London: s. n., 1756), 265–9. A full text of the chapter is conveniently available in McCormick, *Secret Sexualities*, 131–4.
54. [Ward], *A Complete and Humourous Account*, 265.
55. *Ibid.*, 269.
56. [Anon.], *This Is Not the Thing: or, Molly Exalted* ([London: s. n., 1763]).
57. See Lisa Jardine and Alan Stewart, *Hostage to Fortune: The Troubled Life of Francis Bacon* (New York: Hill and Wang, 1998), 464–6.
58. [Thomas Gordon], *Francis, Lord Bacon: or the Case of Private and National Corruption and Bribery Impartially Considered. Addressed to all South-Sea Directors, Members of Parliament, Ministers of State, and Church Dignitaries. By a True-born Englishman* (London: J. Roberts, 1721); [Gordon], *The Conspirators or, the Case of Catiline, As Collected from the Best Historians, Impartially Examined*, 2nd ed. (London: J. Roberts, 1721).
59. [Gordon], *Conspirators*, 25, 28, 32–2.
60. *Ibid.*, 29.
61. [J. Basset?], *Sodom's Catastrophe, a Poem, with the Addition of Other Pieces of Poetry* (London [Birmingham?]: Jacob Robinson, 1748), 42. Even in works from the period dealing with tribadism, the figure of Ganymede appeared as weak and effeminate. William King describes a "little Ganymede" who served

along with Hebe, Jupiter's daughter, in the capacity of cupbearer ([William King], *The Toast. An Heroic Poem in Four Books, Written Originally in Latin by Frederick Scheffer: Now Done into English ... by Peregrine O'Donald* [Dublin: s. n., 1736], 21).

62. [Anon.], *Love-Letters between a Certain Late Nobleman and the Famous Mr. Wilson: Discovering the True History of the Rise and Surprising Grandeur of that Celebrated Beau* (London: s. n., [1723]), t. p. 1, t. p. 2, preface.
63. [Anon.], *The Character of the Times Delineated. Designed for the Use of Those Who Mourn in Secret for the Iniquities of the Nation, and Are Convinced by Sad Experience, that Private Vices are Public and Real Mischiefs* (London: s. n., 1732), t. p. 14.
64. Josiah Woodward, *Sodom's Vices Destructive to other Cities and States: A Sermon Preached before the Right Honorable The Lord Mayor of the City of London* (London: B. Aylmer and A. Bell, 1697), "Dedication," 1, 11, 13.
65. Woodward, *Sodom's Vices*, 17.
66. Wesley, *Serious Thoughts Occasioned by the Earthquake at Lisbon: To which Is Subjoined an Account of all the Late Earthquakes there and in other Places*, 6th ed. (London: s. n., 1756), 4, 28.
67. Coke, *Reports*, 36–7.
68. 28 Elizabeth I, c. 6, pt. 2; Hale, *Historia Placitorum Coronae*, 1: 628, 630–1; Herrup, *House in Gross Disorder*, 28, 174; Antony E. Simpson, "Vulnerability and the Age of Female Consent: Legal Innovation and Its Effect on Prosecutions for Rape in Eighteenth-Century London," in *Sexual Underworlds of the Enlightenment*, eds. G. S. Rousseau and Roy Porter (Manchester: Manchester University Press, 1987), 182, 184, 186. Considerable confusion characterized laws against rape as well as those against sodomy. Matthew Hale thought the age of consent for females in rape cases might be twelve rather than ten years (*Historia Placitorum Coronae*, 630–1). Case law rather than statute law dealt with rape charges, and victims by the eighteenth century found it difficult to determine which of several definitions of carnal knowledge applied to their situations (Simpson, "Vulnerability and the Age of Female Consent," 182).
69. [Anon.], *The Gardner at the Gallows: for Buggerie Laid to His Charge. Being a Narrative of a Strange and Admirable Passage of Gods Providence in the Reprieve of Thomas Rivers ... where Being Tied Up, the Lad and Mother ... They Declare the Wrong They Had Done Him, and Who Thereupon Was Reprieved* [London?: s. n., 1667?]; [Anon.], *Some Particulars Relating to the Life of William Dillon Sheppard*, *passim*; Goldsmith, *Worst of Crimes*, 39, 75, 84–5; Harvey, *Sex in Georgian England*, 124–5; Morris, "Sodomy and Male Honor," 395; Murray, "Homosexual Acts and Selves," 461–2.
70. Roger Morriss, *Cockburn and the British Navy in Transition: Admiral Sir George Cockburn, 1772–1853* (Columbia, SC: University of South Carolina Press, 1997), 53, 121, 203.
71. There is, to my knowledge, only one lengthy record of naval officer chit-chat, but it comes, alas, from the post-Civil War United States Navy rather than from Nelson's navy. See Burg, "Officers, Gentlemen, 'Man-Talk,' and Group Sex in the 'Old Navy,' 1870–1873," *Journal of the History of Sexuality* 11 (July 2002): 439–56.
72. Boteler, *Recollections of My Sea Life*, 64, 98.
73. David Allan, "Some Methods and Problems in the History of Reading: Georgian England and the Scottish Enlightenment," *Journal of the Historical*

Society 3 (Winter 2003): 95; Richard Altick, *The English Common Reader: A Social History of the Mass Reading Public, 1800–1900*, 2nd ed. (Chicago: University of Chicago Press, 1998), 65; Jan Fergus, "Eighteenth-Century Readers in Provincial England: The Customers of Samuel Clap's Circulating Library and Bookshop in Warwick, 1770–1772" in *Papers of the Bibliographical Society of America* 78 (1984): 167.

74. Allan, "Some Methods and Problems," 92–3; Frank Beckwith, "The Eighteenth-Century Proprietary Library," *Journal of Documentation* 3 (1947–8): 84–6, 90; E. Boddy, "The Dalton Book Club," *Library History* 9 (1992), 98; John Feather, *The Provincial Book Trade in the Eighteenth Century* (Cambridge: Cambridge University Press, 1985), 21, 28–9, 41–2; 75, 79, 134–7; Fergus, "Eighteenth-Century Readers," 157–9, 172–6; H. M. Hamlyn, "Eighteenth-Century Circulating Libraries in England," *The Library*, 5th Series, 1 (1946–7): 197, 198; Paul Kaufman, "Eighteenth-Century Book Clubs and Their Role in Social History," *Libri* 14 (1964–5): 2–3, 26–7, *et passim*; James Raven, "The Book Trades," in Isabel Rivers, *Books and Their Readers in Eighteenth-Century England* (Leicester: Leicester University Press, 1982), 3. Daniel Defoe claimed that Bath hosted "one of the finest bookseller's shops in Europe" (*A Tour Thro' the Whole Island of Great Britain ... Interspersed with Useful Observations Particularly Fitted for the Perusal of Such as Desire to Travel over the Island* [London: J. Osborn, *et al.*, 1738], 2: 241, and playwright Richard Brinsley Sheridan also suggested the availability of books in the resort town, writing of two of the local lending libraries, one owned by a Mr. Bull, and the other by a Mr. Frederick (*The Rivals*, ed. with intro. and notes by T. Balston [Oxford: Clarendon Press, 1960], act 1, scene 2).
75. Rodger, *Wooden World*, 166, 252.
76. Altick, *English Common Reader*, 51–3, 70, 75; Feather, "Provincial Book Trade," 7–8; Fergus, "Eighteenth-Century Reader," 159–64, 171; Raven, "Book Trades," 18; Roy McKeen Wiles, "The Relish for Reading in Provincial England Two Centuries Ago," in Paul J. Korshin, ed., *The Widening Circle: Essays on the Circulation of Literature in Eighteenth-Century Europe* (Philadelphia: University of Pennsylvania Press, 1976), 93–4, 97–101. In contrast to works intended for the broadest audiences, copies of Isaac Newton's *Principia*, of which only a few hundred were printed, sold for two guineas in 1713, a quarter century after publication and before another edition was available (James Gleick, *Isaac Newton* [New York: Random House, 2003], 156).
77. Allan, "Some Methods and Problems," 92–3, 100.
78. *Ibid.*, 104, 107, 116. See Stanley Fish, *Is There a Text in This Class: The Authority of Interpretive Communities* (Cambridge, MA: Harvard University Press, 1980), *passim*.
79. Leviticus 20: 13.
80. Romans 1: 26, 27. The same chapter also condemns female homoeroticism with wording that is somewhat more ambiguous than that used in reference to males. For explication on Paul's epistle to the Romans and the applicability of 1: 27 see Bernadette J. Brooten, *Love between Women: Early Christian Responses to Female Homoeroticism* (Chicago: University of Chicago Press, 1996), 242–3, *et passim*, and T. Corey Brennan's review of Brooten in *Bryn Mawr Classical Review* (http://ccat.sas.upenn.edu/bmcr/1997/97.05.07.html [27 April 2007]).

2 Regulating Sodomy in the Pre-Nelson Navy

1. *Laws of War and Ordinances of the Sea Ordered and Established by the Parliament of the Commonwealth of England for the Regulating and Better Government of the Navy's Ships and Ships of War,* (London: John Field, 1652); Christopher Lloyd, *The British Seaman, 1200–1860: A Social Survey* (Rutherford, NJ: Fairleigh Dickinson University Press, 1968), 86–7, 239–40.
2. 13 Charles II c. 9.
3. Stephen P. Adye, *A Treatise on Courts Martial ... To Which is Added I. An Essay on Military Punishments and Rewards. II. Considerations on the Act for Punishing Mutiny and Desertion* (New York: H. Gayne, 1769), *passim*; John McArthur, *A Treatise on the Principles and Practice of Naval Courts-Martial* (London: Longden, Whieldon, and Butterworth, 1792), 20–3.
4. John D. Byrn, *Crime and Punishment in the Royal Navy: Discipline on the Leeward Islands Station, 1784–1812* (Aldershot, UK: Scholar 1989), 12. Full texts of the 1749 *Articles of War* are conveniently available in Byrn, (*Ibid.*, 203–10), in Markus Eder, *Crime and Punishment in the Royal Navy of the Seven Years' War, 1755–1763,* (Burlington, VT: Ashgate, 2004), 158–73 and in the statutes 22 George II. c. 33 and 19 George III. c. 17.
5. Byrn, *Crime and Punishment ... Leeward Islands,* 12.
6. ADM 2/81, 124–5. The Dutch East India Company had more problems with bestiality than the British, or at least they prosecuted it more often. The Company's records from Capetown contain a number of trials over the course of the eighteenth century that featured men having sex with animals, most often with shipboard pigs. See J. Oosterhoff, "Sodomy at Sea at the Cape of Good Hope during the Eighteenth Century," *Journal of Homosexuality* 16 (1/ 2 1988): 230–1.
7. *Anno Regni Caroli II ... Anno Dom 1661 ... An Act for the Establishing Articles and Orders for the Regulating of ... Forces by Sea. Also Part of an Act passed ... Anno Dom. 1720 for Rendering the Said Act More Effectual* (London: Edward Castle, 1727); 19 Geo. III. c. 17; Byrn, *Crime and Punishment ... Leeward Islands,* 12; Lloyd, *British Seaman,* 239; 22 George II. c. 33.
8. [Charles McPherson], *Life on Board a Man-of-War, Including A Full Account of the Battle of Navarino, by a British Seaman* (Glasgow: Blackie Fullerton, 1829), 47.
9. Margarette Lincoln, *Representing the Royal Navy: British Sea Power, 1750–1815* (Burlington, VT: Ashgate, 2002), 117.
10. Eder, *Crime and Punishment ... 1755–1763,* 18–19.
11. Samuel Leech, A *Voice from the Main Deck: Being a Record of the Thirty Years'Adventures of Samuel Leech,* intro. Michael Crawford (Annapolis, MD: Naval Institute Press, 1999), 76; Michael A. Lewis, *A Social History of the Navy, 1783–1815* (London: George Allen, 1960), 23, 228; R. D. Merriman, ed., *Queen Anne's Navy: Documents Concerning the Administration of the Navy of Queen Anne, 1702–1714* (London: Navy Records Society, 1961), 316; *Laws of War,* t. p. 7. Brian Lavery, ed., *Shipboard Life and Organization 1731–1815,* vol. 138, *Publications of the Navy Records Society* (Aldershot, UK: Ashgate, 1998), 41–2. See also John Davis's account of life onboard the fictional HMS *Desdemona* in *The Post-Captain; or The Wooden Walls Well Manned Comprehending a View of Naval Society and Manners,* ed. and intro. from the third edition, 1808, by R. H. Case (London: Scolartes Press, 1928), 36, 48, 62, 243.

12. N. A. M. Rodger, *The Wooden World: An Anatomy of the Georgian Navy.* (London: Collins, 1986), 66.
13. Stewards and trumpeters were also petty officers at various times (Lewis, *Social History of the Navy*, 270; Michael A. Lewis, *The Navy of Great Britain: A Historical Portrait* (London: Allen and Unwin, 1948), 178, although as late as the Napoleonic Wars, one chronicler of naval life referred to them as a lower order of warrant officer (Robert Mercer Wilson, "Remarks on Board His Majesty's Ship *Unité* of 40 Guns," in H. G. Thursfield, ed., *Five Naval Journals*, 1789–1817, vol. 91, *Publications of the Navy Records Society* [London: Navy Records Society, 1951], 250.
14. J. B. Hedderwick, *The* Captain's *Clerk* (London: Hutchinson, 1957), 43; Lewis, *Social History of the Navy*, 88, 263; Michael A. Lewis, *The Navy in Transition: A Social History, 1814–1864* (London: Hodder and Stoughton, 1965), 148; William Richardson, A *Mariner of England: An Account of the Career of William Richardson from Cabin Boy to the Merchant Service to Warrant Officer in the Royal Navy as Told by Himself, ed.* Spencer Childers (London: John Murray, 1908), 308–309; Rodger, *Wooden World*, 76, 264, 267, 338; Brian Vale, *A Frigate of King George: Life and Duty on a British Man of War, 1807–1829* (London: I. B. Tauris, 2001), 11. There was, in practice, considerable flexibility in assignments for standing officers. They often received promotions from smaller to larger ships, and assignments could be traded by those wanting sea duty and those who did not (Rodger, *Wooden World*, 22). Standard distribution of prize money gave 1/8 to the commander-in-chief, 1/4 to the ship's captain, 1/8 to warrant officers, 1/8 to the lieutenants and the master, 1/8 to the petty officers, and 1/4 to the sailors and marines (*Ibid.*, 103, 129).
15. Eder, *Crime and Punishment ... 1755–1763*, 18–19; Rodger, *Wooden World*, 103, 113.
16. *Ibid.*, 25–7, 348–51, *et passim*.
17. *Regulations and Instructions Relating to His Majesty's Service at Sea, Established by His Majesty in Council* (London, 1757),152; Duncan Crewe, *Yellow Jack and the Worm: British Naval Administration in the West Indies, 1739–1748* (Liverpool: Liverpool University Press, 1993), 104–5; Eder, *Crime and Punishment ... 1755–1763*, 11; Lewis, *The Navy in Transition*, 155; William Henry Dillon, *Narrative of My Professional Adventures (1790–1839)*, ed. Michael A. Lewis in vol. 93, *Publications of the Navy Records Society* (London: Navy Records Society,1953), 2: 273; Lewis, *Social History of the Navy*, 88, 90, 135; Lewis, *The Navy of Britain*, 309–317; Merriman, *Queen Anne's Navy*, 196; Rodger, *Wooden World*, 27, 68; Lincoln, *Representing the Royal Navy*, 10; Vale, *Frigate of King George*, 27; Basil Hall, *Fragments of Voyages and Travels by Captain Basil Hall, R. N.* (Edinburgh: Cadell, 1833), 3: 34–5.
18. Lewis, *Social History of the Navy* 87–90; Lloyd, *British Seaman*, 184–6. Captains' servants, boys on track to become commissioned officers, became known as "First Class Volunteers." "Second Class Volunteers" trained to be masters or for service elsewhere (Lewis, *Navy in Transition*, 99–100, 105; Rodger, "Shipboard Life in the Georgian Navy, 1750–1800: The Decline of the Old Order," in *The North Sea: Twelve Essays on Social History of Maritime Labor*, eds. Lewis R. Fischer *et al.* [Stavanger, Norway: Stavanger Maritime Museum/Association of North Sea Societies, 1992], 32–3). See also Rodger, "Officers, Gentlemen and their Educations, 1793–1860," in *Les Empires in*

Guerre et Paix, ed. Edward Freeman (Vincennes: Service Historique de la Marine, 1990), 141–2 and Rodger, "Honor and Duty at Sea, 1660–1815," *Historical Research*, 75 (2002), 440. By 1815 the Marine Society had equipped and sent to sea over 30,000 boys (Lincoln, *Representing the Royal Navy*, 110).

19. Cullen, *Memoirs*, 58; Lewis, *Social History of the Navy*, 24, 270, 271; Lewis, *Navy of Britain*, 178; Rodger, *Wooden World*, illustration between 286–7. James A. Gardner records a midshipman having a cot onboard the *Salisbury* in the 1780s (James A. Gardner, *Above and under the Hatches: Recollections of James Anthony Gardner*, eds. R. Vesey Hamilton and John Knox Laughton [London: Chatham, 2000], 47). John Nicol wrote that his status as a ship's cooper entitled him to mess with the steward, away from ordinary crew members, on board HMS *Proteus* in the 1770s (*The Life and Adventures of John Nicol*, ed. Tim Flannery [Orig. pub. 1822; New York: Atlantic Monthly Press, 1997], 27–8).
20. ADM 1/5266, (Ball–Jones court martial, 9 October 1706).
21. *Ibid.*
22. Netta Murray Goldsmith, *Worst of Crimes: Homosexuality and the Law in Eighteenth–Century London* (Aldershot, UK: Ashgate,1988), 67; Merriman, *Queen Anne's Navy*, 196; Leon Radzinowicz, *The Movement for Reform*, vol. 1, *A History of English Criminal Law and Its Administration from 1750* (London: Stevens and Sons, 1948), 632; Rodger, *Wooden World*, 27.
23. McArthur, *Principles and Practice of Naval Courts Martial*, 137–8.
24. ADM 1/5266 (Ball–Jones court martial, 9 October 1706).
25. Ned Ward, *Wooden World Dissected in the Character of a Ship of War*, forward by Geoffrey Callender (Orig. pub., 1707; 5th ed. 1751; London: Edwin Chappell, 1929), 75. The half-shilling price is provided in a book advertisement on back of the title page of Garrick's *Miss in Her Teens*. Both Geoffrey Callender and N. A. M. Rodger caution researchers against relying too heavily on Ward (Callender, "Introduction," Ward, *Wooden World Dissected*, ix; Rodger, *Wooden World*, 13–14).
26. ADM 1/5267 (Coise-Davis court martial, 19 July 1709).
27. Lewis, *Social History of the Navy*, 88, 225, 240–1, 263, 268; Merriman, *Queen Anne's Navy*, 316; Rodger, *Wooden World*, 20–4, 66–7, 76, 264, 267, 338.
28. Richard Wiseman, *Eight Chirurgical* [*sic*] Treatises, 5th ed. (London: B. Tooke, 1719), Second set of pages carrying nos. 347–8 in Book 3, Chapter 3; ADM 1/5267 (Coise–Davis court martial, 19 July 1709).
29. *Ibid.*; 13 Charles II. c. 9.
30. ADM 1/5265 (Brese-Hoter court martial, 13 April 1704).
31. ADM 1/5266 (Emmeson-Hughes court martial, May 1–2, 1706).
32. ADM 1/5266 (Cartwright-Jones court martial, May 20, 1706).
33. Dillon, *Narrative of My Professional Adventures*, 1: 144, 337; Peter Linebaugh, "The Tyburn Riot against the Surgeons," in *Albion's Fatal Tree: Crime and Society in Eighteenth-Century England*, eds., E. P. Thompson, *et al.* (New York: Pantheon, 1975), 86; Rodger, *Wooden World*, 20–1; Lewis, *Social History of the Navy*, 219, 303; Lewis, *Navy of Britain*, 255–6; Lewis, *Navy in Transition*, 141–3; Gardner, *Above and Under the Hatches*, 223; Merriman, *Navy of Queen Anne*, 219–20. Surgeons and pursers most often had cabins on the orlop deck, far below the waterline where the only light came from candles and lanterns. They shared the deck with storerooms, sail lockers, and the cockpit, where men wounded in battle were brought. Surgeons received their own distinctive

uniforms in 1806, but like pursers, they did not actually receive commissions until 1843. The position of the remaining warrant officers such as the chaplain and schoolmaster was anomalous in some respects. Chaplains did not receive wardroom status until 1812, and had no official uniform until World War I. Schoolmasters did not hold warrants until the reign of William IV. These two "civilian" officers often had cabins, along with the gunner, in the gun room, the after portion of the gun deck separated from the deck itself by a screen or a temporary bulkhead. The degree of comfort available in the gun room varied considerably from ship to ship and probably from decade to decade. One author described it as a Spartan place where the wide sweep of the tiller under the deckhead made it difficult to erect many cabin partitions and numerous denizens thus slung their hammocks in a common area. Another wrote of a gun room of the 1780s "fitted up in luxurious style, with window curtains, blinds, buffets, wine coolers, silver forks and many other appendages of that delicate nature unknown in the good old times" (Gardner, *Above and Under the Hatches*, 20–1). The number of warrant officers with sufficient prestige to mess in the wardroom varied, depending on a number of factors including the size of the ship. Over the years, however, the number generally expanded to include the master and several of the "civilian" warrant officers – purser, surgeon, and the chaplain, though not often the schoolmaster. Pursers, surgeons, and chaplains did not receive quarterdeck status until 1806. Small arms were often stowed in the gunroom, and it sometimes doubled as an officers mess on smaller ships (Zachary B. Friedenberg, *Medicine Under Sail* [Annapolis: Naval Institute Press, 2002], 6, 9; Lewis, *Social History of the Navy*, 234–6, 240, 243, 251, 254, 261; Lewis, *Navy in Transition*, 141–8; Lewis, *Navy of Britain*, 92, 181–2; 234, 257, 268, 277; Lincoln, *Representing the Royal Navy*, 162, 167; Lloyd, *British Seaman*, 34; Gardner, *Above and Under the Hatches*, 20–1, 57, 89–90, 223, 237; Merriman, *Queen Anne's Navy*, 323–4; James Morrison, *The Journal of James Morrison, Boatswain's Mate of the* Bounty, *Describing the Mutiny and Subsequent Misfortunes of the Mutineers, together with an Account of the Island of Tahiti* [Waltham St. Lawrence, UK [?]: Golden Cockerel Press, 1935], 27; Rodger, *Wooden World*, 66–7). On board the fictional *Desdemona* the purser, surgeon, and officer of marines dined amid the gunroom's four eighteen pounders (Davis, *Post-Captain*, 9–10). The master at arms (not to be confused with the master) did not become a warrant officer until 1805 (William Robinson, *Jack Nastyface: Memoirs of a Seaman*, ed. Oliver Warner [Originally published as *Nautical Economy*, London, 1836; reprint, Annapolis, MD: Naval Institute Press, 1973], 34). Edward Mangin commented on the canvas walls of the cabin he was assigned as chaplain of HMS *Gloucester* ("Some Account of the Writer's Situation as a Chaplain in the British Navy," in Thursfield, *Five Naval Journals*, 9–10). Schoolmasters, chaplains, and gunners also had their quarters sectioned off by canvas on some ships according to William H. Dillon (*Narrative of My Professional Adventures*, 1: 13, 17, 21, 214). John Nicol, in a comment reflecting on the skills of Royal Navy surgeons in the late eighteenth century, noted that his Chinese barber's herbal cures were more effective against venereal disease than the medications prescribed by his ship's doctor (*Adventures of John Nicol*, 107).

34. ADM 1/89 (Edward Hawke, *St. George*, Spithead, to John Clevland, Admiralty, London, 20 July 1755); *Commissioned Sea Officers of the Royal Navy, 1660–1815*, eds. David Syrett and R. L. DiNardo (Aldershot, U. K.; Brookfield, VT, U. S. A.: Scolar Press, for the Navy Records Society; Ashgate, 1944), 208.
35. ADM 1/924 (T. Broderick, HMS *Barfleur*, Spithead, to John Clevland, Admiralty, London, 13 June 1757); Rodger, *Wooden World*, 80.
36. ADM 1/924 (T. Broderick, *Barfleur*, Spithead, to John Clevland, Admiralty, London, 13 June 1757).
37. ADM 12/26 (French-Pombol court martial, 21 February 1756), 14.
38. *Ibid.*, 15.
39. Ibid., 14–16. It appears from Admiralty records that the crime of "uncleanness" could connote either improperly conducted excretory activity, a general lack of hygiene, or homoerotic behavior. Sexual "uncleanness" was by far the more serious of the types of offenses, and could result in the perpetrators facing courts martial. In the trial of Christopher Beauchamp and James Bruce, it is obvious that the unclean activity charged against them is mutual masturbation. Most of their alleged sexual activities took place in the starboard roundhouse of their ship. Excretory functions conducted in a roundhouse could not have been a violation of any regulation let alone chargeable under the *Articles of War* since roundhouses were designated locations for urination and defecation (ADM 1/5453 and ADM 1/5354 [Beauchamp-Bruce court martial, 6–15 January 1816], *passim*. William Crutchley admitted engaging in unclean practices with John Westerman under the half-deck of HMS *Africaine*, but added that no sodomy took place. His reference to uncleanness is obviously contained in a sexual context (ADM 1/5453 [Crutchley examination, 16 December 1815]). In the 1816 court martial of John Parsons, one of the *Africaine* crew was accused of uncleanness; his offense was clearly sexual, involving groping, kissing and fondling. The only references to excretions in the trial came when witness Thomas Bottomy was asked if he knew why Parsons was broken from sergeant to private. He replied, "Yes, for dirtiness, pissing in his hammock." The action cost Parsons his rank, but could not approach the level of seriousness necessary to convene a court martial over it (ADM 1/5354 [Parsons 2nd court martial, 16 January 1816], [25–6]). The association of uncleanness with sexual misconduct in the navy was found in English society as well. In the title of Nicholas Bernard's book, *The Case of John Atherton, Bishop of Waterford in Ireland: Who Was Convicted of the Sin of Uncleanness with a Cow, and Other Creatures; for which He Was Hanged at Dublin*, uncleanness has an unmistakable sexual connotation. See also Josiah Woodward's *Sodom's Vices Destructive to Other Cities and States: A Sermon Preached before the Right Honorable The Lord Mayor of the City of London* (London: s.n., 1732),1, 11, 13.

    In contrast to the seriousness with which sexual uncleanness was treated, ordinary uncleanness was a familiar but minor shipboard problem. A naval doctor who had devoted his life to the service, Thomas Trotter, adjudged that, "Seamen are naturally indolent and filthy" (Thomas Trotter, *Medicina Nautica: An Essay on the Diseases of Seamen*, 2nd ed. [London: Longman, 1804], 443). See also Friedenberg (*Medicine under Sail*, 59). Unclean behavior of a non-sexual nature was for summary rather than judicial attention. On board the *Africaine* in 1816, officers took official cognizance of two crewmembers, a seamen and a marine, urinating in unauthorized locations. Emanuel Cross urinated "in the stair" and marine John Parsons "went forward on the main deck on the larboard side and made water between the guns" (ADM 1/2427 [13 October 1815], 6, 15). Neither mariner faced courts martial for "uncleanness" for their untidy actions. Joseph Hubbard, one of the *Africaine*'s boys, deposed to going "forward on the larboard side of the galley to the manger to make water" as if urinating here and there about the ship were an ordinary practice (ADM 1/5453 [Hubbard examination, 15 December 1815], 1). John D. Byrn also discusses several cases of uncleanness. In each instance the unclean behavior is specifically described, pissing onto the deck from the maintop, stinking clothes, and dirtying the ship's side, but none of the guilty mariners faced anything more serious than summary punishment for their offenses (*Crime and Punishment ... Leeward Islands*, 151). Thomas Collings recorded the case of a rating berated and kicked in the mouth for having a dirty kit, but his chastisement went no further (Hedderwick, *Captain's Clerk*, 44). In the set of regulations he drafted while captain of the *Hyperion* in the early nineteenth century, William P. Cumby several times dealt with filth, but saw it as a management problem, not a matter for judicial cognizance. According to the rules he laid down, it could be handled by the boatswain, who was to make sure the forecastle stayed clean, that no clothes were "spread or hung in improper places," and that marines were "not to suffer any dirt to be thrown out of the ports" (Cumby, "Orders and Regulations," in Thursfield, *Five Naval Journals*, 340, 344–5). In English civil society, as in the navy, waste elimination at inappropriate locations while frowned upon did not occasion serious disapprobation. James Lowther, Lord Lonsdale once recounted how the elder lads at his school would not customarily take the trouble to go to the "pissing place" at the far end of the dormitory, but would instead "piss by the little boys' beds" (Sissman, *Boswell's Presumptuous Task*, 169).

40. ADM 1/653 ([?] Smith, HMS *Union*, the Downs, to John Clevland, Admiralty, London, 8 June 1757).
41. *Ibid.*
42. *Ibid.*
43. Arthur N. Gilbert, "Buggery and the British Navy, 1700–1861," 10 *Journal of Social History* (Fall 1976): 77. Gilbert provides no source for the Val case. His citation contains only a reference to the court martial of James Ball on 8 October 1706 (*Ibid.*, 93 n. 37).
44. ADM 1/5300 (Finley-Newton court martial 2 July 1761); ADM 12/26 (Finley-Newton court martial, 2 July 1761), 21–26.
45. ADM 1/5300 (Finley-Newton court martial, 2 July 1761); ADM 12/26 (Finley-Newton court martial, 2 July 1761), 21–26; Roland Pietsch, "Ships' Boys and Charity in the Mid-Eighteenth Century: The London Marine Society (1756–1722)" (Ph. D. diss., University of London, 2003), 203; Rodger, *Wooden World*, 159, 392, n. 31. Hanging was the most usual method of execution in the navy, but on at least one occasion a man convicted of a capital offense was dispatched with firearms. Admiral John Byng, found guilty of violating the twelfth article of war, was shot on the quarterdeck of HMS *Monarch*, 14 March 1757 (Augustus Hervey, *Augustus Hervey's Journal: Being the Intimate Account of the Life of a Captain in the Royal Navy Ashore and*

Afloat, 1746–1759, ed. David Erskine [London: Kimber, 1954], 243; *Commissioned Sea Officers*, 67).
46. Eder, *Crime and Punishment ... 1755–1763*, 3–4, 11; Lincoln, *Representing the Royal Navy*, 41; Dudley Pope, *Life in Nelson's Navy* (Annapolis, MD: Naval Institute Press, 1981), 243.
47. Eder, *Crime and Punishment ... 1755–1763*, 12, 116–18, 121–2, 127, 137–8, 155; Richardson, *Mariner of England*, 117.
48. ADM 51/1264 (*Perdix* log, 28 June 1796); ADM 51/2606 (*Nyaden* log, 11 September 1810, 2 May 1811); Byrn, *Crime and Punishment ... 1784–1812*, 150.
49. *Ibid.*, 124.

3 Ratings with Ratings, Ratings with Boys

1. ADM 1/5302 (Clark-Pearson court martial, 8 February 1763).
2. R. A. J. Walling, *The Story of Plymouth* (New York: Morrow, [1950]), 145.
3. ADM 1/5302 (Clark-Pearson court martial, 8 February 1763); *Regulations and Instructions Relating to His Majesty's Service at Sea, Established by His Majesty in Council* (London: 1752), 4; John Harvey Boteler, *Recollections of My Sea Life from 1880–1830*. ed. by David Bonner-Smith, vol. 82; *Publications of the Navy Records Society* ([London]:Navy Records Society, 1942); J. J. Colledge, *Ships of the Royal Navy: A Complete Record of the Royal Navy from the Fifteenth Century to the Present* (London: Greenhill Books, 1987), 228, 247, 346; F. W. Lipscomb, *Heritage of Sea Power: The Story of Portsmouth* (London: Hutchinson, 1969), 161. The maximum number of officers, usually captains, permitted on courts martial boards was thirteen (22 George. II. c. 33, 15; John McArthur, *A Treatise on the Principles and Practice of Naval Courts-Martial*, [London: Longdon,Whieldon, and Butterworth, 1792], 53), but it often proved impossible to obtain that number even by requiring all those available at any particular location to participate.
4. [William Nugent Glascock], *Naval Sketchbook: or the Service Afloat and Ashore: with Characteristic Reminiscences, Fragments, and Opinions, by an Officer. New ed.*, (London: Colburn and Bently,1831), 2: 36; Henry Keppel, *A Sailor's Life under Four Sovereigns* (London: Macmillan, 1899), 1: 55–6.
5. ADM 1/5302 (Clark-Pearson court martial, 8 February 1763).
6. *Ibid.*; *Regulations and Instructions Relating to His Majesty's Service at Sea, Established by His Majesty in Council*. 9th ed. London: s. n., 1757, 5–6; Markus Eder, *Crime and Punishment in the Royal Navy of the Seven Years' War, 1755–1763* (Burlington, VT: Ashgate, 2004), 50–1, 152, 157; John McArthur, *A Treatise on the Principles and Practice of Naval Courts-Martial*, (London, Wheildon, and Butterworth, 1792), 91, 273; Stephen P. Adye, A *Treatise on Courts Martial ... To Which is Added I. An Essay on Military, Punishments and Rewards. II. Considerations on the Act for Punishing Mutiny and Desertion* (New York: H. Gayne, 1769), 99.
7. (ADM 1/5299 [Billin-Bryan court martial, 13 May 1762], 1; ADM 1/5301 [Billin-Bryan court martial, 13 May 1762], 1; ADM 12/26 (Billin-Bryan court martial, 13 May 1762), 27–33; Colledge, *Ships of the Royal Navy*, 240; 22 Geo. II. c. 33, 15; Eder, *Crime and Punishment ... 1755–1763*, 5–13, 50–1.

8. McArthur, *Principles and Practice of Naval Courts Martial*, 102–3, Appendix pages xx, c; Adye, *Treatise on Courts Martial*, 24; 19 George. III. c. 17, 22–3. The provision in 22 George. II. c. 33, 15 requiring court martial board members to remain on board the ship where the court martial was held throughout the duration of the proceeding caused considerable inconvenience for officers over the years. It was repealed by 19 George. III. c. 17, 22. See the cases of Purser Bartholomew Worth and Master Thomas Biddle who were sent back to England in 1823 along with several witnesses when a court martial board could not be constituted from officers on board ships in the South American Squadron. Both men were finally convicted of smuggling at Portsmouth and dismissed from the service (Brian Vale, A *Frigate of King George: Life and Duty on a British Man of War, 1807–1829* [London: I. B. Tauris, 2001], 111, 113, 135, 169).
9. Eder, *Crime and Punishment ... 1755–1763*, 152; *Regulations and Instructions*, 5–6; McArthur, *Treatise on the Principles and Practice of Naval Courts Martial*, 76–80; Adye, *Treatise on Courts Martial*, 37; 22 Geo. II. c. 33, 17.
10. ADM 1/5299 (Billin-Bryan court martial, 13 May 1762); ADM 1/5301 (Billin-Bryan court martial, 13 May 1762); *Commissioned Sea Officers of the Royal Navy, 1660–1815*. Eds. David Syrett and R. L. DiNardo. (Aldershot, UK; Brookfield, VT, USA: Scolar Press, for the Navy Records Society; Ashgate, 1994), 238.
11. McArthur, *Principles and Practice of Naval Courts Martial*, 104; 22 George II. c. 33, 18. Oaths were prescribed for board members and judge advocates of courts martial (22 George. II. c. 33, 16).
12. ADM 1/5299 (Billin-Bryan court martial, 13 May 1762), 4; ADM 1/5301 (Billin-Bryan court martial, 13 May 1762), 4.
13. ADM 1/5299 (Billin-Bryan court martial, 13 May 1762), 6; ADM 1/5301 (Billin-Bryan court martial, 13 May 1762), 6.
14. ADM 1/5299 (Billin-Bryan court martial, 13 May 1762), 9; ADM 1/5301 (Billin-Bryan court martial, 13 May 1762), 9.
15. ADM 1/5299 (Billin-Bryan court martial, 13 May 1762); ADM 1/5301 (Billin-Bryan court martial, 13 May 1762); ADM 12/26 (Billin-Bryan court martial, 13 May 1762) 27–33.
16. *Ibid.*, 33.
17. Arthur N Gilbert, "Buggery and the British Navy, 1700–1861," *Journal of Social History* 10 (Fall 1976): 75, 87, 92, 92 n.,93, 97 n., 98. The first of the mutinies occurred on a fifth rate, HMS *Winchelsea* in 1793. The next two took place the following year on board the 74-gun HMS *Windsor Castle* and the 74-gun HMS *Culloden*. HMS *Defiance*, another 74, experienced a mutiny in 1795. Five years later, mutineers took over a sixth rate, HMS *Danaë* (Colledge, *Ships of the Royal Navy*), 97, 100, 103, 381, 382; Jonathan Neale, *The Cutlass and the Lash: Mutiny and Discipline in Nelson's Navy*) [London: Pluto Press, 1985], 162–4; N. A. M. Rodger, "Honor and Duty at Sea, 1600–1815" *Historical Research*, 75 (2002): 139–151, 442.
18. G. E. Manwaring and Bonamy Dobrée, *The Floating Republic: An Account of the Mutinies at Spithead and the Nore, 1797* (London: Geoffrey Bles, 1935), 3–7, 118, 126, 236. Jervis's victory against the Spanish Navy off Cape Vincent was far short of a great naval triumph, but Pitt, needing a fillip for the national spirit, magnified the engagement grandly, creating Jervis Earl of St. Vincent

and making Horatio Nelson (whose daring contributed to the fleet's success) a Knight of the Bath (*Ibid.*, 6–7). Manwaring's characterization differs sharply from the triumphalist version provided in John Marshall's biographical sketch of Jervis (*Royal Naval Biography Containing Memoirs of the Flag-Officers, Superannuated Rear-Admirals, Retired-Captains, Post-Captains and Commanders* [London: Longman, 1823–33], 1: 26–8). The most destructive mutiny of 1797, that on board HMS *Hermione* in which ten officers were executed, did not take place until September of that year (Paul A. Gilje, *Liberty on the Waterfront: American Maritime Culture in the Age of Revolution* [Philadelphia: University of Pennsylvania Press, 2004], 139–40; James Dugan, *The Great Mutiny* (New York: Putnam's, 1965), 131, 393–6; Neale, *Cutlass and Lash*, 1–4; Leonard Guttridge, *Mutiny: A History of Naval Insurrection* [Annapolis, MD: Naval Institute Press, 1992], 76–81). For additional discussion on the socio-economic and political causes of the observable increases in crime and punishment during wartime, see Eder, *Crime and Punishment ... 1755–1763*, 8.

19. Gilbert, "Buggery and the British Navy, 1700–1861," *Journal of Social History* 10 (Fall 1976): 72–97, 97, n. 98. Gilbert cites Ad. Mss. 31, 176 *Jervis Order Book*, 29 July 1797 and Ad. Mss. 31, 186, *Journal of St. Vincent*, 3 July 1797; Colledge, *Commissioned Sea Officers*, 392; Dugan, *Great Mutiny*, 30–2, 151; John Marshall, *Royal Naval Biography, Containing Memoirs of the Flag-Officers, Superannuated Rear-Admirals, Retired-Captains, Post-Captains and Commanders*. (London: Longman, 1823–1833), 1: 28.
20. William James, *Old Oak: The Life of John Jervis, Earl of St. Vincent* (London: Longman, 1950), 103–4.
21. ADM 1/5339 (Benson-Francis court martial, 30 June 1797); ADM 12/26 (Benson-Francis court martial, 30 June 1797), 41–2.
22. ADM 1/5299 (Billin-Bryan court martial, 13 May 1762); ADM 1/5301 (Billin-Bryan court martial, 13 May 1762), 6.
23. ADM 12/26 (Billin-Bryan court martial, 30 June 1797), 41.
24. ADM 1/5339 (Benson-Francis court martial, 30 June 1797), 4, 5, 7, 9, 12, 13, 17, *et passim*.
25. ADM 1/5339 (Benson-Francis court martial, 30 June 1797), 2; ADM 12/26 (Benson-Francis court martial, 30 June 1799), 42.
26. ADM 12/26 (Callaghan-McMaster court martial 29 July 1799), 52.
27. ADM 12/26 (Hubbad-Hynes court martial, 10 December 1800) 53–54.
28. ADM 12/26 (Fuller-Greenard court martial, 21 April 1802), 56–57. Uneasiness about the surgeon's qualifications rather than a hatred of sodomy may also have been a reason they ignored the surgeon's testimony. See Peter Cullen, "Memoirs of Peter Cullen, Esquire" in H. G. Thursfield, ed., *Five Naval Journals, 1789–1817*, vol. 91, *Publications of the Navy Records Society* (London: Navy Records Society, 1951). Cullen passed formal examinations at Surgeons' Hall before being certified to serve as a surgeon on a navy ship (49–50). The Medical Board had been licensing surgeons for the navy since the latter years of the eighteenth century (Thomas Trotter, *Medicina Nautica: An Essay on the Diseases of Seamen*, 2nd ed. [London: Longman, 1804], 12, 25, 34).
29. James, *Old Oak*, 134; Dugan, *Great Mutiny*, 117. If in fact Duckworth was a man of forbearance in 1802, he might have learned it from earlier experience when captain of HMS *Leviathan*. In April 1797, shortly after returning from

the West Indies, he and his officers were "disbanded" by his crew, who joined the mutiny at Spithead (Dugan, *Great Mutiny*, 118).

30. ADM 12/26 (Brown-McCarthy court martial, 7 January 1804), 57–58.
31. ADM 2/81 (Blake court martial, 11 August 1758), 124–5; Eder, *Crime and Punishment ... 1755–1763*, 141, 145–6.
32. Testimony varied about Savage's position in relation to the bitts. He was variously described as "under the bitts," "upon the aftermost knee of the bitts," "between the bitts," and "lying flat on the deck with his face downwards between the bitts" (ADM 1/5343 [Morris-Savage court martial, 9 January 1797, *passim*]).
33. ADM 12/26 (Benson-Francis court martial, 30 June 1797), 41–42 .
34. ADM 1/5343 (Morris-Savage court martial, 9 January 1797), 5, 9, 10, 11, 16.
35. *Ibid.*, 19.
36. ADM 12/26 (Falso-Lambert court martial, 3 December 1798), 48, 49.
37. *Ibid.*, 48–50.
38. ADM 12/26 (Douglas-Ware, Harries-Harrison court martial, 16 June 1800), 54–6.
39. ADM 12/21 (Holland-Riley court martial, 11 May 1802), 2–14.
40. *Ibid.*, 213–15.
41. ADM 1/5299 (Billin-Bryan court martial, 13 May 1762); ADM 1/5301 (Billin-Bryan court martial, 13 May 1762); ADM 1/5302 (Clark-Pearson court martial, 8 February 1763); ADM 12/26, (Billin-Bryan court martial, 13 May 1762), 27–33; ADM 12/26, (Clark-Pearson court martial, 8 February 1763 279–80; [Edward Ward], *Adam and Eve Stripped of their Furbelows: or, the Fashionable Virtues and Vices of Both Sexes Exposed to Public View* (London: A. Bettlesworth, [1715] 213; [Edward Ward]. *A Complete and Humorous Account of all the Remarkable Clubs and Societies in the Cities of London and Westminster from the R_____l-S_____y down to the Lumber-Troop*. 7th ed. London: s. n., 1756. 265–9; Josiah Woodward, *Sodom's Vices Destructive to other Cities and States: A Sermon Preached before the Right Honorable The Lord Mayor of the City of London* (London: B. Aylmer and A. Bell, 1697), "Dedication," 1, 11, 13, 17; [Anon.], *Epistle from Little Captain Brazen, to the Worthy Captain Plume. To Which Is Added an Answer to the Said Epistle In the Character of Iago* [Robert Walpole?] *Is Set Forth So As To Be Understood by the Meanest Capacity.* (London: A. Moore [1731]) 7, 8; [Anon.], *This Is Not the Thing*, 1; [Thomas Newcomb], *The Manners of the Age: In Thirteen Moral Satires. Written with a Design to Expose the Vicious and Irregular Conduct of Both Sexes, in the Various Pursuits of Life* (London: Jer. Batley, 1733), 310, 316; Tobias Smollett, *The Adventures of Roderick Random*, ed. Paul Boucé (New York: Oxford University Press, 1979), 310, 316; Tobias Smollett, "*Advice: A Satire*" in *The Works of Tobias Smollet, Poems, Plays, and* The Briton, intro. and notes by Byron Gassman (Athens, GA: University of Georgia Press, 1993), 32; Tobias Smollett, *The Adventures of Peregrine Pickle in which Are Included Memories of a Lady of Quality*, ed. and intro., James L. Clifford (New York: Oxford University Press, 1964), 242–3, 366. See also, Lincoln, *Representing the Royal Navy*, 30–1.
42. William Henry Dillon, A *Narrative of My Professional Adventures (1790–1839)*, 2 vols. Edited by Michael A. Lewis. Vol. 93, *Publications of the Navy Records Society*. London: Navy Records Society, 1953. 1: 371–2, 2: 83; [McPherson],

Life on Board a Man-of-War, Including A Full Accouont of the Battle of Navarino by a British Seaman. (Glasgow: Blackie Fullerton 1829), 170; Robert Mercer Wilson, "Remarks on Board His Majesty's Ship *Unité* of 40 Guns," in Thusfield, Five Naval Journals 188.

43. One possible exception to this was the case of Captain Richard Matson who, after being acquitted of sodomy in 1799, resigned from the Royal Navy and retired to the countryside where, according to a transcriber's note included with his trial record, it is alleged he continued to seek out male sex partners in preference to the women who would likely have been available to a retired captain living on shore (ADM 12/26, Matson court martial, 18 July 1799), 51–52 See also, Chapter 5.
44. ADM 12/21 (McMahan court martial, 2 January 1798), 210–11.
45. ADM 1/5397 (Grimshaw-Scott court martial, 21 June 1809), 7, 9–14, 17, 25.
46. *Ibid.*, 26–7.
47. *Ibid.*, 27–8.
48. *Ibid.*, 3.
49. ADM 1/5397 (Colquhoun-Fleming court martial, 23 June 1809), i–ii, 2, 17.
50. Cullen, "Memoirs," in Thursfield, *Five Naval Journals*, 54; Michael A. Lewis, *The Navy in Transition: A Social History, 1814–1864* (London: Hodder and Stoughton, 1965), 161; Lincoln, *Representing the Royal Navy*, 162.
51. ADM 1/5397 (Colquhoun-Fleming court martial, 23 June 1809), iii, 2–3, 5–6, 9–10.
52. ADM 1/5478 (McGee-Peach court martial, 17 July 1832), 2.
53. *Ibid.*, 7, 8.
54. *Ibid*, 11–12.
55. *Ibid.*, 12, 13.
56. *Ibid.*, 13.
57. ADM 12/26 (Douglas-Ware court martial, 16 June 1800), 55; Boteler, *Recollections of My Sea Life*, 25, 34.
58. Quoted from Lincoln, *Representing the Royal Navy*, 26–7. Her source for the material is *Sailor's Letters* (Nettleton, UK: Plymouth, [1800?]).
59. ADM 12/26 (Carter court martial, 15 May 1804), 9–10, 293.
60. ADM 1/5299 (Billin-Bryan court martial, 13 May 1762), 10; ADM 1/5301 (Billin-Bryan court martial, 13 May 1762), 10; ADM 1/5302 (Clark-Pearson court martial, 8 February 1763), 1; ADM 12/26 (Cross-Spencer court martial, 9 September 1775), 273–4; (Macdonald-Mitchell court martial, 12 November 1762), 278–7; Clark-Pearson court martial, 8 February 1763), 279–80; (Read-Tattersall court martial, 4 July 1796), 288–91; (Manning court martial, 14 December 1802), 292.
61. ADM 1/5299 (Billin-Bryan court martial, 13 May 1762), 4; ADM 1/5301 (Billin-Bryan court martial, 13 May 1762), 4; ADM 12/26 (Billin-Bryan court martial, 13 May 1762), 32.
62. ADM 12/26 (Billin-Bryan court martial, 13 May 1762), 32.
63. ADM 1/5343 (Morris-Savage court martial, 9 January 1797), 7; ADM 12/26 (Benson-Francis court martial, 30 June 1797), 42.
64. *Ibid.*, 2; ADM 12/26 (Morris-Savage court martial, 9 January 1798), 42.
65. William Blackstone, *Ehrlich's Blackstone*, vol. 2, ed. by J. W. Ehrlich (New York: Capicon Books, 1959) 2: 408;William Eden, *Principles of Penal Law*, (London: B. White and T. Cadell, 1771), 242.

66. Garrick, *Miss in Her Teens: Or, The Medley of Lovers* (London: s. n., 1747), later ed., (London: Alexander Cleugh), 1789, 23; Nathaniel Lancaster, The *Pretty Gentleman: Softness of Manners Vindicated from the False Ridicule Exhibited under the Character of William Fribble, Esq.* (London: M. Cooper 1747), 6, 8–9, 10–11; Johann William von Archenholz, *A Picture of England* (London: s. n., 1797), 197; John Wesley, *Serious Thoughts Occasioned by the Earthquake at Lisbon: To which Is Subjoined an Account of all the Late Earthquakes there and in other Places*, 6th ed. (London: s. n., 1756), 4, 28.
67. ADM 1/5299 (Billin-Bryan court martial, 13 May 1762); ADM 1/5301 (Billin-Bryan court martial, 13 May 1762).
68. ADM 12/26 (Hubbard-Hynes court martial, 10 December 1800), 53–4.
69. See Stephen Zeeland, *Sailors and Sexual Identity: Crossing the Line between "Straight" and "Gay" in the U. S. Navy* (New York: Haworth, 1995), 31; Zeeland, *The Masculine Marine: Homoeroticism in the U. S. Marine Corps* (New York: Haworth, 1996), 3–4, 9–10.
70. Dillon, *Narrative of My Professional Adventures*, 2: 124–5.
71. ADM 1/5296 (Bicks-Booth court martial, 10 December 1757); ADM 12/26 (Bicks-Booth court martial, 27 June 1757), 13–14.
72. ADM 1/5296 (Colquhoun-Fleming court martial, 23 June 1809).
73. ADM 1/5296 (Bicks–Booth court martial, 27 June 1757); ADM 12/26 (Bicks-Booth court martial, 27 June 1757), 13–14.
74. *Ibid.* 13. The ellipsis in the quotation reads, "He [Bicks] was even caught in the fact [*sic*] by some of the crew who called others to witness it." The writer of the summary of the trial transcript is in error. The record indicates there were no witnesses to any of the acts of sodomy Bicks engaged in with Booth. All eye-witness testimony to sexual activities in the transcript relate to Bicks and Touhead, when both men were chained to the same bolt (ADM 1/5296 [Bicks-Booth court martial, 10 December 1757].
75. Gilbert, "Buggery and the British Navy," 77.
76. ADM 12/26 (Tremissen-Veaux court martial, 12 December 1759), 17.
77. Ibid., 16–21; Roland Pietsch, "Ships' Boys and Charity in the Mid-Eighteenth Century: The London Marine Society (1756–1772)" (Ph. D. diss., University of London, 2003)," 204.
78. ADM 12/21 (Palmer court martial, 19 August 1779), 205–7.
79. Gilbert, "Buggery and the British Navy," 78. Gilbert cites ADM 12/24 (Dickie court martial, 13 August 1801), 271–273.
80. ADM 12/26 (Billin-Bryan court martial, 27 July 1761), 26; Pietsch, "Ships' Boys and Charity," 204.
81. ADM 12/26 (Chilton court martial, 3 November 1762), 33–5; Pietsch, "Ships' Boys and Charity," 202–203; Colledge, *Ships of the Royal Navy*, 311.
82. ADM 12/26 (Jenness court martial, 25 August 1798), 46–8.
83. ADM 1/5399 (Black-Phillips court martial, 19 September 1709), iii, 2–5.
84. *Ibid.*, 7–9.
85. *Ibid.*, 8.
86. *Ibid.*, 13, 17.
87. Gilbert, "Buggery and the British Navy," 76–7.
88. *Ibid.*; ADM 1/5399 (James-Martin court martial, 22 September 1809).
89. ADM 12/26 (Brown-McCarthy court martial, 27 June 1804), 57–8.
90. ADM 1/5399 (North court martial, 6 September 1809), 1–3, 7–10.
91. *Ibid.*, 7–11.

4 Officers and Boys at Sea

1. ADM 12/24 (Dickie court martial, 13 August 1801), 271–2.
2. *Ibid.*, 271.
3. John Harvey Boteler, *Recollections of My Sea Life from 1808–1830*, ed. by David Bonner-Smith, vol. 82, *Publications of the Navy Records Society*. ([London]: Navy Records Society, 1942), 34, 86, 228, 236–7, *et* passim; Michael A. Lewis, "Chapter Introduction" to Dillon, *Narrative of my Professional Adventures (1790–1839)*, 2 vols., ed. by Michael A. Lewis, vol. 93, *Publications of the Navy Records Society* (London Navy Records Society, 1953), 1: 321–2; Margarette Lincoln, *Representing the Royal Navy: British Sea Power 1750–1815* (Burlington, VT: Ashgate, 2002), x, 3, 16, 17–18, 52; J. J. Colledge, *Ships of the Royal Navy: A Complete Record of the Royal Navy from the Fifteenth Century to the Present* (London: Greenhill Books, 1987), 33; *Commissioned Sea Officers of the Royal Navy, 1660–1815*, ed. by David Syrett and R. L. DiNardo (Aldershot, UK; Brookfield, VT, USA: Scolar Press, for the Navy Records Society, Ashgate,1994), 357; [Charles McPherson], *Life on Board of a Man-of-War, Including A Full Account of the Battle of Navarino, By a British Seaman* (Glasgow: Blackie Fullerton, 1829) 128; N. A. M. Roger, *The Wooden World: An Anatomy of the Georgian Navy*. (London: Collins, 1986), 247–8, *et passim* Robert Mercer Wilson, "Remarks on Board His Majesty's Ship *Unité* of 40 Guns," in H. G. Thursfield ed., *Five Naval Journals, 1789–1817*, vol. 91, *Publications of the Navy Record Society* (London: Navy Records Society, 1951), 145; "William Boyce (1711–1779)," *Eighteenth-Century English Music*. http://www.rslade. btinternet.co.uk/boyce/ index.html (27 July 2004). Brain Vale, *A Frigate of King George: Life and Duty on a British Man of War, 1807–1829* (London: I. B. Tauris, 2001), 121. Even situations perhaps entirely innocent could spawn shipboard rumors. Frederick Hoffman in his memoirs wrote of how in 1794 his ship captured a French brig and took on board a Capuchin friar and two officers "for what purpose we could never find except to give them a cruise. The friar, who was a quiet, fat, rather good-looking man, messed in the cabin." Hoffman slyly located the origins of any suspicions that might have circulated among the crew with the midshipmen. "The wicked mids," he explained, said the cleric's purpose was "to 'confess' the captain" (*A Sailor of King George: The Journals of Captain Frederick Hoffman, RN, 1793–1814*, eds. A. Beckford Bevan and H. B. Wolryche-Whitmore [Annapolis, MD: Naval Institute Press, 1998], 52).
4. ADM 12/26 (Beale court martial, 7 March 1759), 275.
5. *Ibid.*, 276.
6. ADM 1/5301 (Orde court martial, 1 February 1762), 1–5; ADM 1/5301 (Angel court martial, 12 January 1762), letter of Rice Price; *Commissioned Sea Officers*, 35.
7. ADM 1/5301 (Orde court martial, 1 February 1762), 5.
8. ADM 1/5301 (Angel court martial, 12 January 1762), letter of Rice Price.
9. ADM 1/5301 (Orde court martial, 1 February 1762), 5.
10. *Ibid.*, 4.
11. *Ibid.*, 1; ADM 1/5301 (Angel court martial, 12 January 1762), 1, supplementary pages; David P. Henige, *Colonial Governors from the Fifteenth Century to the Present: A Comprehensive List* (Madison, WI: University of Wisconsin Press, 1970), 36.
12. ADM 1/5301 (Angel court martial, 12 January 1762), supplementary pages.

13. ADM 1/5301 (Orde court martial, 1 February 1762), 6.
14. *Ibid.*, 6.
15. ADM 1/5301 (Angel court martial, 12 January 1762), supplementary pages, 1.
16. *Ibid.*, 2–7.
17. *Ibid.*, 18–22; Daniel Baugh, *British Naval Administration in the Age of Walpole* (Princeton, NJ: Princeton University Press, 1965), Appendix II.
18. ADM 1/5301 (Angel court martial, 12 January 1762), 21–4.
19. *Ibid.*, 8–10, 11–15.
20. *Ibid.*, 12.
21. *Ibid.*, 15.
22. *Ibid.*, 11–15.
23. ADM 1/5301 (Orde court martial, 1 February 1762), 12.
24. ADM 1/5301 (Angel court martial, 12 January 1762), 26–30 (1–5 of Angel's statement).
25. Rictor Norton, *Mother Clap's Molly House: The Gay Subculture in England, 1700–1830* (London Gay Mens' Press, 1992), 134–45.
26. ADM 1/5301 (Angel court martial, 12 January 1762), 18.
27. *Ibid.*, 18–22.
28. *Ibid.*, 12–15.
29. *Ibid.*, 15.
30. *Ibid.*, 22–3.
31. *Ibid.*, 12–15.
32. *Ibid.*, 1–3.
33. Markus Eder, *Crime and Punishment in the Royal Navy of the Seven Years' War 1755–1763*, 111; [J. Delafons], *Treatise on Naval Courts Martial* (s. l.: s. n., 1805), 260–1; *Commissioned Sea Officers*, 179; David Hannay, *Naval Courts Martial* (Cambridge, UK: Cambridge University Press, 1914), xlv.
34. ADM 1/5301 (Orde court martial, 1 February 1762), 1; [Delafons], *Treatise on Naval Courts Martial*, 262. The British captured Martinique from France in 1762, but it was returned shortly thereafter.
35. ADM 1/5301 (Angel court martial, 12 January 1762), supplementary pages; ADM 1/5301 (Orde court martial, 1 February 1762), 1–2.
36. *Ibid.*, 1–2, 15.
37. *Commissioned Sea Officers*, 339.
38. PRO 30/20/8, letter of G. B. Rodney, on board HMS *Marlborough*, Martinique, 31 January 1762 to Henry Angel, on board *Stag*; PRO 30/20/8 letter of G. B. Rodney, on board *Marlborough*, Martinique, 10 February 1762 [to John Clevland, Secretary of the Admiralty, London].
39. N. A. M. Rodger notes that Angel resigned his commission, although this is not entirely clear from Rodney's letters (*Wooden World*, 80).
40. PRO 30/20/8, letter of G. B. Rodney, on board *Marlborough*, Martinique, 31 January 1762 to Henry Angel, on board *Stag*.
41. *Ibid.*
42. PRO 30/20/8 letter of G. B. Rodney, on board *Marlborough*, Martinique, 10 February 1762 [to John Clevland, Secretary of the Admiralty, London].
43. *Commissioned Sea Officers*, 26.
44. ADM 1/5301 (Orde court martial, 1 February 1762), 1.
45. Lieutenant Archibald Cowan, on board the *Blanche*, to Commodore [Horatio] Nelson, 24 August 1796, in ADM 1/5337 (Sawyer court martial, 18 October

1796), 3–4; Lieutenant Archibald Cowan, on board the *Blanche*, to Captain Charles Sawyer, on board the *Blanche*, 6 September 1796, in ADM 1/5337 (Sawyer court martial, 18 October 1796), 9; Horatio Nelson, Porto Ferrajo, Elba, to Sir Gilbert Elliot, 26 September 1796, in Horatio Nelson, *Dispatches and Letters of Vice Admiral Lord Viscount Nelson*, with notes by Nicholas Harris Nicolas (London: Henry Colburn, 1845) 2: 280–1; Horatio Nelson, Bastia, Corsica, to Admiral Sir John Jervis, 14 October 1796, in *Dispatches and Letters of ... Nelson*, 7: cxxii; Roger Morriss, *Cockburn and the British Navy in Transition: Admiral Sir George Cockburn, 1772–1853* (Columbia, SC: University of South Carolina Press, 1997), 34–6.

46. Lieutenant Archibald Cowan, on board the *Blanche*, to Captain George Cockburn, on board HMS *La Minerve*, 10 September 1796, in ADM 1/5337 (Sawyer court martial, 18 October 1796), 12–13. Cockburn, too, was aware of Sawyer's family connections (Captain George Cockburn, on board *La Minerve*, to Captain Charles Sawyer, on board the *Blanche*, September 10, 1796, in ADM 1/5337 (Sawyer court martial, 18 October 1796), 14–16.
47. The defense is contained in "Paper No. 1" included as part of ADM 1/5337 (Sawyer court martial, 18 October 1796).
48. ADM 1/5337 (Sawyer court martial, 18 October 1796), "Paper No. 1."
49. ADM 1/5337 (Sawyer court martial, 18 October 1796); ADM 12/26 (Sawyer court martial, 18 October 1796), 285–8; ADM 12/27E (Sawyer court martial, 18 October 1796), 183; Jacob Nagle, *The Nagle Journal: A Diary of the Life of Jacob Nagle, Sailor from the Year 1775–1841*, ed. by John C. Dann (New York: Weidenfield and Nicholson 1988), 192, 204; *Commissioned Sea Officers*, 101, 366, 388.
50. Horatio Nelson, Bastia, Corsica, to Admiral Sir John Jervis, 19 October 1796, in *Dispatches and Letters of ... Nelson*, 7: cxxiv.
51. ADM 12/26 (Allen-court martial, 22–4 April 1797), 36; ADM 1/5339 (Allen court martial, 22–4 April 1797), 2–4.
52. *Ibid.*, 4–5.
53. ADM 12/26 (Allen-court martial, 22–4 April 1797), 37–39; ADM 1/5339 (Allen court martial, 22–4 April 1797), 3, 6–7, 14, 18.
54. ADM 12/26 (Allen court martial, 22–4 April 1797), 37, 38; Colledge, *Ships of the Royal Navy*, 283.
55. ADM 12/26 (Allen court martial 22–4 April 1797), 40–41; ADM 1/5339 (Allen court martial, 22–4 April 1797), 1–3, 7–8, 9, 10, 17, 19–20.
56. *Ibid.*, 9.
57. *Ibid.*, 11.
58. *Ibid.*, 11–18.
59. ADM 12/26 (Allen court martial, 22–4 April 1797), 40–1; ADM 1/5339 (Allen court martial, 22–4 April 1797), 1–3, 7–8, 9, 10, 17, 19–20. Allen's execution took place on 22 April 1797 according to *Commissioned Sea Officers*, 4, 82. ADM 51/1298 (HMS *Adventure* log) gives the 15 May date. Dudley Pope, *Life in Nelson's Navy* (Annapolis, MD: Naval Institute Press 1981), 243; A. D. Harvey, "Prosecutions for Sodomy in England at the Beginning of the Nineteenth Century," *Historical Journal*, 21 (1978), 940; Keppel, *Sailor's Life under Four Soverigns* (London: Macmillian, 1899), 1: 55–6.
60. ADM 12/26 (Matson court martial, 18 July 1799), 51; Colledge, *Ships of the Royal Navy*, 100.

61. ADM 12/26 (Matson court martial, 18 July 1799), 51.
62. *Ibid.*, 52.
63. *Ibid.*, 51–2.
64. ADM 1/5383 (William Berry court martial, 2–3 October 1807), 4–5, 8–11, 23, *et passim*.
65. J. B. Hedderwick, The *Captain's Clerk* (London: Hutchinson, 1957), 29.
66. ADM 1/5383 (William Berry court martial, 2–3 October 1807), 8–9. A. D. Harvey, *Sex in Georgian England: Attitudes from the 1720s to the1820s*, (London: Duckworth) 1994, 114. John Nicol wrote of women on board the 74-gun HMS *Goliath* at the Battle of the Nile working as powder monkeys along with the boys. Some of them were wounded during the battle, one succumbed to her injuries, and one bore a son while the battle raged (*Life and Adventures of John Nicol*, ed. by Tim Flannery [Originally published, 1822; New York: Atlantic Monthly Press, 1997], 174–5). Women also worked as powder monkeys or messengers on at least one occasion in the French navy as well (Gordon Taylor, *The Sea Chaplains: A History of the Chaplains of the Royal Navy* [New York: Oxford University Press, 1978], 218); Samuel Leech recorded two children being born on his warship in 1811, although he also voiced his displeasure at having females on board. "A man of war is no place for a woman," he complained (Leech, *Voice from the Main Deck: Being a Record of the Thirty Years'Adventures of Samuel Leech*, intro. by Michael Crawford [Annapolis, MD: Naval Institute Press, 1999], 56–7). At least one sea-going woman apparently agreed with him. John H. Boteler reported a purser's wife hanging herself from a shipboard beam (*Recollections of My Sea Life from 1808–1830*, ed. by David Bonner-Smith, vol. 82, *Publications of the Navy Records Society* [London : Navy Records Society, 1942], 87). James Durand, an American impressed into British service told of a woman on board his ship, the *Vengeance*, who lost an arm to fire from a shore battery during an attack on Stonington, Connecticut in August of 1814 (*An Able Seaman of 1812: His Adventures on* Old Ironsides *and as an Impressed Sailor in the British Navy* [New Haven, CT: Yale University Press, 1926], 77, 119); Chaplain Edward Mangin wrote of a baby born on board HMS *Gloucester* in 1802 (Mangin, "Some Account of the Writer's Situation," in Thursfield, *Five Naval Journals*, 14); Charles McPherson told of nine wives of petty officers on board HMS *Genoa* who tended wounded men in the cockpit during the Battle of Navarino (*Life on board a Man-of-War*, 151–2). Another nautical writer, William N. Glascock wrote of a petty officer's wife on board a warship in one of his humorous essays ([Glascock], *Naval Sketchbook: The Service Afloat and Ashore: With Characteristic Reminiscences, Fragments, and Opinions by a Officer*, new ed. [London: Colburn and Bently, 1831], 1: 30, 88, 93–4, 114–16). For more information on wives sailing on board warships at sea, see Dillon, *Narrative of My Professional Adventures*, 2 vols., ed. by Michael A. Lewis, vol. 93 *Publications of the Navy Records Society* (London: Navy Records Society, 1953), 2: 329–30; J. B. Hedderwick, *Captain's Clerk* (London: Hutchinson, 1957) 38–40, 45, 62, 75–6, 88; Peter Kemp, *The British Sailor: A Social History of the Lower Deck* (London: Dent, 1970), 167–73; Margaret S. Creighton and Lisa Norling, eds., *Iron Men, Wooden Women: Gender and Seafaring in the Atlantic World, 1700–1920* (Baltimore: Johns Hopkins University Press, 1996), 1–33; Old Sailor [Barker, Matthew Henry], *Greenwich Hospital: A Series of Naval*

Sketches Descriptive of the Life of a Man-of-War's Man, by an Old Sailor (London: James Robins, 1826), 31, 69–70.

67. ADM 1/5383 (William Berry court martial, 2–3 October 1807), 5–6, 10–12, 18–19. The term "shaking" also found its way into United States Navy slang by the nineteenth century. See B. R. Burg, *An American Seafarer in the Age of Sail: The Erotic Diaries of Philip C. Van Buskirk, 1851–1870* (New Haven, CT: Yale University Press, 1995), 26, 27.
68. ADM 1/5383 (William Berry court martial, 2–3 October 1807), 8, 17.
69. *Ibid.*, 6.
70. *Ibid.*, 6, 12–14.
71. *Ibid.*, 15–18. William Berry's statement is contained in Appendix B of the trial record.
72. *Ibid.*, 16–18.
73. *Ibid.*, 18–22, Appendix A.
74. *Ibid.*, 18–20, 22, Appendix C.
75. *Ibid.*, 23, Appendix D; Hoffman, *A Sailor of King George*, 146.
76. ADM 1/5383 (William Berry court martial, 2–3 October 1807), 23, Appendix B; *Commissioned Sea Officers*, 32.
77. ADM 12/26 (Blow court martial, 1 January 1780), 209.
78. ADM 12/26 (Sargent court martial, 9 December 1799), 291.

5 Warrant Officers, Petty Officers, and their Boys

1. ADM 12/26 (Falso-Lambert court martial, 3 December 1798), 50, ADM 12/26 (Sawyer court matial, 18 October 1796), 285–8; ADM 1/5337 (Sawyer court martial, 18 October 1796); Jacob Nagle, *The Nagle Journal: A Diary of the Life of Jacob Nagle, Sailor from the Year 1775–1841*, ed. by John C. Dann (New York: Weidenfield and Nicholson, 1988), 192, 204.
2. ADM 1/5266 (Ball-Jones court martial, 9 October 1706); ADM 1/5267 (Coise-Davis court martial, 19 July 1709); ADM 12/26 (Bicks-Booth court martial, 27 June 1757), 13; *Commissioned Sea Officers of the Royal Navy, 1660–1815, ed. by David Syrett and R. L. DiNardo* (Aldershot, UK; VT, USA: Scholar Press, for the Navy Records Society: Ashgate, 1994), 54, 238–9; Samuel Leech, *Voice from the Main Deck: Being a Record of the Thirty Years Adventures of Samuel Leech*, intro. by Michael Crawford (Annapolis, MD: Naval Institute Press, 1999), 56. According to William Spavens, who served during the Seven Years War, warrant officers were hanged from the starboard main yard arm. Ordinary sailors convicted of capital crimes were hanged at a fore yardarm (*The Narrative of William Spavens, a Chatham Pensioner, Written by Himself. A Unique Lower Deck View of the Navy of the Seven Years War* [Orig. pub. 1796; London: Chatham, 1998], 66). In another reference to the place where men were hanged, John Nicol recorded that a marine convicted of allowing crewmembers access to the spirit room was hanged from a fore yardarm (*Life and Adventures of John Nicol*, ed. by Tim Flannery [Orig. pub. 1822; (New York: Atlantic Monthly Press, 1997)], 46–7). Over half a century later, another carpenter, James Hyndman of HM Sloop *Wasp* was found drunk and in bed with one of the boys belonging to the crew. He lost his position as carpenter and was ordered to serve before the mast in 1813. The full record of the proceeding

against him is lost. A surviving summary contains only a half dozen words (ADM 12/27F (77).

3. ADM 1/5301 (Garbut-Pyle court martial, 23 October 1762), 1.
4. ADM 1/5301 (Garbut-Pyle court martial, 23 October 1762), 5.
5. *Ibid.*; Michael A. Lewis, *The Navy in Transition: A Social History 1814–1864* (London: Hodder and Stoughton, 1965), 152.
6. ADM 1/5301 (Garbut-Pyle court martial, 23 October 1762); *Commissioned Sea Officers*, 181; J. J. Colledge, *Ships of the Royal Navy: A Complete Record of the Royal Navy from the Fifteenth Century to the Present* (London: Greenhill Books, 1987), 330.
7. ADM 1/5301 (Garbut court martial, 23 October 1762).
8. *Ibid.*
9. *Ibid.*
10. *Ibid.*
11. ADM 1/5369 (Ambler court martial, 22 April 1805); ADM 12/26 (Ambler court martial, 22 April 1805), 58–71; ADM 1/5376 (Graham court martial, 9 December 1806). *N. A. M. Rodger, The Wooden World: An Anatomy of the Georgian Navy* (London: Collins, 1986), 28–9. In addition to the midshipman and mates who would rise in the naval hierarchy, there were persons in both ranks who although able and experienced held no expectation of ever receiving commissions or warrants (*Ibid.*, 29). *Tisiphone* is referred to in the court martial record as a sloop (ADM 1/5369 [Ambler court martial, 22 April 1805]; 12/26, 58). She is listed as a sixth-rate ship of twenty guns in Colledge's *Ships of the Royal Navy* (351). The reason for the discrepancy is that ships under thirty-two guns, sixth rates by navy regulations, were called sixth rates only when commanded by post-captains. When commanded by lieutenants or commanders they were denominated sloops (*Oxford Companion to Ships and the Sea*, ed. Peter Kemp [New York: Oxford University Press, 1994], 664, 692).
12. ADM 1/5369 (Ambler court martial, 22 April 1805); ADM 12/26 (Ambler court martial, 22 April 1805), 58–9. John Marshall, *Royal Naval Biography Containing Memories of the Flag-Officers, Superannuated Rear-Admirals, Retired-Captains, Post-Captains and Commanders* (London: Longman 1823–1833), 198, 199. The rear admiral was Sir John Sutton. The "lord" in all likelihood was Thomas Cochrane, Earl of Dundonald, who held the rank of captain in 1805 (*Commissioned Sea Officers*, 87, 333, 428). The *Salvador del Mundo* fell into British hands at the Battle of St. Vincent in 1797 (Bernard Ireland, *Naval Warfare in the Age of Sail: War at Sea, 1756–1815* [New York: Norton, 2000], 144).
13. ADM 1/5369 (Ambler court martial, 22 April 1805), 3–4.
14. *Ibid.*, 5. Captain Basil Hall, while not specifying a minimum age for boys, maintained that there was always ample work for them on board a sloop of war (Basil Hall, *Fragments of Voyages and Travels by Captain Basil Hall, RN* [Edinburgh: Cadell, 1833], 50).
15. ADM 1/5369 (Ambler court martial, 22 April 1805), 9.
16. *Ibid.*, 6.
17. *Ibid.*, 7.
18. *Ibid.*, 9.
19. *Ibid.*, 6, 11.
20. *Ibid.*, 11, 12, 13.
21. *Ibid.*, 12, 13, 14.

22. ADM 12/26 (Ambler court martial, 22 April 1805), 70.
23. *Ibid*, 71.
24. ADM 1/5376 (Graham court martial, 9 December 1806), 1, 2, 4, 5; Colledge, *Ships of the Royal Navy*, 149.
25. ADM 1/5376 (Graham court martial, 9 December 1806), 5–8.
26. *Ibid.*, 8.
27. *Ibid.*, 8, 12–17. "Sing out" was the naval jargon for "cry out" (Albert Borowitz, *The Thurtell-Hunt Murder Case; Dark Mirror to Regency England* [Baton Rouge, LA: Louisiana State University Press, 2006], 155).
28. *Ibid.*, 6–7, 11, 13–15; *Commissioned Sea Officers*, 33.
29. ADM 1/5376 (Graham court martial, 9 December 1806), 18–21.
30. *Ibid.*, 8–12.
31. *Ibid.*, 11.
32. *Ibid.*, 12.
33. *Ibid.*, 16–17, 19–21; *Commissioned Sea Officers*, 366.
34. ADM 1/5376 (Graham court martial, 9 December 1806), 22.
35. Markus Eder, *Crime and Punishment in the Royal Navy of the Seven Years' War ... 1755–1763* (Burlington, VT: Ashgate, 2004), 85; J. C. Sainty, compiler, *Admiralty Officials, 1660–1870*, vol. 4, *Office-Holders in Modern Britain* (London: University of London, Institute for Historical Research, 1975), 128.
36. Michael A. Lewis, *A Social History of the Navy 1783–1815* (London: Allen and Unwin, 1948), 240–1; Rodger, *Wooden World*, 20–4, 268. Masters became wardroom officers in the mid eighteenth century, but did not have uniforms until 1787. Their uniforms did not distinguish them from other warrant officers until 1807. In 1808 they were officially ranked as lieutenants, following the lowest commissioned lieutenants in precedence but still outranking surgeons. They were not appointed by commission until 1843 (Lewis, *Navy in Transistion*, 138–9).
37. Patrick O'Brian, *Master and Commander* (Orig. pub. 1970; New York: W. W. Norton, 1990), 197.
38. ADM 1/5390 (McCasky court martial, 29 December 1808), 19–23.
39. *Ibid.*, 26.
40. *Ibid.*, 1–14, 48; William O'Byrne, *A Naval Biographical Dictionary Comprising the Life and Services of Every Living Officer in Her Majesty's Navy* (London: John Murray, 1849), 207.
41. ADM 1/5390 (McCasky court martial, 29 December 1808), 29–38.
42. *Ibid.*, 13–14, 23, 25, 29, 43.
43. *Ibid.*, 38–41, 44–6.
44. *Ibid.*, 44–6.
45. *Ibid.*, 45.
46. *Ibid.*, 45–55.
47. ADM 12/21 (McMahan court martial, 2 January 1798), 211–12.
48. *Ibid.*; Arthur N. Gilbert, "Buggery and the British Navy, 1700–1861," *Journal of Social History*, 10 (Fall 1976), 78.
49. ADM 1/5473 (Maxwell court martial, 2 January 1829), i–iii, 1–2.
50. *Ibid.*, ii–iii, 1–2.
51. *Ibid.*, 3.
52. *Ibid.*, 3–6, 47.
53. *Ibid.*, 7–16.

54. ADM 1/5473 (Maxwell court martial, 2 January 1829), 24–30.
55. *Ibid.*, 16, 29, 30, 42, 58.
56. *Ibid.*, 9, 15, 22, 57, *et passim*.
57. *Ibid.*, 11–14, 24–7, 29, 31.
58. *Ibid.*, 11, 16–18, 21, 26–7, 43, 46–7, 54–6, 58, 62; Rodger, *Wooden World*, 41, 348, 363; Colledge, *Ships of the Royal Navy*, 358.
59. ADM 1/5473 (Maxwell court martial, 2 January 1829), 62.
60. *Ibid.*, iii, 1, 20.
61. *Ibid.*, 34–6, 47–8; N. A. M. Rodger, "Shipboard Life in the Georgian Navy, 1750–1800: The Decline of the Old Order," in *The North Sea: Twelve Essays on Social History of Maritine Labor*, ed. by Lewis R. Fischer, *et al.* (Stavanger, Norway: Stavanger Maritine Museum/Association of North Sea Societies, 1992), 34. See William Blackstone, *Ehrlich's Blackstone*, ed. J. W. Ehrlich (New York: Capricon Books, 1959), 2: 408; Mathew Hale, *Historia Placitorum Coronae: The History of the Pleas of the Crown* (Dublin: E. Lynch, 1778), 1: 628; John McArthur, *A Treatise on the Principles and Practice of Naval Courts-Martial* (London: Longden Whieldon, and Butterworth, 1792), 20–3.
62. ADM 1/5473 (Maxwell court martial, 2 January 1829), 38, 46.
63. *Ibid.*, 48–9.
64. *Ibid.*, 36–38, 48.
65. *Ibid.*, 48.
66. *Ibid.*, 8–16, 38–40, 40–5, 51–62.
67. Anne Gilmour-Bryson, "Sodomy and the Knights Templar," *Journal of the History of Sexuality*, 7 (October 1966), 157–60, 162–6; Rodger, *Wooden World*, 69–71; Carolyn Bingham, "Seventeenth-century Attitudes toward Deviant Sex" 1 *Journal of Interdisciplinary History* (Spring 1971), 447–72.

6 Sodomy, Indecency, and HMS *Africaine*

1. ADM 1/2427 (9 October 1815). Edward Rodney was the youngest son of Admiral George B. Rodney (*Dictionary of National Biography*, eds. Leslie Stephen and Sidney Lee [London: Oxford University Press, 1921–2], 47: 86). Emanuel Cross's name is also given as Cruz in the Beauchamp-Bruce court martial record. His color and origins in Santo Domingo are noted in Beauchamp defense narrative (ADM 1/5453 [Beauchamp-Bruce court martial, 6–15 January 1816], 11, 12, 38, 46, 49); ADM 51 /2086 (*Africaine* log, 8 December 1816).
2. ADM 1/5453, (Crutchley examination, 16 December 1815). Christopher Beauchamp was accused of violating the second article of war numerous times between April 1812 and October of 1815 as well as violating the thirty-fifth article by committing acts prohibited at sea while on shore (ADM 1/1259 [Order for Beauchamp court martial]; ADM 1/5453 [Beauchamp-Bruce court martial, 6–15 January 1816], 25–6). The first lieutenant was probably George Rich Andrews, who died in 1813. He was succeeded as first lieutenant by William Sturgess (ADM 1/1259 [Report on *Africaine* discipline], 2–3, 5–6, 8–10); *Commissioned Sea Officers of the Royal Navy, 1660–1815*, ed. by David Syrett and R. L. DiNardo (Aldershot, UK: Scolar Press, for the Navy Records Society; VT, USA: Ashgate, 1994), 7.
3. ADM 1/1259 (Report on *Africaine* discipline), 4–5, 10–11, 13, 16–17.

4. *Ibid.*, 3–4, 5–6, 10, 13–14, 16.
5. ADM 1/2427 (9, 11, 13 October 1815; 2, 3 November 1815; 5 December 1815), 1–16 *passim*. Jean's given name is Frank in ADM 1/2427 (9 October, 2 November 1815), but he is entered as Francisco Jean when testifying against James Bruce and Christopher Beauchamp (ADM 1/5453 [Beauchamp–Bruce court martial, 6–15 January 1816], 7, 19). His non-British origins and imperfect English are also noted in the Beauchamp-Bruce court martial record (ADM 1/5453, 2, 7, 19, 25) and in Beauchamp's defense narrative (ADM 1/5453, 46). Gilbert claims he spoke Italian (Arthur N. Gilbert, The *Africaine* Courts-Martial: A Study of Buggery in the Royal Navy, *Journal of Homosexuality* 1 [1974]: 111–12), but Portuguese is more likely (ADM 1/5453 [Beauchamp-Bruce court martial, 6–15 January 1816], 7, 19; ADM 1/5453 [Tall-Treake court martial, 2–4 January 1816], 15).
6. N. A. M. Rodger, *The Wooden World: An Anatomy of the Georgian Navy* (London: Collins, 1986), 188–204, 348–51; John Tapson, "John Tapson Journal," 1 January 1812, 24 July 1814. William L. Clements Library, University of Michigan, Ann Arbor, Michigan. Seraco places the number of crewmen at 250 (ADM 1/5453 [Charles-Seraco court martial, 1–2 January 1816], 14). The *Africaine* had been captured from the French in the Mediterranean by HMS *Phoebe* in 1801, but she may have been retaken by the French and then recaptured by the British (J. J. Colledge, *Ships of the Royal Navy: A Complete Record of the Royal Navy from the Fifteenth Century to the Present* (London: Greenhill Books, 1987), 24. See also Brain Vale, *A Frigate of King George: Life and Duty on a British Man of War, 1807–1829* (London: I. B. Tauris, 2001), 44.
7. ADM 1/5354 (Parsons 2nd court martial, 16 January 1816), 1, 5, 8.
8. ADM 1/2427, *passim* (ADM 51/2086 (*Africaine* log, 8 December 1815); ADM 1/5453 (Beauchamp-Bruce court martial, 6–15 January 1806), 2, 21. The number of men in several of the job classifications can shift slightly, for some men are sometimes listed in different employments from one document to the next. Slight variations from document to document also exist for the given names of some of the men. The same mariner, for example, might be identified as both James and John, depending on the source.
9. ADM 1/2427 (13 October 1815); Gilbert, "*Africaine*," 113.
10. ADM 1/2427 (13 October 1815); Gilbert, "*Africaine*," 113.
11. ADM 1/2427 *passim*.
12. *Ibid.*, 9 October, 2 November, 5 December 1815; ADM 1/5453 (Charles-Seraco court martial, 1–2 January 1816), 8.
13. ADM 1/1259 (Edward Thornborough, *Queen Charlotte*, Portsmouth, to J[ohn] W[ilson] Coker, Secretary of the Admiralty, [London], 3 January 1816); ADM 1/1259 (Order 3 for court martial of Rafaelo Seraco); ADM 1/2427 (9, 11 October, 2 November 1815); ADM 1/5453 (Charles-Seraco court martial, 1–2 January 1816), 8; ADM 1/5453 (Seraco-Treake court martial, 22 January 1816), [33].
14. ADM 1/2427, 9, 11 October, 2 November, 5 December 1815; ADM 1/5453 (Hubbard examination, 15 December 1815), 1, 3–4; ADM 1/5453 (Tall-Treake court martial, 2–4 January 1816), 5; ADM 1/5453 (Hubbard-Treake court martial, 5 January 1816), 2, 15; ADM 1/2086 (*Africaine* log, 8 December 1815); Gilbert, "*Africaine*," 112. Occasionally, boys worked as messengers rather than having specific assignments to officers or midshipmen (Robert Mercer Wilson,

"Remarks on Board His Majesty's Ship *Unité* of 40 Guns," in H. G. Thursfield, ed., *Five Naval Journals.1789–1817*, vol. 91, *Publications of the Navy Records Society* (London: Navy Records Society, 1951), 249).

15. ADM 1/5453 (Hubbard examination, 15 December 1815), 1–2.
16. ADM 1/2427 (2 November 1815); ADM 1/5453 (Hubbard examination, 15 December 1815).
17. ADM 1/5453 (Hubbard-Treake court martial, 5 January 1816), 7–8.
18. ADM 1/2427 (9 October, 2 November 1815); ADM 1/5453 (Seraco-Treake court martial, 22 January 1816), 12, 16.
19. ADM 1/2427 (13 October 1815).
20. ADM 1/5453 (Tall-Treake court martial, 2–4 January 1816), 11–12.
21. *Ibid.* ADM 1/2427 (9, 11 October 1815).
22. *Ibid.* (11, 13 October, 3 November 1815).
23. *Ibid.* (13 October, 3 November 1815). When he gave testimony against Bruce, Beauchamp, Treake, and Tall, Jean was identified at least three times as a cook's mate or undercook (ADM 1/5453 [Beauchamp-Bruce court martial, 6–15 January 1806], 2, 21; ADM 1/5453 [Tall-Treake court martial, 2–4 January 1816], 3).
24. ADM 1 /2427(11 October 1815).
25. *Ibid.* (2 November 1815); ADM 1/5453 (Hubbard examination, 15 December 1815), 2, 4.
26. *Ibid.*, 4.
27. *Ibid.*
28. ADM 1/5453 (Beauchamp-Bruce court martial, 6–15 January 1816), 20.
29. ADM 1/1259 (Edward Thornborough, *Queen Charlotte*, Portsmouth, to J. W. Coker, Secretary of the Admiralty, [London], 3 January 1816); ADM 1/5453 (Tall-Treake court martial, 5 January 1816), 2, 5–6, 7, 9, 11–12; ADM 1/5453 (Seraco-Treake court martial, 22 January 1816), 30.
30. Gilbert, "*Africaine*", 115–16; ADM 1/5453 (Charles-Seraco court martial, 1–2 January 1816), 5–7; ADM 1/5453 (Hubbard-Treake court martial, 5 January 1816, 2, 10); ADM 1/5453 (Tall-Treake court martial, 2–3 January 1816), 2–4, 6, 10.
31. ADM 1/2427,1–16; ADM 1/5354 (Parsons 2nd court martial, 16 January 1816), 12; ADM 1/5453 (Charles-Seraco court martial, 1–2 January 1816), 2, 3, 5–6; ADM 1/5453 (Treake-Hubbard court martial, 2–4 January 1816), 2–3, 4, 5, 7, 8–9, 10; ADM 1/5453 (Tall-Treake court martial, 5 January 1816), 2–3, 6–7, 16; ADM 1/5453 (Seraco-Treake court martial, 22 January 1816), [2–3, 7–8, 17, 18, 22–6, 29, 38]; Gilbert, "*Africaine,*" 115–16
32. ADM 1/5453 (Tall-Treake court martial, 2–4 January 1816), 9, 16; ADM 1/5453 (Hubbard-Treake court martial, 5 January 1816), 4–6; ADM 1/5453 (Seraco-Treake court martial, 22 January 1816), 32, 34–5. James Harris, the *Africaine*'s carpenter explained to one court martial that the billboard was never actually shipped, but that the stop for it was eleven inches wide and anyone on it could hang onto the chains (ADM 1/5453 [Hubbard-Treake court martial, 5 January 1816], 9). Presumably, with a base almost a foot wide and using the fore chains for handholds, two men could engage in buggery with a measure of privacy and without the danger of falling into the sea, at least in calm weather.
33. ADM 1/5453 (Tall–Treake court martial, 2–4 January 1816), 8, 12. On recognition signs and signals, see Nicholas C. Edsall, *Towards Stonewall: Homosexuality*

and Society in the Modern Western World (Charlottesville, VA: University of Virginia Press, 2003), 8.

34. ADM 1/5453 (Parsons 2nd court martial, 16 January 1816), 12–14.
35. ADM 1/5453 (Tall-Treake court martial, 2–4 January 1816), 4; ADM 1/5453 (Hubbard-Treake court martial, 5 January 1816), 4–5, 10; ADM 1/5453 (Seraco-Treake court martial, 22 January 1816), [25–6, 37]; ADM 1/5453 (Beauchamp-Bruce court martial, 6–15 January 1806), 22.
36. ADM 51/2086 (*Africaine* log, 8 December 1815).
37. Michael A. Lewis, *The Navy in Transition: A Social History 1814–1864*, (London: Hodder and Stoughton, 1965), 63–71; George Peard, *To the Pacific and Arctic with Beechey: The Journal of Lt. George Peard of HMS* Blossom, *1825–1828*, ed. Barry M. Gough (Cambridge: Cambridge University Press, 1973), 5–6; Margarette Lincoln, *Representing the Royal Navy: British Sea Power* (Burlington, VT: Ashgate, 2002), 186, 189.
38. Gilbert, "*Africaine,*" 113–14; Colledge, *Ships of the Royal Navy*, 279.
39. Gilbert, "*Africaine,*" 113–14.
40. ADM 1/5453 (Crutchley examination, 16 December 1815), 1.
41. ADM 1/2427 (13 October 1815).
42. ADM 1/5453 (Tall-Treake court martial, 2–4 January 1816), 5; ADM 1/5453 (Hubbard-Treake court martial, 5 January 1816), 2.
43. *Ibid.*, 2.
44. ADM 1/5453 (Crutchley examination, 16 December 1815); ADM 51/2086 (*Africaine* log, 1 February 1816); Gilbert, *Africaine*, 119.
45. ADM 1/5453 (Crutchley examination, 16 December 1815); Gilbert, *Africaine*, 119.
46. ADM 1/5453 (Seraco-Treak court martial, 22 January 1816), 30–2, 35–6; ADM 1/5453 (Parsons 2nd court martial, 16 January 1816), 15–16.
47. ADM 1/2427 (13 October 1815).
48. ADM 1/5354 (Parsons 2nd court martial, 16 January 1816), 2; ADM 1/ 5453 (Beauchamp-Bruce court martial, 6–15 January 1806), 7.
49. ADM 1/5453 (Parsons 2nd court martial, 16 January 1816), 9–10.
50. Gilbert, "*Africaine,*" 115; ADM 1/5453 (Bruce-Beauchamp court martial, 6–15 January 1806), 12–20. Cross spent eight weeks in irons at one point in the cruise for "having done something with a soldier [William Dane, actually a marine] at Trincomalee." He was charged with "having pulled down the trousers of the soldiers [*sic*] (ADM 1/5453 [Beauchamp-Bruce court martial, 6–15 January 1806], 25–6); ADM 1/5453 (Charles-Seraco court martial, 1–2 January 1816), 20.
51. Gilbert, "*Africaine,*" 114–15, 119; ADM 1/5453 (Charles-Seraco court martial, 1–2 January 1816), 8; ADM 1/5453 (Hubbard-Treak court martial, 5 January 1816), 10–11. A claim by Cross that he had been offered a pardon was vehemently denied by several witnesses (ADM 1/5453 [Beauchamp-Bruce court martial, 6–15 January 1806], 26–31). In the several pages cited with the number 29, the National Archives number for the Beauchamp-Bruce court martial changes from ADM 1/5453 to ADM 1/5354. The remainder of the documents can be found under ADM 1/5354.
52. Beauchamp is listed as a midshipman most often in the records of the case (ADM 1 /2427 [3 November 1815]; ADM 1/5354 [Broome statement]), although one document identifies him as a master's mate (ADM 1/5453

[Beauchamp-Bruce court martial, 6–15 January 1806], 1). Beauchamp identifies himself at separate locations as both a midshipman and a master's mate in his defense narrative (ADM 1/5453 [Beauchamp defense narrative], 49, 54, 55). The two were not mutually exclusive, one being a rank and the other a job title, and distinctions between the two might have been slight, blurred, or non-existent in terms of pay, privileges, messing, and quartering arrangements on board a smaller ship like the *Africaine* (Lewis, *Navy in Transition*, 158–9). Bruce is classified as a midshipman in every reference to his rank.

53. ADM 1/5453 (Beauchamp–Bruce court martial, 6–15 January 1806), 3.
54. Lewis, *Navy in Transition*, 158, 165.
55. ADM 1/5453 (Beauchamp-Bruce court martial, 6–15 January 1806), 4–6, 7.
56. *Ibid.*, 12–27.
57. ADM 1/5453 (Beauchamp defense narrative), 1–2.
58. *Ibid.*, 3.
59. *Ibid.*, 8.
60. *Ibid.*, 49.
61. *Ibid.*, 26–7.
62. *Ibid.*, 22, 50–1, 54–5. Greetham was Deputy Judge Advocate of the Fleet from 6 November 1804 to 23 July 1831 (J. C. Sainty, compiler, *Admiralty Officials, 1660–1870*, vol. 4, *Office-Holders in Modern Britain*, London: University of London, Institute for Historical Research, 1975), 128.
63. ADM 1/5453 (Beauchamp defense narrative), 58–9.
64. *Ibid.*, 59–60.
65. *Ibid.*, 60–4; ADM 1/5453 (Bruce defense narrative) 2–3; ADM 1/5354 (Broome statement); ADM 1/5354 (Beauchamp-Bruce court martial, 6–15 January 1806), unnumbered sheet at end of document.
66. Lincoln, *Representing the Royal Navy*, 3–4, 20–1, 36, 151, 152.
67. ADM 1/5354 (Beauchamp-Bruce court martial, 6–15 January 1806), 36.
68. Gilbert, "*Africaine*," 111–13, 115–19; ADM 1/5453 (Charles-Seraco court martial, 2 January 1816, 3, 14), 3, 14; ADM 1/5453 (Hubbard-Treak court martial, 5 January 1816), 11–12; ADM 1/5453 (Tall–Treak court martial, 2–4 January 1816), 1, 17 [misnumbered as 7]; ADM 1/5453 (Seraco-Treak court martial, 22 January 1816), *passim*. Treak would have been condemned to death a third time in his trial with Hubbard, but the court, knowing that he already had garnered two death sentences deemed a third mere wasted effort (ADM 1/5453 [Hubbard-Treak court martial, 5 January 1816], 11).
69. ADM 1/5453 (Tall-Treak court martial, 2–4 January 1816), unnumbered fourth preliminary page to court martial record.
70. ADM 51/2086 (*Africaine* log).
71. ADM 1/1259 (Edward Thornborough, *Queen Charlotte*, Portsmouth,to J. W. Coker, Secretary of the Admiralty, 1 February 1816 [London]).
72. ADM 1/1259 (Edward Thornborough, *Queen Charlotte*, Portsmouth, to J. W. Coker, Secretary of the Admiralty, [London], 3 February 1816); ADM 1/1259 (Report on *Africaine* discipline), 1–2, 6–8, 11–12, 14–19; The three captains were Robert Alexander, William Bowles, and Alexander Renton Sharpe (ADM 1/1259 [Report on *Africaine* discipline], 21).
73. Colledge, *Ships of the Royal Navy*, 24.

7 The Last Sex Court Martial

1. Brain Vale, *A Frigate of King George: Life and Duty on a British Man of War, 1807–1829*, 121.
2. ADM 1/5473 (Maxwell court martial, 2 January 1829); ADM 1/5484 (Morgan court martial, 2–4 April 1838); ADM 1/5478 (McGee–Peach court martial, 17 July 1832). See also Chapter 5. Parliament removed sodomy from the list of capital crimes in 1861.
3. ADM 1/5484 (Morgan court martial, 2–4 April 1838), 6, 8.
4. *Ibid.*, 6, 14.
5. *Ibid.*, 58, 62, 65, 66. Frere's promotion to lieutenant came in May of 1838 (William O'Byrne, *Naval Biographical Dictionary Comprising the Life and Services of Every Living Officer in Her Majesty's Navy* (London: John Murray, 1849), 381).
6. ADM 1/5484 (Morgan court martial, 2–4 April 1838), ii, 6, 60, 62, 64, 65, 68; O'Byrne, *Naval Biographical Dictionary*, 782.
7. ADM 1/5484 (Morgan court martial, 2–4 April 1838), 7, 8, 15, 16, 12, 18, 19, 39, 48, 49, 59, 60, 61, 63, 64, 77, *et passim*; J. J. Colledge, *Ships of the Royal Navy: A Complete Record of the Royal Navy from the Fifteenth Century to the Present* (London: Greenhill Books, 1987), 260; N. A. M. Rodger, *The Wooden World: An Anatomy of the Georgian Navy*, (London: Collins, 1986), 348–9.
8. ADM 1/5484 (Morgan court martial, 2–4 April 1838), 7, 15–16, 39–40, 53, 54.
9. *Ibid.*, 7, 15, 16, 55, 56, 57. Midshipman John Boyd later claimed D'arcy told him Morgan's first act of indecency occurred on the voyage out from England. Lieutenant James Charles Prevost agreed that Morgan's indelicate act took place on a gangway, but he was not certain whether it was the port or starboard gangway (*Ibid.*, 18, 48).
10. *Ibid.*, 63–4.
11. *Ibid.*, 8, 77.
12. *Ibid.*, 16–17, 24, 54, 56–7, 76. Four years after the Morgan court martial, Prevost would wed Ellen Mary Moresby, the daughter of his captain during the years he served on board the *Pembroke* (O'Byrne, *Naval Biographical Dictionary*, 925).
13. ADM 1/5484 (Morgan court martial, 2–4 April 1838), 16. The correct date for the letter was more likely 31 March 1838 (*Ibid.*, 76).
14. *Ibid.*, 60–1.
15. *Ibid.*, 29, 30, 37, 39, 45, 62, 64–5, 69, 89.
16. *Ibid.*, 43,
17. *Ibid.*, 9–10, 20, 21–2, 25, 41–3, 44, 50, 51, 52, 53–4, 61–2, 68–9. Boyd had not yet become a passed midshipman in 1838. He did not successfully complete his examinations until the following year (O'Byrne, *Naval Biographical Dictionary*, 78).
18. ADM 1/5484 (Morgan court martial, 2–4 April 1838), 11, 28, 42, *et passim*.
19. *Ibid.*, 42.
20. *Ibid.*, 41–2.
21. *Ibid.*, 41.
22. *Ibid.*, 42–3.
23. *Ibid.*, 13–14, 28, 30, *et passim*; Lieutenant Richard Morgan, *Pembroke* to Captain Fairfax Moresby, *Pembroke*, 25 March 1838 in ADM 1/5484 (Morgan court martial, 2–4 April 1838), 3.

24. Byrne lists the admiral as Robert not Richard Stopford (*Naval Biographical Dictionary*, 1127).
25. Fairfax Moresby, *Pembroke* to Richard Stopford, *Princess Charlotte*, 26 March 1838; Richard Stopford, *Princess Charlotte*, to Fairfax Moresby, *Pembroke*, 27 March 1838; Fairfax Moresby, *Pembroke*, to Richard Stopford, *Princess Charlotte*, undated [27 or 28 March 1838] all in ADM 1/5484 (Morgan court martial, 2–4 April 1838), 3–5.
26. *Ibid.*, 1–5, 31–2.
27. *Ibid.*, 33–4, 35, 38, 43, 78–9.
28. *Ibid.*, 17, 21, 25, 27–8, 33, 35, 36, 38, 43, 51, 53–4, 57, 78–9.
29. *Ibid.*, 73, 75, 82–3, 88, 90–2, 93–4, 95.
30. *Ibid.*, 84.
31. *Ibid.*, 79–80.
32. *Ibid.*, 86–7, 93, 94; O'Byrne, *Naval Biographical Dictionary*, 352.
33. ADM 1/5484 (Morgan court martial, 2–4 April 1838), 74–7, 81, *et passim*.
34. *Ibid.*, 77–8, 88–9, 90–2, 95.
35. *Ibid.*, iv, 96.
36. Henry Baynham, *From the Lower Deck: The Old Navy, 1780–1840* (London: Hutchinson, 1969), 116. As N. A. M. Roger suggests, a word of caution is always in order when evaluating officers' characterizations of their crews. The depth of knowledge on the subject is neither wide nor deep ("Shipboard Life In The Georgian Navy, 1750–1800: The Decline Of The Old Order," in *The North Sea: Twelve Essays on Social History of Martime Labor*, ed. Lewis R. Fischer, *et al.* (Stavanger, Norway: Stavanger Maritime Museum/ Association of North Sea Societies, 1992), 30).
37. Edward Mangin, "Some Account of the Writer's Situation as a Chaplain in the British Navy," in H. G. Thursfield, ed., *Five Naval Journals, 1789–1817*, vol. 91, *Publications of the Navy Record Society* (London: Navy Records Society, 1951), 9.
38. John Cremer, *Ramblin' Jack: The Journal of Captain John Cremer, 1770–1774*, ed. R. Reynell Bellamy (London: Johathan Cape, 1936), 41; William Henry Dillon, *A Narrative of My Professional Adventures (1790–1839)*, ed. Michael A. Lewis, vol. 93, *Publications of the Navy Records Society* (London: Navy Records Societey, 1953), 1: 14,214–15; 1: 14, 214–15; M. D. Hay, *Landsman Hay: The Memoirs of Robert Hay, 1789–1847* (London: Rupert Hart-Davis, 1953), 37–8, 51, 60, 124; Isaac Land, "Domesticating the Maritime: Culture, Masculinity and Empire in Britain, 1770–1820" (Ph. D. diss., University of Michigan), 1999, 22; Margarette Lincoln, *Representing the Royal Navy: British Sea Power, 1750–1815* (Burlington, VT: Ashgate, 2002), 22, 152–5; Samuel Leech, *Voice from the Main Deck: Being a Record of the Thirty Years Adventures of Samuel Leech*, intro. by Michael Crawford (Annapolis, MD: Naval Intitute Press, 1999), 16, 36, 47, 70, 86, 102–3; [Charles McPherson], *Life on Board a Man–of–War, Including A Full Account of the Battle of Navarino, by a British Seaman* (Glasgow: Blackie Fullerton, 1829), 22; Robert M. Wilson, "Remarks on Board His Majesty's Ship *Unité* of 40 Guns," in Thursfield, *Five Naval Journals* 131–2, 144. The same situation prevailed on board American ships during in the late eighteenth century. See Jesse Lemish, "Jack Tar in the Streets: Merchant Seamen in the Politics of Revolutionary America," *William and Mary Quarterly* 25 (July 1968): 371–2.

39. ADM 1/5382 (Sand court martial, 10 July 1807); Cremer, *Ramblin' Jack*, 53; James Morrison, *The Journal Of James Morrison, Boatswain's Mate of the Bounty, Describing The Mutiny and Subsequent Misfortunes of the Mutineers, Together with an Account of the Island of Tahiti* (Waltham St. Lawernce, UK[?], Golden Cockerel Press, 1935), 9–10, 19, 37, 41; J. B. Hedderwick, *Captain's Clerk* (London: Hutchinson, 1957), 69; William Richardson, *Mariner of England: An Account of the Career of William Richardson from Cabin Boy to the Merchant Service to Warrant Officer in the Royal Navy as Told by Himself*, ed. by Spencer Childers. (London: John Murray, 1908), 200.
40. Mangin, "Some Account of the Writer's Situation," in Thursfield, 8, 11, 14, 17, 18, 37. Mangin's complaints about officers were shared by other seagoing clergymen, and the socially and spiritually debilitating atmosphere for men of God, combined with the insalubrious conditions on board ships, surely discouraged men from taking up naval service. Not only were the accommodations for chaplains uncomfortable and mess arrangements beneath what men of the cloth thought they deserved, but chaplains endured humiliation even when carrying out bodily functions. A seventeenth–century wag writing in the fashion of Swift articulated the complaints of naval parsons in a poem where a ship's cleric, while acknowledging he must dine separately from his superiors in rank, begs permission of the lieutenants to be allowed to use the commissioned officers' toilet located aft at the quarter gallery:

> You that can grant or can refuse the power
> Low from the stern to drop the golden shower,
> ... ...
> E'r taught the difference, to commissions due,
> Presumptuous I aspired to mess with you:
> But since the difference known 'twixt sea and shore,
> That mighty happiness I urge no more,
> An humble boon and of a different kind,
> (Grant heaven a different answer it may find)
> Attends you now – excuse the rhyme I write,
> And tho' I mess not with you – let me sh-te ([Anon.], "A Sea Chaplain's Petition to the Lieutenants in the Ward-Room for the Use of the Quarter Gallery," in *The Annual Register, or a View of the History, Politics, and Literature of the Year 1758* [London: J. Dodsley, 1759], 442).

The cleric went on to explain his humiliation of one ordained by the Church of England having to share a "house of office" with those of lower station:

> And if my Muse can aught of truth divine,
> The boon the Muse petitions shall be mine:
> For sure this answer would be monstrous odd,
> Sh-te with the common tars, thou man of God. (*Ibid.*, 443)

When William Nelson sought an appointment as a ship's chaplain in 1781, his famous brother Horatio discouraged him. "As to my real opinion" he wrote, "whether or not you will like it, I say as I always did, that it is five to one you will not (being a Navy Chaplain)." At another point he wrote, explaining, "I hope you have lost all ideas of going to sea, for the more I see of chaplains of men of war, the more I dread seeing my brother in such a disagreeable station in life." (Gordon Taylor, *The Sea Chaplains: A History of the Chaplains of the Royal Navy* (New York: Oxford University Press, 1978), 187–8).

Often navy chaplains were men who could not secure appointments ashore. Admiral John Jervis complained in the early 1790s to both the Admiralty and the Archbishop of Canterbury about "roué parsons" who should not be in the navy. Yet for a few the service had at least some attraction. A number of clerics joined ships fitting out, took leave before they sailed, and collected their wages while their floating parishes were at sea (Waldo E. L. Smith, *The Navy and Its Chaplains in the Age of Sail* [Toronto: Ryerson, 1961], 98; Taylor, *Sea Chaplains*, 170, 187–8, 220). Thomas Masterman Hardy, of Trafalgar fame, complained in 1801 that if the chaplain of his ship HMS *Isis* did not report on board he could no longer carry him on the books (A. M. Broadley and R. G. Bartelot, *Nelson's Hardy: His Life, Letters, and Friends* [London: John Murray, 1909], 82); Those who actually sailed could not have found the labors demanded of them particularly arduous. Often the question was asked among naval men, "Who does the least work in the ship – the chaplain or the captain of marines?" (Taylor, *Sea Chaplains*, 180).

Complaints about the dearth of chaplains in the navy dated back at least to the tenure of Samuel Pepys as Secretary of the Admiralty in the seventeenth century. Still, no provisions for recruiting chaplains were made. Throughout the eighteenth century they were hired by captains who desired their presence. Chaplains received the same wages as seamen, though they supplemented their incomes with the involuntary contributions crewmen were forced to pay for their support. After the wages of sailors were raised following the mutinies in 1797, the increase did not extend to naval clerics. When the influence of evangelicals began to take hold, the situation of chaplains improved. By the turn of the century they were allowed to mess with the officers on some ships, and in 1806 the navy provided its first job description for chaplains in the new *Regulations and Instructions* adopted that year. At about this time, they were also allowed to supplement their pay £20 per year by serving as schoolmasters. In 1812 the Admiralty established regular pay and pension systems for chaplains, regularized their appointments to ships, created an administrative structure for superintending their work, and began actively to recruit them. Even with an increased pay scale, official recognition, improved living conditions, and the 1824 regulation making them the equals in rank (though subordinate to lieutenants), there was no rush of qualified men to join the fleet. Despite the restricted number of openings for clergyman on land during the late Georgian and early Victorian eras, recruiting chaplains for the Royal Navy remained always a difficult business (Richard Charles Blake, "Aspects of Religion in the Royal Navy, 1770–1870" [M. Phil. diss., University of Southampton], 6, 15, 19, 78, 103, 130–5; A. G. Kealy, *Chaplains of the Royal Navy, 1626–1903* [Portsmouth: Wilkins and Son, (1905?)], 5, 8, 14, 19, 22, 25; Smith, *Navy and Its Chaplains*, 67, 71, 111–12, 127–8, 135; Taylor, *Sea Chaplains*, 147, 169–70, 221, 230–3, 237–41). It was not until 1843 that chaplains received appointment by commission rather than by warrant. They officially acquired uniforms only in 1940. (*Ibid.*, 230, 262).

41. *Regulations and Instructions Relating to His Majesty's Service at Sea, Established by His Majesty in Council*, 9th ed. (London: s. n., 1757), 46; John D. Byrn, *Crime and Punishment in the Royal Navy: Discipline on the Leeward Islands Station, 1784–1812* (Aldershot, UK: Scolar, 1989), 149; Marge Darby, *What Caused the Mutiny on the Bounty* (Sidney: Angus and Robertson, 1965), 10, 43; Lincoln, *Representing the Royal Navy*, 22, 152–5; Spavens, *The Narrative of William Spavens, a Chatham Pensioner, Written by Himself: A Unique Lower Deck View of the Navy of the Seven Years War* (Orig. pub. 1796; London: Chatham, 1998), 4; John Nicol, *The Life and Adventures of John Nicol*, ed. by Tim Flannery (Org. pub., 1822; New York: Atlantic Monthly Press, 1997) 5, 28, *et passim*.
42. [William Nugent Glascock], *Naval Sketchbook: or the Service Afloat and Ashore with Characteristic Reminiscences, Fragments, and Opinions by an Officer*, (New ed.; London: Colburn and Bently), 1: 143.
43. Land, "Domesticating the Maritime," 249, 254.
44. Blake, "Aspects of Religion in the Royal Navy," 12, 94–101; William P. Cumby, "Orders and Regulations for the Government and Discipline of His Majesty's Ship *Hyperion*, William Pryce Cumby, Captain," in Thursfield, *Five Naval Journals, passim*; Dillon, *Narrative of My Professional Adventures*, 1: 95, 96, 97; Roald Kverndal, *Seamens' Missions: Their Origin and Early Growth: A Contribution to the Church Maritime* (Pasadena, CA: William Carey, 1986), 105; Jeffrey Raigersfeld, *The Life of a Sea Officer*, ed. L. G. Carr-Laughton (London: Cassell, 1929), 11, 81; William Richardson, *A Mariner of England: An Account of the Career of William Richardson from Cabin Boy to the Merchant Service to Warrant Officer in the Royal Navy as Told by Himself*, ed. by Spencer Childers (London: John Murray,1908), 105–6; Waldo, *Navy and Its Chaplains*, 89–90.
45. ADM 1/5484 (Morgan court martial, 2–4 April 1838), iv. 74, 75, 96. For only a smattering of the mass of material available on the role of influence in naval careers, see Thomas Cochrane, *Autobiography of a Seaman* (London: Richard Bentley, 1860), 2: 138, 260–3; Dillon, *Narrative of My Professional Adventures*, 5, 15, 150; Hedderwick, *Captain's Clerk*, 69–70, 90–1; Richardson, *Mariner of England*, 128; Thursfield, "Introduction" to Charles Abbot, "Journal of a Voyage to China in HMS *Alceste* Kept by Charles Abbot, Midshipman," in Thursfield, *Five Naval Journals*, 278; Roger Morriss, *Cockburn and the British Navy in Transition: Admiral Sir George Cockburn 1772–1853* (Columbia, SC: University of South Carolina Press, 1997), 11, 28, 38, 176, 218; N. A. M. Rodger, "Honor and Duty at Sea 1660–1815," *Historical Research*, 75 (2002) 441; Rodger, "Officers, Gentlemen, and their Educations, 1793–1860," in *Les Empires in Guerre et Paix*, ed. by. Edward Freeman (Vincennes: Service Historique de la Marine, 1990), 140, 143; Rodger, "Shipboard Life, in the Georgian Navy, 1750–1800: The Decline of the Old Order," in *The North Sea: Twelve Essays on Social History of Maritime Labor*, ed. by Lewis R. Fischer, *et al.* (Stavanger, Norway: Stavanger Maritime Museum/Association of North Sea Societies, 1992), 32–3. Even John Harvey Boteler, a well-connected Tory boasting a distinguished naval ancestry, found himself unable to get a ship when a Whig ministry rose to power. His brother, the only Whig in the family, had no comparable difficulty (Boteler, *Recollections of My Sea Life*, 248). For information on the courts martial of Richardson and Cleghorn, see Thursfield, "Introduction" to Wilson, "Remarks on Board," in Thursfield, *Five Naval Journals*, 125–6.

46. Olive Anderson, "The Growth of Christian Militarism in Mid-Victorian Britain," *English Historical Review*, 86 (January 1971): 46–73; Kverndal, *Seamens' Missions*, 12–13, 25; Taylor, *Sea Chaplains*, 233, 267.
47. Kverndal, *Seamens' Missions*, 30, 71, 80–90, 105, 109, 124, 129, 154, 297, 340–6. It was not only officers who saw benefits in the new religious influence in the navy. It also improved living and working conditions for the ratings (Rodger, "Shipboard Life," 34–6). There was a close connection in the thinking of evangelicals between improving the morals of mariners and suppressing the slave trade (Frederick C. Leiner, *The End of Barbary Terror: America's 1815 War Against the Pirates of North Africa* [New York: Oxford University Press, 2006], 161–171).
48. Blake, "*Aspects of Religion in the Royal Navy*" 10, 14, 20, 21, 34, 103, 194–5; Kverndal, *Seamens' Missions*, 102, 109, 285–90, 308, 717, 815; *Commissioned Sea Officers*, 299.
49. Christians zealous for propagating the faith also published books intended to assist sailors with their devotions such as *The Seaman's Devotional Assistant* (1821) and *The Sailor's Hymn Book* the following year. Between 1820 and 1826 at least four magazines appeared that intended to appeal to sailors' spirituality. (Blake, "Aspects of Religion in the Royal Navy," 22, 278–9, 306–25).
50. Old Quartermaster [Bechervaise], *Thirty-six Years of a Seafaring Life* (Portsea, UK: Woodward, 1839), 114; Blake, "Aspects of Religion in the Royal Navy," iii, 11, 16, 17, 20, 47, 76, 80, 81, 161–2, 240, 264; Peter Cullen, *Memoirs of Peter Cullen, Esq.*, in Thursfield, *Five Naval Journals*, 58; [Glascock], *Naval Sketchbook*, 2:151–8, 159–60, 165; Kverndal, *Seamens' Missions*, 107, 130–1, 132, 232–3, 265, 364–71, Leech, *Voice from the Main Deck*, 80; Lincoln, *Representing the Royal Navy*, 22, 109, 118, 132, 193, 198; Land, "Domesticating the Maritime," 27, 243; [McPherson], *Life on board a Man-of-War*, 47; Jacob Nagle, *The Nagle Journal: A Diary of the Life of Jacob Nagle, Sailor, from the Year 1775–1841*, ed. by John C. Dann (New York: Weidenfield and Nicholson, 1988), xxiii–xxiv; Charles Pemberton, *The Autobiography of Pel. Verjuice*, ed. by Eric Partridge (London : Scolartis, 1929), 223; Rodger, "Honor and Duty at Sea," 445–6; Wilson, "Remarks on board", in Thursfield, *Five Naval Journals*, 58, 123, 140, 177, 187–8. The missionary zeal which so affected the navy throughout the nineteenth century was also being expended with equal enthusiasm on the British army during the same period (Anderson, "Growth of Christian Militarism" *passim*. See also, Jane Samson, "The 1834 Cruise of the HMS Alligator: The Bible and the Flag," *The Northern Mariner/La Marin Du Nord* 3 (October 1993), 46.
51. Randolph Trumbach, *Sex and the Gender Revolution*, vol. 1, *Hetrosexualilty and the Third Gender in Enlightenment London* (Chicago: University of Chicago Press, 1998), 24–6, 30–1.
52. ADM 1/5397 (Colquhoun-Fleming court martial, 23 June 1809).
53. ADM 1/5473 (Maxwell court martial, 2 January 1829), 24–30.
54. *Ibid.*, 16, 29, 30, 42, 58.
55. *Ibid.*, 15, 22.
56. ADM 1/5484 (Morgan court martial, 2–4 April 1838), 74.

Works Cited

Unpublished materials

National Archives, Kew, UK

ADM 1/89 (Edward Hawke, *St. George*, Spithead, to John Clevland, Admiralty, London, 20 July 1755).

ADM 1/307 (G. B. Rodney, *Marlborough*, Fort Royal, Martinique, to [John Clevland, Admiralty, London], 10 February 1762).

ADM 1/653 (G. Smith, *Union*, The Downs, to John Clevland, Admiralty, London, 8 June 1757).

ADM 1/924 (T. Broderick, *Barfleur*, Spithead, to John Clevland, Admiralty, London, 13 June 1757).

ADM 1/1259 (Order for Beauchamp court martial).

ADM 1/1259 (Report on *Africaine* discipline).

ADM 1/1259 (Edward Thornborough, *Queen Charlotte*, Portsmouth, to J. W. Coker, Admiralty, London, 3 January 1816).

ADM 1/1259 (Edward Thornborough, *Queen Charlotte*, Portsmouth, to J. W. Coker, Admiralty, London, 3 February 1816).

ADM 1/1259 (Order for court martial of Rafaelo Seraco).

ADM 1/2427 (9, 11, 13 October 1815; 2, 3 November 1815; 5 December 1815).

ADM 1/5265 (Brese-Hoter court martial, 13 April 1704).

ADM 1/5266 (Ball-Jones court martial, 9 October 1706).

ADM 1/5266 (Cartwright-Jones court martial, 20 May 1706).

ADM 1/5266 (Emmeson-Hughes court martial, 1–2 May 1706).

ADM 1/5267 (Coise-Davis court martial, 19 July 1709).

ADM 1/5296 (Bicks-Booth court martial, 10 December 1757).

ADM 1/5299 (Billin-Bryan court martial, 13 May 1762).

ADM 1/5300 (Finley-Newton court martial, 2 July 1761).

ADM 1/5301 (Angel court martial, 12 January 1762), ADM 1/5301 (Billin-Bryan court martial, 13 May 1762).

ADM 1/5301 (Garbut-Pyle court martial, 23 October 1762).

ADM 1/5301 (Orde court martial, 1 February 1762).

ADM 1/5302 (Clark-Pearson court martial, 8 February 1763).

ADM 1/5337 (Sawyer court martial, 18 October 1796).

ADM 1/5337 (Archibald Cowan, *Blanche*, [Mediterranean] to [Horatio] Nelson, [Mediterranean], 24 August 1796, in Sawyer court martial).

ADM 1/5337 (Archibald Cowan, *Blanche*, [Mediterranean] to Charles Sawyer, *Blanche*, [Mediterranean], 6 September 1796, in Sawyer court martial).

ADM 1/5337 (George Cockburn, *La Minerve*, [Mediterranean], to Charles Sawyer, *Blanche*, [Mediterranean], 10 September 1796, in Sawyer court martial).

ADM 1/5339 (Allen court martial, 22–24 April 1797).

ADM 1/5339 (Benson-Francis court martial, 30 June 1797).

ADM 1/5343 (Morris-Savage court martial, 9 January 1798).

ADM 1/5354 (Broome statement).

ADM 1/5354 (Parsons 2nd court martial, 16 January 1816).
ADM 1/5369 (Ambler court martial, 22 April 1805).
ADM 1/5376 (Graham court martial, 9 December 1806).
ADM 1/5382 (Sand court martial, 10 July 1807).
ADM 1/5383 (Berry, William, court martial, 2–3 October 1807).
ADM 1/5390 (McCasky court martial, 29 December 1808).
ADM 1/5397 (Colquhoun-Fleming court martial, 23 June 1809).
ADM 1/5397 (Grimshaw-Scott court martial, 21 June 1809).
ADM 1/5399 (Black-Phillips court martial, 19 September 1809).
ADM 1/5399 (James-Martin court martial, 22 September 1809).
ADM 1/5399 (North court martial, 6 September 1809).
ADM 1/5453 (Beauchamp-Bruce court martial, 6–15 January 1816).
ADM 1/5453 (Beauchamp defense narrative).
ADM 1/5453 (Bruce defense narrative).
ADM 1/5453 (Charles-Seraco court martial, 1–2 January 1816).
ADM 1/5453 (Crutchley examination, 16 December 1815).
ADM 1/5453 (Hubbard examination, 15 December 1815).
ADM 1/5453 (Hubbard-Treake court martial, 5 January 1816).
ADM 1/5453 (Parsons 1st court martial, 6 January 1816).
ADM 1/5453 (Seraco-Treake court martial, 22 January 1816).
ADM 1/5453 (Tall-Treake court martial, 2–4 January 1816).
ADM 1/5473 (Maxwell court martial, 2 January 1829).
ADM 1/5478 (McGee-Peach court martial, 17 July 1832).
ADM 1/5484 (Morgan court martial, 2–4 April 1838).
ADM 1/5484 (Richard Morgan, *Pembroke* to Fairfax Moresby, *Pembroke*, 25 March 1838, in Morgan court martial, 3).
ADM 1/5484 (Fairfax Moresby, *Pembroke* to Richard Stopford, *Princess Charlotte*, 26 March 1838, in Morgan court martial, 3–5).
ADM 1/5484 (Fairfax Moresby, *Pembroke* to Richard Stopford, *Princess Charlotte*, 27 or 28 March 1838, in Morgan court martial, 3–5).
ADM 1/5484 (Richard Stopford, *Princess Charlotte* to Fairfax Moresby, *Pembroke*, 27 March 1838, in Morgan court martial, 3–5).
ADM 2/81 (Blake court martial, 11 August 1758), 124–125.
ADM 12/21 (McMahan court martial, 2 January 1798), 210–211.
ADM 12/21 (Palmer court martial, 19 August 1779), 205–207.
ADM 12/21 (Holland-Riley court martial, 11 May 1802), 213–15.
ADM 12/24 (Dickie court martial, 13 August 1801), 271–273.
ADM 12/26 (Allen court martial, 22–4 April 1797), 35–41.
ADM 12/26 (Beale court martial, 7 March 1759), 275–276.
ADM 12/26 (Ambler court martial, 22 April 1805), 58–71.
ADM 12/26 (Benson-Francis court martial, 30 June 1797), 41–42.
ADM 12/26 (Berry, Michael, court martial, 2 July 1761), 26.
ADM 12/26 (Billin-Bryan court martial, 13 May 1762), 27–33.
ADM 12/26 (Bicks-Booth court martial, 27 June 1757), 13–14.
ADM 12/26 (Blow court martial, 1 January 1780), 209.
ADM 12/26 (Brown-McCarthy court martial, 7 January 1804), 57–58.
ADM 12/26 (Carter court martial, 15 May 1804), 293.
ADM 12/26 (Chilton court martial, 3 November 1762), 33–35.
ADM 12/26 (Clark-Pearson court martial, 8 February 1763), 279–280.

ADM 12/26 (Cross-Spencer court martial, 9 September 1775), 273–4.
ADM 12/26 (Douglas-Ware, Harries-Harrison courts martial, 16 June 1800), 54–56.
ADM 12/26 (Falso-Lambert court martial, 3 December 1798), 48–50.
ADM 12/26 (French-Pomble court martial, 21 February 1756), 14–16.
ADM 12/26 (Finley-Newton court martial, 2 July 1761), 21–26.
ADM 12/26 (Fuller-Greenard court martial, 21 April 1802), 56–57.
ADM 12/26 (Harries-Harrison court martial. See ADM 12/26 Douglas-Ware court martial), 54–56.
ADM 12/26 (Hubbard-Hynes court martial, 10 December 1800), 53–54.
ADM 12/26 (Jenness court martial, 25 August 1798), 46–48.
ADM 12/26 (Macdonald-Mitchell court martial, 12 November 1762), 278–9.
ADM 12/26 (Manning court martial, 14 December 1802), 292.
ADM 12/26 (Callaghan-McMaster court martial, 29 July 1799), 52.
ADM 12/26 (Matson court martial, 18 July 1799), 50–52.
ADM 12/26 (Morris-Savage court martial, 9 January 1798), 42–45.
ADM 12/26 (Read-Tattersall court martial, 4 July 1796), 288–91.
ADM 12/26 (Sargent court martial, 9 December 1799), 291.
ADM 12/26 (Sawyer court martial, 18 October 1796), 285–288.
ADM 12/26 (Tremissen-Veaux court martial, 12 December 1759), 16–21.
ADM 12/27E (Sawyer court martial, 18 October 1796), 183.
ADM 12/27F (Hyndman court martial, 22 November 1813), 77.
ADM 36/13833 (*Centurion* muster book).
ADM 51/155 (*Centurion* log).
ADM 51/1264 (*Perdix* log).
ADM 51/1298 (*Adventure* log).
ADM 51/2086 (*Africaine* log).
ADM 51/2606 (*Nyaden* log).
PRO 30/20/8 (G. B. Rodney, *Marlborough*, Martinique to Henry Angel, *Stag*, Martinique, 31 January 1762).
PRO 30/20/8 (G. B. Rodney, *Marlborough,* Martinique to John Clevland, Admiralty, London, 10 February 1762).

William L. Clements Library, University of Michigan, Ann Arbor, Michigan

Tapson, John. "John Tapson Journal." 25 April 1806–28 December 1814.

Statutes

25 Henry VIII, c. 6.
28 Henry VIII, c. 6.
31 Henry VIII, c. 7.
33 Henry VIII, c. 17.
2 and 3 Edward VI, c. 17.
5 Elizabeth I, c. 17.
25 Elizabeth I, c. 6, pt. 2.
28 Elizabeth I, c. 6, pt. 2.
13 Charles II, c. 9.
22 George II, c. 33.
19 George III, c. 17.

Dissertations

Blake, Richard Charles. "Aspects of Religion in the Royal Navy, 1770–1870." M. Phil. diss., University of Southampton, 1980.

Land, Isaac E. "Domesticating the Maritime: Culture, Masculinity, and Empire in Britain, 1770–1820." Ph. D. diss., University of Michigan, 1999.

Pietsch, Roland. "Ships' Boys and Charity in the Mid-Eighteenth Century: The London Marine Society (1756–1772)." Ph. D. diss., University of London, 2003.

Primary materials

Abbot, Charles. "Journal of a Voyage to China in HMS. *Alceste* Kept by Charles Abbot, Midshipman." In Thursfield, *Five Naval Journals*.

Adye, Stephen P. *A Treatise on Courts Martial ... To Which is Added: I. An Essay on Military Punishments and Rewards. II. Considerations on the Act for Punishing Mutiny and Desertion*. New York: H. Gayne, 1769.

Anno Regni Caroli II ... Anno Dom 1661 ... An Act for the Establishing Articles and Orders for the Regulating of ... Forces by Sea. Also Part of an Act passed ... Anno Dom. 1720 for Rendering the Said Act More Effectual. London: Edward Castle, 1727.

Anno Regni Georgii ... At the Parliament Begun and Holden at Westminster the Tenth Day of November, Anno Dom. 1747 in the Twenty-first Year of the Reign of Our Sovereign Lord George the Second ... An Act for Amending, Explaining and Reducing into One Act of Parliament, the Laws Relating to the Government of His Majesty's Ships, Vessels, and Forces by Sea. Also an Act Made in 19 Geo. III to Explain and Amend the Said Act. London: Charles Eyre, 1794.

[Anon.] *Account of the Proceedings against Capt. Edward Rigby ... for Intending to Commit the Abominable Sin of Sodomy on the Body of one William Minton*. [London?]: F. Collins, 1698.

[Anon.]*The Arraignment and Conviction of Mervin Lord Audley, Earl of Castlehaven ... As also the Beheading of the Said Earle Shortly After on Tower Hill*. London, 1642.

[Anon.] *The Bloody Register ... A Select and Judicious Collection of the Most Remarkable Trials for Murder, Treason, Rape, Sodomy, Highway Robbery, Piracy ... From the Year 1700 to the Year 1764, Inclusive*. London: E. and M. Viney, 1764.

[Anon.]. *The Case of Sodomy, in the Tryal of Mervin Lord Audley, Earl of Castlehaven, for Committing a Rape. And Sodomy with Two of His Servants*. London: John Morphew, 1708.

[Anon.]. *The Character of the Times Delineated. Designed for the Use of Those Who Mourn in Secret for the Iniquities of the Nation, and Are Convinced by Sad Experience that Private Vices are Public and Real Mischiefs*. London: s. n., 1732.

[Anon.]. *College Wit Sharpened on the Head of a House .... Addressed to the Two Famous Universities of S-d-m and G-m-rr-h*. London: J. Wadham, 1739.

[Anon.]. *The Duel: A Poem Inscribed to the Right Honorable W*[illiam] *P*[ulteney], *Esq*. London, 1731.

[Anon.]. *An Epistle from Little Captain Brazen to the Worthy Captain Plume. To Which Is Added an Answer to the Said Epistle In Which the Character of Iago* [Robert Walpole?] *Is Set Forth So As To Be Understood by the Meanest Capacity*. London A. Moore, [1731].

[Anon.]. *A Faithful Narrative of the Proceeding in a Late Affair between the Rev. Mr. John Swinton, and Mr. George Baker, Both of Wadham College, Oxford: Wherein the Reasons*

That Induced Mr. Baker to Accuse Mr. Swinton of Sodomitical Practices ... Are Set Down .... To Which Is Prefixed a Particular Account of the Proceedings Against Robert Thistlethwaite, Late Doctor of Divinity and Warden of Wadham College for a Sodomitical Attempt on Mr. W. French. London: Britannia, 1739.

[Anon.]. *A Full and Genuine Narrative of the Confederacy Carried on By Cather, Cane, Alexander, Nixon, Patterson, Falconer, and Smith ... Against the Hon. Edward Walpole, Esq. Charging Him With ... Sodomy, ... Together with an Account of their Remarkable Trial and Conviction*. London: J. Fox and B. Tovey, 1751.

[Anon.]. *The Gardner at the Gallows: for Buggerie Laid to His Charge. Being a Narrative of a Strange and Admirable Passage of Gods Providence in the Reprieve of Thomas Rivers ... where Being Tied Up, the Lad and Mother ... They Declare the Wrong They Had Done Him, and Who Thereupon Was Reprieved*. [London?: s. n., 1667].

[Anon.]. *Hell Upon Earth; Or the Town in an Uproar. Occasioned by the Late Horrible Scenes of Forgery, Perjury, Street-Robbery, Murder, Sodomy, and Other Shocking Impieties*. London: J. Roberts and A. Dodd, 1729.

[Anon.]. *The Life and Death of John Atherton, Lord Bishop of Waterford and Lysmore ... Who for Incest, Buggery and Many Other Enormous Crimes After Having Lived a Vicious Life Dyed a Shameful Death: And Was on the Fifth of December Last Past Hanged on the Gallows Green at Dublin*. London: s. n., 1641.

[Anon.]. *Love-Letters between a Certain Late Nobleman and the Famous Mr. Wilson: Discovering the True History of the Rise and Surprising Grandeur of that Celebrated Beau*. London: s. n., 1723.

[Anon.]. *Plain Reasons for the Growth of Sodomy in England: To Which Is Added the Petit Maitre, an Odd Sort of Unpoetical Poem in the Trolly-lolly Style*. London: A. Dodd and E. Nutt, [1730?].

[Anon.]. *The Political Balance, for 1754. The Mock-Patriot, for 1753. To Which Is Added, the Case of John Atherton, Bishop of Waterford in Ireland, Who was Convicted of Bestiality With a Cow and Other Creatures*. Dublin: s. n., 1661; reprint, London: Rodger Lapis and Judas Alcock, 1754.

[Anon.]. "A Sea Chaplain's Petition to the Lieutenants in the Ward-Room for the Use of the Quarter Gallery." In *The Annual Register, or a View of the History, Politics, and Literature of the Year 1758*. London: J. Dodsley, 1759, 442.

[Anon.]. *Select Trials at the Sessions-House in the Old-Bailey, for Murder Robberies, Rapes, Sodomy, Coining .... In Four Volumes From the Year 1720 to this Time*. London: J. Applebee, 1742.

[Anon.]. *Some Particulars Relating to the Life of William Dillon Sheppard, Who Was Executed ... for Sodomy on Monday the 1st of June, 1761*. Bristol: E. Ward, [1761].

[Anon.]. *This Is Not the Thing: or, Molly Exalted*. [London]: s. n., [1763].

[Anon.]. *The Trial and Conviction of Several Reputed Sodomites Before the Right Honorable, the Lord Mayor, and Recorder of London, at Guildhall, the 20*th *Day of October 1707*. London: J. Morphew, 1707.

[Anon.]. *The Trial of Charles Bradbury, for the Detestable Crime of Sodomy Said to Be Committed on the Body of James Hearne at Justice Hall on the Old Bailey on Thursday the 11th of September, 1755*. London: M. Cooper, 1755.

[Anon.]. *The Trial of Lord Audley, Earl of Castlehaven, for Inhumanely Causing his Own Wife to be Ravished and for Buggery*. London: s. n., 1679.

[Anon.]. *A Trip Through London Containing Observations on Men and Things*. London: J. Roberts, *et al.*, 1728.

[Anon.]. *The Tryal and Condemnation of Mervin, Lord Audley Earl of Castle-Haven ... for Abetting a Rape upon his Countess, Committing Sodomy with His Servants, and*

Commanding and Countenancing the Debauching of His Daughter. London: s. n., 1699.

[Anon.]. *The Trial of Mervin Lord Audley, Earl of Castlehaven, for a Rape and Sodomy*. London: E. Curll, 1719.

[Anon.]. *The Whole Proceedings on the Wicked Conspiracy Carried on Against the Hon. Edward Walpole, Esquire by John Cather, Adam Nixon, Daniel Alexander, Patrick Cane alias Kane and Others*. London: H. Gifford, 1751.

[Anon.]. *The Woman-Hater's Lamentation: or, A New Copy of Verses on the Fatal End of Mr. Grant, a Woollen-Draper, and Two Others that Cut their Throats or Hanged Themselves in the Counter; With the Discovery of Near Hundred More that Are Accused of Unnatural [sic] Despising the Fair Sex, and Intriguing With One Another*. London: s. n., 1707.

Archenholz, Johann Wilhelm von. *A Picture of England*. London: s. n., 1797.

[Basset, J?]. *Sodom's Catastrophe, a Poem with the Addition of Other Pieces of Poetry*. London [Birmingham?]: Jacob Robinson, 1748.

Baynham, Henry. *From the Lower Deck: The Old Navy 1780–1840*. London: Hutchinson, 1969.

Bechervaise, John. See Old Quartermaster.

Bernard, Nicholas. *The Case of John Atherton, Bishop of Waterford in Ireland: Who Was Convicted of the Sin of Uncleanness with a Cow, and Other Creatures; for which He Was Hanged at Dublin*. London: E. Curll, 1710.

Blackstone, William. *Ehrlich's Blackstone*. Vol. 2, Edited by J. W. Ehrlich. New York: Capricorn Books, 1959.

Boteler, John Harvey. *Recollections of My Sea Life from 1808–1830*. Edited by David Bonner-Smith. Vol. 82, *Publications of the Navy Records Society*. [London]: Navy Records Society, 1942.

Burton, Robert. *Anatomy of Melancholy*. London, 1621; reprint, New York: New York Review of Books, 2001.

Cannon, Thomas. *Ancient and Modern Pederasty Investigated and Exemplified*. [London?], s. n., 1749. [No copies of this work are extant.]

Cobbett, Thomas and T. B. Howell, eds. *Cobbett's Complete Collection of State Trials and Proceedings for High Treason and other Crimes and Misdemeanors from the Earliest Period to the Present Time*. 33 vols. London: R. Bagshaw, 1809–1826.

Cochrane, Thomas. *Autobiography of A Seaman*. London: Richard Bentley, 1860.

Coke, Edward. *The Third Part of the Institutes of the Laws of England Concerning High Treason and other Pleas of the Crown, and Criminal Cases*. London: s. n., 1648.

——. *Reports of Sir Edward Coke. Diverse Resolutions and Judgments Given upon Solemn Arguments, and with Great Deliberation and Conference with the Learned Judges in Cases of Law*. London: Henry Twyford and Thomas Dring, 1658.

Colt, Henry Dutton, *A Full and True Account of the Discovery and Apprehending of a Notorious Gang of Sodomites in St. James's: With the Examination and Commitment of Two of them to Newgate, by Sir Henry Dutton Colt*. London: T. Bland, 1709.

Cremer, John. *Ramblin' Jack: The Journal of Captain John Cremer, 1770–1774*. Edited by R. Reynell Bellamy. London: Jonathan Cape, 1936.

Cullen, Peter. "Memoirs of Peter Cullen, Esq." In Thursfield, *Five Naval Journals*.

Cumby, William P. "Orders and Regulations for the Government and Discipline of His Majesty's Ship *Hyperion*, William Pryce Cumby, Captain." In Thursfield, *Five Naval Journals*.

D'Anvers, Caleb [William Pulteney]. *A Proper Reply to a Late Libel: Entitled Sedition and Defamation Displayed, In a Letter to the Author*. London: s. n., 1731.

Davis, John. *The Post-Captain; or The Wooden Walls Well Manned Comprehending a View of Naval Society and Manners*. Edited with an introduction from the 3rd edition, 1808 by R. H. Case. Reprint, London: Scolartes Press, 1928.

Defoe, Daniel. *A Tour Thro' the Whole Island of Great Britain ... Interspersed with Useful Observations Particularly Fitted for the Perusal of Such as Desire to Travel over the Island*. London: J. Osborn, *et al.*, 1738.

——. "The True-Born Englishman: A Satyr." Vol. 2, *Poems on Affairs of State: Augustan Satirical Verse, 1660–1714*. Edited by Frank H. Ellis. New Haven, CT: Yale University Press, 1970.

[Delafons, J.], *Treatise on Naval Courts Martial*. S. l.: s. n., 1805.

Dillon, William Henry. *A Narrative of My Professional Adventures, (1790–1839)* 2 vols. Edited by Michael A. Lewis. Vol. 93, *Publications of the Navy Records Society*. London: Navy Records Society, 1953.

Durand, James. *An Able Seaman of 1812: His Adventures on* Old Ironsides *and as an Impressed Sailor in the British Navy*. New Haven, CT: Yale University Press, 1926.

Eden, William. *Principles of Penal Law*. London: B. White and T. Cadell, 1771.

Gardner, James A. *Above and Under the Hatches: Recollections of James Anthony Gardner* Edited by R. Vesey Hamilton and John Knox Laughton. London: Chatham, 2000.

Garrick, David. *Miss in Her Teens: Or, The Medley of Lovers*. London: s. n., 1747. Later edition. London: Alexander Cleugh, 1789.

[Glascock, William Nugent]. *Naval Sketchbook: or the Service Afloat and Ashore: with Characteristic Reminiscences, Fragments, and Opinions, by an Officer*. New edition. London: Colburn and Bently, 1831.

[Gordon, Thomas]. *The Conspirators or, the Case of Catiline, As Collected from the Best Historians, Impartially Examined*, 2nd edition. London: J. Roberts, 1721.

——. *Francis, Lord Bacon: or the Case of Private and National Corruption and Bribery Impartially Considered. Addressed to all South-Sea Directors, Members of Parliament, Ministers of State, and Church. By a True-born Englishman*. London: J. Roberts, 1721.

Hale, Matthew. *Historia Placitorum Coronae: The History of the Pleas of the Crown*. [Dublin: E. Lynch, 1778].

Hall, Basil. *Fragments of Voyages and Travels by Captain Basil Hall*, R. N. Edinburgh: Cadell, 1833.

Hargrave, Francis. "Preface." Vol. 1, *A Complete Collection of State Trials and Proceedings for High Treason and Other Crimes and Misdemeanors; The Fourth Edition Commencing with the Eleventh Year of the Reign of King Richard II and Ending with the Sixteenth Year of the Reign of George III*. London: T. Wright, 1776–1781.

Hay, M. D. *The Memoirs of Robert Hay, 1789–1847*. London: Rupert Hart-Davis, 1953.

Hervey, Augustus. *Augustus Hervey's Journal: Being the Intimate Account of the Life of a Captain in the Royal Navy Ashore and Afloat, 1746–1759*. Edited by David Erskine. London: Kimber, 1954.

——. *Lord Hervey and His Friends, 1726–38: Based on Letters from Holland House, Melbury, and Ickworth*. Edited by the Earl of Ilchester. London: John Murray, 1950.

——. *Memoirs of the Reign of King George II from His Accession to the Death of Queen Caroline*. Edited by John Wilson Croker. New York; Scribner and Welford, 1844.

Hoffman, Fredrick, *A Sailor of King George: The Journals of Captain Frederick Hoffman, RN, 1793–1814*. Edited by A. Beckford Bevan and H. B. Wolryche-Whitmore. Annapolis, MD: Naval Institute Press, 1998.

[Holloway, Robert]. *The Phoenix of Sodom, or the Vere Street Coterie, Being an Expedition of the Gambols Practiced by the Ancient Lechers of Sodom and Gomorrah Embellished and Improved with the Modern Refreshments in Sodom*. London: J. Cook, 1813.

Keppel, Henry. *A Sailor's Life under Four Sovereigns*. London: Macmillan, 1899.

[King, John], *Bishop Atherton's Case Discussed in a Letter to the Author of a Late Pamphlet, Entitled The Case of John Atherton, Bishop of Waterford in Ireland, Fairly Represented*. London: E. Curll, 1711.

——. *The Case of John Atherton, Bishop of Waterford in Ireland: Fairly Represented. Against a Late Partial Edition of Dr. Barnard's Relation, and Sermon at His Funeral*. London: Luke Stokoe, 1710.

[King, William]. *The Toast. An Heroic Poem in Four Books, Written Originally in Latin by Frederick Scheffer: Now Done into English ... by Peregrine O'Donald*. Dublin: s. n., 1736.

Lancaster, Nathaniel. *The Plan of an Essay upon Delicacy: With a Specimen of the Work in Two Dialogues*. London: R. Dodsley, 1748.

——. *The Pretty Gentlemen: or, Softness of Manners Vindicated from the False Ridicule Exhibited under the Character of William Fribble, Esq*. London: M. Cooper, 1747.

Laws of War and Ordinances of the Sea Ordered and Established by the Parliament of the Commonwealth of England for the Regulating and Better Government of the Navy's Ships and Ships of War. London: John Field, 1652.

Leech, Samuel. *A Voice from the Main Deck: Being a Record of the Thirty Years' Adventures of Samuel Leech*. Introduction by Michael Crawford. Annapolis, MD: Naval Institute Press, 1999.

Mangin, Edward. "Some Account of the Writer's Situation as a Chaplain in the British Navy." In Thursfield, H. G. ed. *Five Naval Journals*.

Marshall, John. *Royal Naval Biography Containing Memoirs of the Flag Officers, Superannuated Rear-Admirals, Retired-Captains, Post-Captains and Commanders*. London: Longman, 1823–1833.

McArthur, John. *A Treatise on the Principles and Practice of Naval Courts-Martial*. London: Longden, Whieldon, and Butterworth, 1792.

[McPherson, Charles], *Life on Board a Man-of-War, Including A Full Account of the Battle of Navarino, by a British Seaman*. Glasgow: Blackie Fullerton, 1829.

Morrison, James. *The Journal of James Morrison, Boatswain's Mate of the* Bounty, *Describing the Mutiny and Subsequent Misfortunes of the Mutineers, together with an Account of the Island of Tahiti*. Waltham St. Lawrence, UK: Golden Cockerel Press, 1935.

Nagle, Jacob. *The Nagle Journal: A Diary of the Life of Jacob Nagle, Sailor, from the Year 1775 to 1841*. Edited by John. C. Dann. New York: Weidenfield and Nicholson 1988.

Nelson, Horatio. *The Dispatches and Letters of Vice Admiral Lord Viscount Nelson*. With notes by Nicholas Harris Nicolas. 7 vols. London: Henry Colburn, 1845–1846.

[Newcomb, Thomas]. *The Manners of the Age: In Thirteen Moral Satires. Written with a Design to Expose the Vicious and Irregular Conduct of Both Sexes, in the Various Pursuits of Life*. London: Jer. Batley, 1733.

Nicol, John. *The Life and Adventures of John Nicol*. Edited by Tim Flannery. Originally published, 1822; New York: Atlantic Monthly Press, 1997.

O'Byrne, William. *A Naval Biographical Dictionary Comprising the Life and Services of Every Living Officer in Her Majesty's Navy*. London: John Murray, 1849.

Old Quartermaster [John Bechervaise]. *Thirty-six Years of a Seafaring Life*. Portsea, UK: Woodward, 1839.

Original Weekly Journal. London. 20 June 1719, 4 July 1719, 25 July 1719.

Peard, George. *To the Pacific and Arctic with Beechey: The Journal of George Peard of H. M. S.* Blossom, *1825–1828*. Edited by Barry M. Gough. Cambridge: Cambridge University Press, 1973.

Pemberton, Charles. *The Autobiography of Pel. Verjuice*. Edited by Eric Partridge. London: Scolartis, 1929.

Prynne, William. *Histrio-Mastix: The Players Scourge*. London: Michael Sparks, 1633.

Pulteney, William. See Caleb D'Anvers.

Radicante, Alberto. *An Account of the Troubles Contained in This Pamphlet, the Author (Who Wrote It in Italian) Was Obliged to Fly the Kingdom; the Translator Was Sent to Newgate, and the Publisher Confined to the Fleet. A Philiosophical* [*sic*] *Dissertation on Death Composed for the Consolation of the Unhappy. By a Friend to Truth*. London: s. n., 1732.

——. *A Philiosophical* [*sic*] *Dissertation on Death Composed for the Consolation of the Unhappy. By a Friend to Truth*. London: W. Mears, 1732.

Raigersfeld, Jeffrey. *The Life of a Sea Officer*. Edited by L. G. Carr-Laughton. Originally published, 1830; London: Cassell, 1929.

Regulations and Instructions Relating to His Majesty's Service at Sea, Established by His Majesty in Council. 9th edition. London: s. n., 1757.

Richardson, William. *A Mariner of England: An Account of the Career of William Richardson from Cabin Boy to the Merchant Service to Warrant Officer in the Royal Navy as Told by Himself*. Edited by Spencer Childers. London: John Murray, 1908.

Robinson, William. *Jack Nastyface: Memoirs of a Seaman*. Edited by Oliver Warner. Originally published as *Nautical Economy*, 1836; reprint, Annapolis, MD: Naval Institute Press, 1974.

Sheridan, Richard Brinsley. *The Rivals*. Edited with an introduction and notes by T. Balston. Oxford: Clarendon Press, 1960.

Smollett, Tobias. *The Adventures of Peregrine Pickle in which Are Included Memoirs of a Lady of Quality*. Edited with an introduction by James L. Clifford. New York: Oxford University Press, 1964.

——. *The Adventures of Roderick Random*. Edited by Paul Gabriel Boucé. New York: Oxford University Press, 1979.

——. *Advice: A Satire*. In *The Works of Tobias Smollett, Poems, Plays, and* The Briton. Introduction and notes by Byron Gassman. Athens, GA: University of Georgia Press, 1993.

Spavens, William. *The Narrative of William Spavens, a Chatham Pensioner, Written by Himself. A Unique Lower Deck View of the Navy of the Seven Years War*. Originally published, 1796; reprint, London: Chatham, 1998.

Thompson, G[eorge], Torbay, to Mrs. Thompson, 9 September 1797. In Thursfield, *Five Naval Journals*.

Thursfield, H. G., ed. *Five Naval Journals, 1789–1817*. Vol. 91, *Publications of the Navy Records Society*. London: Navy Records Society, 1951.

Trotter, Thomas. *Medicina Nautica: An Essay on the Diseases of Seamen*. 2nd ed. London: Longman, 1804.

[Ward, Edward]. *Adam and Eve Stript of their Furbelows: or, the Fashionable Virtues and Vices of Both Sexes Exposed to Public View*. London: A. Bettlesworth, [1715].

——. *A Complete and Humorous Account of all the Remarkable Clubs and Societies in the Cities of London and Westminster from the R_____l-S_____y down to the Lumber-Troop*. 7th edition. London: s. n., 1756.

——. *The Modern World Disrobed: Adam and Eve Stript of their Furbelows: or, the Fashionable Virtues and Vices of Both Sexes Exposed to Public View*. London: J. Baker, Woodward and J. Morphew, 1708.

——. *Wooden World Dissected in the Character of a Ship of War*. Forward by Geoffrey Callender. Originally published, 1707. 5th edition., 1751; reprint, London: Edwin Chappell, 1929.

Wesley, John. *Serious Thoughts Occasioned by the Earthquake at Lisbon: To which Is Subjoined an Account of all the Late Earthquakes There and in other Places*. 6th edition. London: s. n., 1756.

[Paul Whitehead?], *The State of Rome under Nero and Domitian: A Satire Containing a List of Nobles, Senators, High Priests, Great Ministers of State, Etc., Etc., Etc., Etc. by Messers Juvenal and Persius*. London: C. Corbett, 1739.

Wilson, Robert Mercer. "Remarks on Board His Majesty's Ship *Unité* of 40 Guns." In Thursfield, *Five Naval Journals*.

Wiseman, Richard. *Eight Chirurgical* [*sic*] Treatises. 5th ed. London: B. Tooke, 1719.

Woodward, Josiah. *Sodom's Vices Destructive to Other Cities and States: A Sermon Preached before the Right Honorable The Lord Mayor of the City of London*. London: B. Aylmer and A. Bell, 1697.

Articles

Allan, David. "Some Methods and Problems in the History of Reading: Georgian England and the Scottish Enlightenment." *Journal of the Historical Society* 3 (Winter 2003): 91–124.

Anderson, Olive. "The Growth of Christian Militarism in Mid-Victorian Britain." *English Historical Review* 86 (January 1971): 46–73.

Beckwith, Frank. "The Eighteenth-Century Proprietary Library", *Journal of Documentation* 3 (1947–1948): 81–98.

Bingham, Carolyn. "Seventeenth-century Attitudes toward Deviant Sex." *Journal of Interdisciplinary History* 1 (Spring 1971): 447–472.

E. Boddy, "The Dalton Book Club," *Library History*, 9 (1992): 97–105.

Brennan, T. Cory. Review of *Love between Women: Early Christian Responses to Female Homoeroticism* by Bernadette J. Brooten. *Bryn Mawr Classical Review* (http://ccat.sas.upenn.edu/bmcr/1997/97.05.07.html [27 April 2007]).

Burg. B. R. "Ho Hum, Another Work of the Devil: Buggery and Sodomy in Early Stuart England." *Journal of Homosexuality* 6 (Fall/Winter 1980/81): 69–78.

——. "Officers, Gentlemen, 'Man-Talk,' and Group Sex in the 'Old Navy,' 1870–1873," *Journal of the History of Sexuality* 11 (July 2002): 439–456.

Callender, Geoffrey. Introduction. In Edward Ward. *Wooden World Dissected in the Character of a Ship of War*.

Cohen, Ed. "Legislating the Norm: From Sodomy to Gross Indecency." *South Atlantic Quarterly* 88 (Winter 1989): 181–217.

Fergus, Jan. "Eighteenth-Century Readers in Provincial England: The Customers of Samuel Clap's Circulating Library and Bookshop in Warwick, 1770–1772." In *Papers of the Bibliographical Society of America* 78 (1984): 155–213.

Gilbert, Arthur N. "The *Africaine* Courts Martial: A Study of Buggery in the Royal Navy." *Journal of Homosexuality* 1 (1974): 111–122.

——. "Buggery and the British Navy, 1700–1861." *Journal of Social History* 10 (Fall 1976): 72–97.

Gilmour-Bryson, Anne. "Sodomy and the Knights Templar." *Journal of the History of Sexuality* 7 (October 1966): 151–183.

Hamlyn, H. M. "Eighteenth-Century Circulating Libraries in England." *The Library*. 5th series, 1 (1946–1947): 197–222.

Harvey, A. D. "Prosecutions for Sodomy in England at the Beginning of the Nineteenth Century." *The Historical Journal* 21 (1978): 939–948.

Hitchcock, Tim. "Redefining Sex in Eighteenth-Century England." *History Workshop Journal* 41 (Spring) 1996): 72–90.

Jackson, Holbrook. "Introduction to the 1932 Edition." In Robert Burton, *Anatomy of Melancholy*. New York: New York Review of Books, 2001.

Kaufman, Paul. "Eighteenth-Century Book Clubs and Their Role in Social History," *Libri* 14 (1964–65): 1–31.

Lemish, Jesse. "Jack Tar in the Streets: Merchant Seamen in the Politics of Revolutionary America." *William and Mary Quarterly* 25 (July 1968): 371–372.

Linebaugh, Peter. "The Tyburn Riot against the Surgeons." In *Albion's Fatal Tree: Crime and Society in Eighteenth-Century England*. Edited by E. P. Thomson, *et al*. New York: Pantheon, 1975.

McIntosh, Mary. "The Homosexual Role." *Social Problems* 16 (Fall 1968): 182–192.

Morris, Polly. "Sodomy and Male Honor: The Case of Somerset, 1740–1850." *Journal of Homosexuality* 16 (1/2 1988): 383–406.

Murray, Stephen O. "Homosexual Acts and Selves in Early Modern Europe." *Journal of Homosexuality* 16 (1988): 457–477.

Oosterhoff, J. "Sodomy at Sea at the Cape of Good Hope during the Eighteenth Century." *Journal of Homosexuality* 16 (1/2 1988): 229–235.

Raven, James. "The Book Trades." In Isabel Rivers. *Books and Their Readers in Eighteenth-Century England*. Leicester: Leicester University Press, 1982.

Rodger, N. A. M. "Honor and Duty at Sea, 1660–1815." *Historical Research*. 75 (2002): 139–151.

——. "Officers, Gentlemen and their Educations, 1793–1860." In *Les Empires in Guerre et Paix*. Edited by. Edward Freeman. Vincennes: Service Historique de la Marine, 1990. 139–151.

——. "Shipboard Life in the Georgian Navy, 1750–1800: The Decline of the Old Order." In *The North Sea: Twelve Essays on Social History of Maritime Labor*. Edited by Lewis R. Fischer, *et al*. Stavanger, Norway: Stavanger Maritime Museum/ Association of North Sea Societies, 1992.

Rousseau, G. S. "The Pursuit of Homosexuality in the Eighteenth Century: 'Utterly Confused Category' and/or Rich Repository?" *Eighteenth-Century Life* 9 (May 1985): 132–68.

Samson, Jane. "The 1834 Cruise of HMS *Alligator*: The Bible and the Flag," *The Northern Mariner/Le Marine du Nord* 3 (October 1993): 37–47.

Senelick, Lawrence. "Mollies or Men of Mode? Sodomy and the Eighteenth-Century London Stage." *Journal of the History of Sexuality* 1 (July 1990): 33–67.

Simpson, Antony E. "Vulnerability and the Age of Female Consent: Legal Innovation and Its Effect on Prosecutions for Rape in Eighteenth-Century

London." In *Sexual Underworlds of the Enlightenment*. Edited by G. S. Rousseau and Roy Porter. Manchester: Manchester University Press, 1987.

Trumbach, Randolph. "Sodomitical Subcultures, Sodomitical Roles, and the Gender Revolution of the Eighteenth Century: The Recent Historiography. *Eighteenth-Century Life* 9 (May 1985): 109–121.

Wiles, Roy McKeen. "The Relish for Reading in Provincial England Two Centuries Ago." In Paul J. Korshin, ed. *The Widening Circle: Essays on the Circulation of Literature in Eighteenth-Century Europe*. Philadelphia: University of Pennsylvania Press, 1976.

"William Boyce (1711–1779)." *Eighteenth-Century English Music*. http://www.rslade.btinternet.co.uk/boyce/index.html (27 July 2004).

Books

Altick, Richard. *The English Common Reader: A Social History of the Mass Reading Public, 1800–1900*. 2nd edition. Chicago: University of Chicago Press, 1998.

Baugh, Daniel. *British Naval Administration in the Age of Walpole*. Princeton, NJ: Princeton University Press, 1965.

Borowitz, Albert. *The Thurtell-Hunt Murder Case: Dark Mirror to Regency England*. Baton Rouge, LA: Louisiana State University Press, 1987.

Bray, Alan. *Homosexuality in Renaissance England*. London: Gay Men's Press, 1982.

Broadley, A. M. and R. G. Bartelot. *Nelson's Hardy: His Life, Letters, and Friends*. London: John Murray, 1909.

Brooten, Bernadette J. *Love between Women: Early Christian Responses to Female Homoeroticism*. Chicago: University of Chicago Press, 1996.

Browning, Reed. *Political and Constitutional Ideas of the Court Whigs*. Baton Rouge, LA: Louisiana State University Press, 1982.

Burg, B. R. *An American Seafarer in the Age of Sail: The Erotic Diaries of Philip C. Van Buskirk, 1851–1870*. New Haven, CT: Yale University Press, 1995.

——. *Gay Warriors: A Documentary History from the Ancient World to the Present*. New York: New York University Press, 2002.

Byrn, John D., Jr. *Crime and Punishment in the Royal Navy: Discipline on the Leeward Islands Station, 1784–1812*. Aldershot, UK: Scolar, 1989.

Carvajal, Fredrico Garza. *Butterflies Will Burn: Persecuting Sodomites in Early Modern Spain and Mexico*. Austin, TX: University of Texas Press, 2003.

Colledge, J. J. *Ships of the Royal Navy: A Complete Record of the Royal Navy from the Fifteenth Century to the Present*. London: Greenhill Books, 1987.

Commissioned Sea Officers of the Royal Navy, 1660–1815. Edited by David Syrett and R. L. DiNardo. Aldershot, UK; Brookfield, VT, USA: Scolar Press, for the Navy Records Society; Ashgate, 1994.

Creighton, Margaret and Lisa Norling, eds. *Iron Men, Wooden Women: Gender and Seafaring in the Atlantic World, 1700–1920*. Baltimore: Johns Hopkins University Press, 1996.

Cressy, David. *Transvestites and Transgressions in Tudor England*. New York: Oxford University Press, 2000.

Crewe, Duncan. *Yellow Jack and the Worm: British Naval Administration in the West Indies, 1739–1748*. Liverpool: Liverpool University Press, 1993.

Darby, Marge. *What Caused the Mutiny on the Bounty*. Sidney: Angus and Robertson, 1965.

Dickinson, H. T. "Introduction." In *Proper Reply*. No. 2 in *British Ideas and Issues, 1660–1820: A Series of Reprinted Books and Pamphlets, Walpole's Friends and Foes*. New York: AMS, 1998.

Dictionary of National Biography. Edited by Leslie Stephen and Sidney Lee. Vol. 47. London: Oxford University Press, 1921–2.

Dugan, James. *The Great Mutiny*. New York: Putnam's, 1965.

Eder, Markus. *Crime and Punishment in the Royal Navy of the Seven Years' War, 1755–1763*. Burlington, VT: Ashgate, 2004.

Edsall, Nicholas C. *Toward Stonewall: Homosexuality and Society in the Modern Western World*. Charlottesville, VA: University of Virginia Press, 2003.

Elton, G. R. *Star Chamber Stories*. London: Methuen, 1958.

Feather, John. *The Provincial Book Trade in the Eighteenth Century*. Cambridge: Cambridge University Press, 1985.

Fish, Stanley. *Is There a Text in this Class: The Authority of Interpretive Communities*. Cambridge, MA: Harvard, 1980.

Freeman, Terrance M. *Dramatic Representations of British Soldiers and Sailors on the London Stage, 1660–1800: Britons Strike Home*. Lewiston, NY: E. Mellen, 1995.

Foucault, Michel. *The History of Sexuality: Volume I, An Introduction*. Translated by Robert Hurley. New York: Vintage, 1980.

Friedenberg, Zachary B. *Medicine Under Sail*. Annapolis, MD: Naval Institute Press, 2002.

Gilje, Paul A. *Liberty on the Waterfront: American Maritime Culture in the Age of Revolution*. Philadelphia: University of Pennsylvania Press, 2004.

Gleick, James. *Isaac Newton*. New York: Random House, 2003.

Goldsmith, Netta Murray. *The Worst of Crimes: Homosexuality and the Law in Eighteenth-Century London*. Aldershot, UK: Ashgate, 1998.

Goodich, Michael. *The Unmentionable Vice: Homosexuality in the Later Medieval Period*. Santa Monica, CA: ABC Clio, 1979.

Guttridge, Leonard. *Mutiny: A History of Naval Insurrection*. Annapolis, MD: Naval Institute Press, 1992.

Halperin, David M. *How to Do the History of Homosexuality*. Chicago: University of Chicago Press, 2002.

Halsbard, Robert. *Lord Hervey: Eighteenth-Century Courtier*. Oxford: Clarendon Press, 1973.

Hannay, David. *Naval Courts Martial*. Cambridge: Cambridge University Press, 1914.

Harvey, A. D. *Sex in Georgian England: Attitudes from the 1720s to the 1820s*. London: Duckworth, 1994.

Hedderwick, J. B. *The Captain's Clerk*. London: Hutchinson, 1957.

Henige, David P. *Colonial Governors from the Fifteenth Century to* the *Present: A Comprehensive List*. Madison, WI: University of Wisconsin Press, 1970.

Herrup, Cynthia B. *A House in Gross Disorder: Sex, Law, and the* 2nd *Earl of Castlehaven*. New York: Oxford University Press, 1999.

Hitchcock, Tim. *English Sexualities, 1700–1800*. New York: St. Martin's 1997.

—— and Michèle Cohen. *English Masculinities, 1660–1800*. London: Longmans, 1999.

Hyde, H. Montgomery. *The Cleveland Street Scandal*. New York: Coward, McCann, 1976.

Ireland, Bernard. *Naval Warfare in the Age of Sail: War at Sea 1756–1815*. New York: Norton, 2000.

James, William. *Old Oak: The Life of John Jervis, Earl of St. Vincent*. London: Longman, 1950.

Jardine, Lisa and Alan Stewart. *Hostage to Fortune: The Troubled Life of Francis Bacon*. New York: Hill and Wang, 1998.

Jenkins, Philip. *Moral Panic: Changing Concepts of the Child Molester in Modern America*. New Haven, CT: Yale University Press, 1998.

Kealy, A. G. *Chaplains of the Royal Navy, 1626–1903*. Portsmouth, UK: Wilkins and Son, [1905?].

Kemp, Peter. *The British Sailor: A Social History of the Lower Deck*. London: Dent, 1970.

King, Thomas A. *The Gendering of Men, 1600–1750*. Vol. 1, *The English Phallus*. Madison, WI: University of Wisconsin Press, 2004.

Kverndal. Roald. *Seamens' Missions: Their Origin and Early Growth: A Contribution to the Church Maritime*. Pasadena, CA: William Carey, 1986.

Lavery, Brian, ed. *Shipboard Life and Organization 1731–1815*. Vol. 138, Publications of the Navy Records Society. Aldershot, UK: Ashgate, 1998.

Leiner, Frederick C. *The End of the Barbary Terror: America's 1815 War Against the Pirates of North Africa*. New York: Oxford University Press, 2006.

Lewis, Michael A. *The Navy in Transition: A Social History, 1814–1864*. London: Hodder and Stoughton, 1965.

——. *The Navy of Britain: A Historical Portrait*. London: Allen and Unwin, 1948.

——. *A Social History of the Navy, 1783–1815*. London: George Allen, 1960.

Lincoln, Margarette. *Representing the Royal Navy: British Sea Power, 1750–1815*. Burlington, VT: Ashgate, 2002.

Lipscomb, F. W. *Heritage of Sea Power: The Story of Portsmouth*. London: Hutchinson, 1969.

Lloyd, Christopher, *The British Seaman, 1200–1860: A Social Survey*. Rutherford, NJ: Fairleigh Dickenson University Press, 1968.

McCormick, Ian, ed.. *Secret Sexualities: A Sourcebook of Seventeenth- and Eighteenth-Century Writing*. New York: Routledge, 1977.

Manwaring, G. E. and Bonamy Dobrée. *The Floating Republic: An Account of the Mutinies at Spithead and the Nore, 1797*. London: Geoffrey Bles, 1935.

Merriman, R. D., ed. *Queen Anne's Navy: Documents Concerning the Administration of the Navy of Queen Anne, 1702–1714*. London: Navy Records Society, 1961.

Morriss, Roger. *Cockburn and the British Navy in Transition: Admiral Sir George Cockburn, 1772–1853*. Columbia, SC: University of South Carolina Press, 1997.

Neale, Jonathan. *Cutlass and the Lash: Mutiny and Discipline in Nelson's Navy*. London: Pluto Press, 1985.

Norton, Rictor. *Mother Clap's Molly House: The Gay Subculture in England, 1700–1830*. London: Gay Mens' Press, 1992.

O'Brian, Patrick. *Master and Commander*. Originally published, 1970; New York: Norton, 1990.

Old Sailor [Barker, Matthew Henry], *Greenwich Hospital: A Series of Naval Sketches Descriptive of the Life of a Man-of-War's Man, by an Old Sailor*. London: James Robins, 1826.

Oxford Companion to Ships and the Sea. Edited by Peter Kemp. New York: Oxford University Press, 1994.

Pedicord, Harry William. *The Theatrical Public in the Time of Garrick*. New York: King's Crown, 1954.

Pope, Dudley. *Life in Nelson's Navy*. Annapolis, MD: Naval Institute Press, 1981.

Porter, Roy and Leslie Hall. *The Facts of Life: The Creation of Sexual Knowledge in Britain, 1650–1950*. New Haven, CT: Yale University Press, 1995.

Radzinowicz, Leon. *The Movement for Reform*. Vol. 1, *A History of English Criminal Law and Its Administration from 1750*. London: Stevens and Sons, 1948.

Rodger, N. A. M. *The Wooden World: An Anatomy of the Georgian Navy*. London: Collins, 1986.

Sainty, J. C., compiler. *Admiralty Officials, 1660–1870*. Vol 4, *Office-Holders in Modern Britain*. London: University of London, Institute for Historical Research, 1975.

Sissman, Adam. *Boswell's Presumptuous Task: The Making of the Life of Dr. Johnson*. New York: Farrar, Straus, and Giroux, 2000.

Smith, Bruce R. *Homosexuality in Shakespeare's England*. Chicago: University of Chicago Press, 1991.

Smith, Waldo E. L. *The Navy and Its Chaplains in the Age of Sail*. Toronto: Ryerson, 1961.

Taylor, Gordon. *The Sea Chaplains: A History of the Chaplains of the Royal Navy*. New York: Oxford University Press, 1978.

Trumbach, Randolph. *Sex and the Gender Revolution*. Vol. 1, *Heterosexuality and the Third Gender in Enlightenment London*. Chicago: University of Chicago Press, 1998.

Vale, Brian. *A Frigate of King George: Life and Duty on a British Man of War, 1807–1829*. London: I. B. Tauris, 2001.

Wagner, Peter. *Eros Revived: Erotica of the Enlightenment in England and America*. London: Secker and Warburg, 1988.

Walling, R. A. J. *The Story of Plymouth*. New York: Morrow, [1950].

Zeeland, Stephen. *The Masculine Marine: Homoeroticism in the U. S. Marine Corps*. New York: Haworth, 1996.

——. *Sailors and Sexual Identity: Crossing the Line between "Straight" and "Gay" in the U. S. Navy*. New York: Haworth, 1995.

Index

LaVergne, TN USA
27 September 2009
159139LV00003B/5/P
9 780230 522282